Philosophical Perspectives
in Artificial Intelligence

HARVESTER STUDIES IN COGNITIVE SCIENCE

GENERAL EDITOR Margaret A. Boden, Reader in Philosophy and Psychology, University of Sussex.
LINGUISTICS CONSULTANT Gerald Gazdar, Lecturer in Linguistics, University of Sussex.
Harvester studies in Cognitive Science is a new series which will explore the nature of knowledge by way of a distinctive theoretical approach – one that takes account of the complex structures and interacting processes that make thought and action possible.

Philosophical Perspectives in Artificial Intelligence

EDITED BY

MARTIN RINGLE

Department of Computer Science, Vassar College

THE HARVESTER PRESS

This edition first published in Great Britain in 1979 by
THE HARVESTER PRESS LIMITED
Publisher: John Spiers
17 Ship Street, Brighton, Sussex

British Library Cataloguing in Publication Data
Philosophical perspectives in artificial intelligence. –
(Harvester studies in Cognitive Science)
1.   Artificial intelligence
I.   Ringle, Martin
001.53'5'01   Q335

ISBN 0-85527-901-X

Printed in Great Britain by
Redwood Burn Limited, Trowbridge and Esher

Contents

For my family

Contributors CONTRIBUTORS

Daniel C. Dennett is Professor of Philosophy at Tufts University. He is the author of *Content and Consciousness* (1969) and *Brainstorms: Philosophical Essays on Mind and Psychology* (1978), and has contributed articles to many journals and anthologies in philosophy and cognitive science.

Hubert L. Dreyfus is Professor of Philosophy at the University of California at Berkeley. A long-time critic of Artificial Intelligence, Dreyfus has served as a consultant to the Rand Corporation and a Visiting Scientist to the Yale Artificial Intelligence Program. He is the author of *What Computers Can't Do.*

Wendy Lehnert is Assistant Professor of Computer Science at Yale University. She has done extensive work in the area of natural language processing and is the author of *The Process of Question Answering.*

John McCarthy is Professor of Computer Science and Director of the Artificial Intelligence Laboratory at Stanford University. A pioneer in the field of AI, McCarthy is the author of the original LISP programming language which has been extensively used in natural language processing research. He has contributed numerous articles to journals in computer science.

John McDermott is Assistant Professor of Computer Science at Carnegie-Mellon University. He holds a doctorate in philosophy from Notre Dame University. Since 1974 he has been active in the application of 'production system' theory to the development of expert-level cognitive behavior in computer systems.

Zenon W. Pylyshun is Professor of both Psychology and Computer Science at the University of Western Ontario. He has been a Visiting Scholar in Cognitive Science at M.I.T. and has written and lectured extensively on cognitive psychology and Artificial Intelligence.

Kenneth M. Sayre is Professor of Philosophy at the University of Notre Dame. A pioneer in the philosophical exploration of Artificial Intelligence, he is the author of numerous books and articles, including *Recognition: A Study in the Philosophy of Artificial Intelligence, Consciousness: A Philosophic Study of Minds and Machines,* and *Cybernetics and the Philosophy of Mind.*

Roger C. Schank is Professor of Computer Science and Director of the Artificial Intelligence Project at Yale University. His theory of "conceptual dependency" has had a profound impact in the area of natural language processing. He is the author of numerous articles, technical papers and books, including, *Computer Models of Thought and Language* (edited with K. Colby), *Conceptual information Processing*, and *Scripts, Plans, Goals and Understanding* (with R. Abelson).

Thomas W. Simon is Assistant Professor of Philosophy at the University of Florida at Gainesville. He has written numerous articles in the area of cybernetic systems and computer models. Co-founder and former president of the Society for the Interdisciplinary Study of The Mind, Simon has been active in the interdisciplinary study of language. He is the editor of *Language, Mind and Brain*.

Martin Ringle is Assistant Professor of Computer Science at Vassar College. He has lectured extensively on the interface between philosophy and artificial intelligence and has served as Chairman of the National Symposium for Philosophy and Computer Technology. Co-founder of the Society for the Interdisciplinary Study of the Mind (with Thomas W. Simon), he is editor of the Society journal, the *SISTM Quarterly*, and the monograph series in "Language, Mind, and Brain". He has been a National Endowment for the Humanities Summer Fellow in Philosophy at Indiana University and a Woodrow Wilson Fellow at the State University of New York at Binghamton. His essays in this area include, "Artificial Intelligence as a Micro-Theory Approach to Language" and "Obstacles to a Unified Theory of Language Processing: The Problem of Context".

Acknowledgements

The contributors gratefully acknowledge the assistance they have received from the following agencies: Chapter 2, Al Newell, Herb Simon, and the artificial intelligence research team at MIT; chapter 3, Pergamon Press for permission to reprint diagrams from K. Colby, *Artificial Paranoia*; chapter 4, the Advanced Research Projects Agency of the U.S. Department of Defense and the Office of Naval Research (Contract N00014-75-C-1111); chapter 5, members of the IPS project at Carnegie-Mellon University, including C. Forgy, P. Langley, A. Newell, K. Ramakrishna, and M. Rychener; chapter 10, Professor Martin Ringle and Professor Franz Oppacher.

PREFACE

When philosophy was first practised by the ancient Greeks, there was little that fell beyond its scope. Evidence of this is found each time one opens a college text and discovers, in the introduction, that Aristotle was the 'father of biology', or the 'father of literary criticism', or the 'father of logic and rhetoric'. Since that time, however, the content of philosophy has been systematically carved up to create the autonomous disciplines we know today. By the early part of this century, there was little left to study in philosophy beyond ethics, metaphysics, logic, epistemology, and, of course, religion.

With the persistence of Diogenes, philosophers took to stalking their campuses in search of an honest philosophical problem. The outcome of such forays became the now-familiar 'philosophy of science', 'philosophy of history', 'philosophy of law', 'philosophy of art', and all the other eclecticisms prefaced by the magical words, 'philosophy of. . .' It was not long before philosophers had repossessed their former chattels.

A subject as timely and as fascinating as artificial intelligence could hardly escape notice by the itinerant philosopher. The study of machine mentality offers a tremendous number of new possibilities for the understanding of human mentality, at the same time that it threatens many of our cherished philosophical beliefs about consciousness and human intelligence. The impact of artificial intelligence has been extensively felt in the literature, symposia, and discussions of philosophers.

The purpose of this anthology is to bring the dialogue between philosophy and artificial intelligence up-to-date. The essays which are included here represent a variety of viewpoints from both philosophers and artificial intelligence experts. Some papers are analytical, some are critical, and some report on recent work in artificial intelligence. Hopefully, the philosopher will gain some insight into the state-of-the-art and the state-of-the-attitude in artificial intelligence while the AI worker will learn something about the philosophical issues which relate to his research.

The essays have been trimmed in both size and style to a form which should make them equally accessible to philosophers, AI researchers, and anyone else who is interested in the subject. The more demanding reader will find this volume useful as a guide to the issues which are more extensively dealt with in the technical literature of each of the disciplines.

Some of the material included here is drawn from the first annual conference of the Society for the Interdisciplinary Study of the Mind (SISTM), which was hosted by the State University College at New Paltz, New York. I would like to thank Bill Cadden of IBM (Kingston) and Bob Davidson, Ned Conway, and Phil Semprevivo of New Paltz College for their invaluable assistance in making the conference possible. I would also like to thank my colleagues, John Kirk and Tony Preus, and my students, Joe Loehr, George Lithco, Sandy Keegan and Donna Toth, for the support and inspiration which they lent to that conference.

I am grateful to Maggie Boden for her helpful suggestions on many of the papers, to Tom Simon, president of SISTM, for his widsom, tenacity, and special guidance in the preparation of this volume, to my wife Cathy, who lent both her professional expertise to the production of the manuscript and her human compassion to the preservation of my sanity; and to my colleagues and good friends in the philosophy department at Eau Claire, Wisconsin, Phil Griffin, Dick Behling, Ron Koshoshek and Nancy Sixel. A very special thanks also to Gerald M. Weinberg of Ethnotech, Inc., the late Theodore M. Mischel of the State University of New York at Binghamton, and Michael A. Arbib of the University of Massachusetts for having, in one way or another, guided me into the interdisciplinary study of philosophy and artificial intelligence.

Phillipsport, N.Y.   M.H.R.
1978

PART I
INTRODUCTION

CHAPTER 1

PHILOSOPHY AND ARTIFICIAL INTELLIGENCE
Martin Ringle

A BRIEF HISTORY

The degree to which two disciplines interact is usually in direct proportion to their mutual proximity, in terms of origins, issues, and methodologies. In these respects, philosophy and artificial intelligence could scarcely be farther apart. Despite this fact, however, they have had a great deal to do with one another since the latter took hold, some thirty years ago.

Artificial intelligence (AI) made its debut to the academic community in 1950, the year that Alan Turing published his classic, 'Computing Machinery and Intelligence'. Although research into the design and capabilities of electronic computers began somewhat earlier, it was not until the appearance of this article that the concept of an intelligent artifact assumed the trappings of bona fide scientific inquiry. The question which Turing raised in that article, though emanating from mathematics and computer science, was essentially philosophical: Can machines think? The answer called for a logical and semantic analysis of the concepts of 'thought', 'intelligence', 'consciousness', and 'machine', rather than an empirical assessment of computer behaviour.

Turing's arguments in favour of intelligent machines initiated a flurry of objections from philosophers and marked the first phase of philosophy/AI interaction. The earliest debates focused on the problem of applying mentalistic terms to machines.

Ordinarily, when we say that a machine 'thinks' or that an electric eye 'sees', we put the terms 'think' and 'see' in quotation marks, as I have done, to call attention to the fact that we are using them metaphorically. Such usage is based primarily ·on observed behavioural analogues between people and machines. Prior to the development of the electronic computer,

1

there was little temptation to question this convention. The problem arises when we attempt, as Turing did, to remove the quotation marks and blur the distinction between human and machine attributes. The theoretical danger which such a move incurs is that we may begin to lose sight of the singularly complex nature of human mentality, thus committing ourselves to an over simplified psychological paradigm. To argue, for example, that 'seeing' is exclusively a physical process involving the excitation of photo-receptors by light, is to omit the cognitive component which distinguishes sensation from perception. A similar error may be made if we construe calculation or computation as the exclusive ingredient of thought. Philosophers such as Scriven (1953), Ziff (1964), and Taylor (1966) were quick to attack the idea of 'artificial intelligence' on the grounds that it violated accepted semantic analyses of the relevant terms.

A deeper issue, however, derived from the fact that the criteria offered for the application of psychological predicates appeared to be chiefly behavioural. Even granting Turing's assumption that a machine could completely imitate human (linguistic) behaviour, the question still remains as to whether or not such imitation provides sufficient grounds for the ascription of mental attributes. Gunderson (1964) pointed out that overt behaviour could not, by itself, do more than suggest a certain type of analogy, viz:

> . . .perhaps comparable net results achieved by machines and human beings is all that is needed to establish an analogy between them, but it is far from what is needed to establish that one sort of subject (machines) can do the same thing that another sort of subject (human beings or other animals) can do. Part of what things do is how they do it. To ask whether a machine can think is in part to ask whether machines can do things in certain ways. (p.65)

While arguments of this sort flowed rather freely among philosophers, the response from the early AI community was barely audible. With the exception of such spokesmen as Turing and McKay (1965), the primary concern of pioneer computer scientists was the development of working computer systems, not the adjudication of philosophical problems. The potential for efficient, intelligent data processing by machine was so great, and the technical obstacles so formidable, that few computer scientists had the inclination to occupy themselves with either psychological or philosophical hypotheses.

Philosophers, however, continued to indulge their appetites for artificial intelligence. The tide of philosophical skepticism was abruptly reversed with the insight that AI had something special to offer in two key areas of investigation: (a) the ontological problem of the relationship between minds and bodies; and (b) the epistemological problem of the analysis of mentalistic terms.

Hilary Putnam was among the first to shift the focus from AI back to philosophy itself. In a seminal article entitled 'Minds and Machines' (1960), Putnam adroitly imported a variety of AI concepts to give a new wrinkle to the Cartesian problem of dualism. Using the notions of 'Turing Machine,' 'programming,' 'logical state,' 'machine table,' etc., Putnam mapped out the analogy between the software/hardware dichotomy and the mental/physical dichotomy. His goal was not to solve the Cartesian problem but rather to dissolve it, by likening human mentality to computer software. If, he argued, there were no conceptual problems in relating programming to hardware then equally there should be no problems in relating human mental attributes to bodies. The argument was, in effect, a *reductio ad absurdum*; to suggest that there *were* conceptual problems in the relation of software to hardware would be to admit that humans (and animals) lacked a monopoly on mentality.

Putnam's thesis quickly drew fire from philosophers who viewed it as a resurrection of traditional mechanism. In the ensuing controversy the thesis was repeatedly modified and augmented to handle sophisticated objections. Despite its changes, however, it served to light the way for a new avenue of analysis with respect to mentalistic terms such as 'consciousness', 'perception', 'deduction', and the like.

When we use these terms in ordinary discourse we frequently cover a wide range of concepts, none of which is particularly well-defined. The effort to formalize their meaning leads, not unexpectedly, in the direction of measurement and observation. Quantification, in this instance, can assume two principal forms, which may be described as centralist and peripheralist

(Dennett, 1969: 41ff.). The centralist attempts to analyse mentalistic terms by first identifying mental phenomena with states or processes of the central nervous system. This approach, often referred to as the 'neural identity thesis,' is an extreme form of reductive materialism. The peripheralist follows a similar path and attempts to forge an identification between mentalistic phenomena and observable behaviours.

The problem with both of these approaches derives from the conceptual difficulty of capturing the full meaning of a mentalistic term in the logic of a physicalistic language. As Hamlyn (1957), Mischel (1963) and others pointed out, the chasm between the theoretical framework of mental events, involving reasons, intentions, beliefs, etc., and the theoretical framework of physical events, involving spatio-temporal causes-and-effects, is too wide to permit anything more than a crude one-to-many correspondence. The mapping of one-to-one identities is totally out of the question, given the present sophistication of either the behavioural or the neural sciences.

This leaves the epistemologist with an unpleasant pair of alternatives: either support an untenable (and unilluminating) form of mental-physical identification, or abandon the goal of attaining detailed analyses of mentalistic terminology.

Fortunately, artificial intelligence offers a third alternative. The conceptual foundation of artificial intelligence, as Putnam clearly saw, includes a level which is neither physical, in the traditional sense of the term, nor mental in the precise sense of 'human mentality.' AI workers deal with things like 'information,' 'programs,' 'feedback,' 'data structures,' and the like, which are representative of a level of analysis roughly midway between the standard levels occupied by minds and bodies. While the leap from, e.g. 'believing it will rain today,' to 'neurons k_1 through k_n firing at t_j' is logically prohibited, the leap from such a belief-statement to a description of a 'cognitive set relating to time and weather', is not. Though clearly mentalistic in content, the locutions of the artificial intelligence idiom are untainted by the opacity of ordinary mentalistic discourse and can be intelligibly related to a physicalistic framework. At the same time, they offer a means of decomposing what have been, traditionally, monolithic concepts.

Philosophers such as Sayre (1965, 1969) and Dennett (1969)

enthusiastically applied this new level of analysis to concepts such as recognition, consciousness, awareness, imagery, thinking, reasoning, intentional action and language use. At roughly the same time, AI workers such as McCarthy, Hayes (1969) and Minsky (1968) began to express an interest in some of the same applications of AI to philosophical problems, albeit from the opposite perspective.

Interdisciplinary co-operation, however, was not universal. Anti-mechanists once again voiced their objections to artificial intelligence, in the person of Hubert Dreyfus. In a series of caustic papers and books (Dreyfus, 1965; 1967; 1972) Dreyfus attacked the aims, achievements, and basic presuppositions of the artificial intelligence community. His arguments were based largely on the epistemological principles implied by the information-processing approach, rather than on the semantic implications of ascribing mental properties to machines. As such, they marked an interesting step forward in philosophical criticism. Unfortunately, the tone of Dreyfus' analyses was, by his own admission (1972: xxxiv) polemical rather than neutral. This proved to be a mixed blessing: on the one hand, it served to ignite a controversy which drew a great deal of attention to the philosophy AI/interface; on the other hand, it resulted in so much heated rhetoric that many of the valuable philosophical points were overlooked. With the exception of a few AI workers, such as Joseph Weizenbaum (1976), the AI community recoiled from the dialogue with philosophy and turned their attention back to empirical problems.

Mutual interest of artificial intelligence workers and philosophers in problems of intelligence and consciousness once again kindled co-operation and, during recent years, the dialogue has been re-established. Books such as Kenneth Sayre's *Cybernetics and the Philosophy of Mind*, (1976), Margaret Boden's *Artificial Intelligence and Natural Man*, (1977) and Bertram Raphael's *The Thinking Computer* (1976) each raise a number of stimulating questions concerning the frontier in philosophy and artificial intelligence and are indicative of the new move towards co-operation. While the AI systems of today may still be 'embryonic' with respect to their ultimate potential, they are sophisticated enough to provide us with a valuable means of investigating epistemic activities.

THE AIMS OF ARTIFICIAL INTELLIGENCE

As a newly developed study, AI has not yet coalesced into a well-defined discipline with a universally-agreed-upon description. A good deal of the criticism, and perhaps some of the credit, directed at AI stems from a confused, or at least debatable, assessment of what AI actually attempts to do. AI workers themselves have recently taken time to carefully consider the overall purpose of their studies. (Cf. Newell, 1973; also the papers by Schank, Pylyshyn, and Lehnert in this volume). It will be useful for us to take a brief look at the constellation of activities which relate to the heading, 'artificial intelligence'. The taxonomy that I would like to propose includes the following four divisions: (a) AI technology; (b) AI simulation; (c) AI modelling; and (d) AI theory. Though terms like 'modelling' and 'simulation' have been used extensively in AI literature, they have yet to be canonically distinguished in a way which is agreeable to everyone. The meanings which I shall assign to these terms should not be understood as their prevailing usage, either inside or outside of the AI community. (Pylyshyn and Simon, for example, offer alternative descriptions; Cf. their papers, this volume).

(a) While the entire spectrum of electronic data processing may be described by the term 'artificial intelligence,' only a small portion of computer science is denoted by that term. The ascription of the title of AI is usually based on the nature of the task involved; pattern recognition of printed characters counts as AI, cataloguing payroll checks does not. There is no precise criterion for deciding whether or not a particular computer system is an AI system, but the rule-of-thumb is that anything which would require human mental processes is an example of AI. The definition of 'human mental processes' is purposely left open to draw attention to the time-dependency of the criterion.

Traditionally, the category has been satisfied by projects for game-playing, pattern recognition, problem solving, theorem proving, and the like. The salient feature of AI, in the broadest sense of the term, is that a computer system is developed which is capable of performing in an intelligent fashion. The task which it performs need not be one which is typically performed by humans; its internal data structures need not be analogous to human psychological structures; and its operating principles need not shed light on the theory of human intelligence.

A program such as DENDRAL (Buchanan, Sutherland, Feigenbaum, 1969), which is used in the chemical analysis of mass spectrograms, is clearly an example of artificial intelligence technology, despite the fact that it neither derives from nor explains any special human psychological processes.

When a system demonstrates intelligent behaviour, irrespective of whether its data structures relate in any way to human data structures or whether its tasks relate in any way to ordinary human capacities, we may designate that system as a piece of AI technology, *per se*. Since there is no claim being made that AI technology resembles or describes human processes, there can be no criticism *vis-a-vis* its bearing on psychology. AI technology is a purely pragmatic undertaking and must be judged in the same way that any technology is judged—on pragmatic criteria of reliability, versatility, and cost-effectiveness. We may also note that while the success of AI technology may provide support for the claims of AI theory, the opposite is not true. A failure of AI technology cannot serve as evidence for the invalidity of AI theory any more than a failure of a particular automotive design can undermine a principle of autodynamics. This evidential asymmetry is especially important since so many of the criticisms of AI theory have been based on the results of projects in AI technology. Arguments of this sort may be grouped with the classic, 'if man were meant to fly he would have been born with wings' argument.

(b) The second category of AI is one which I call simulation. Unlike AI technology, AI simulation (as the name indicates) does make a claim to resemblance, in this case resemblance to human beings. The easiest way to classify simulation is on the basis of a similarity in the overt behaviour of a computer system and a person.

When AI first became a technological reality, many people were swept away with its awesome potential. While some computer scientists worked feverishly to create robot missile guidance systems and other instruments of power and destruction, a few provided a pleasant counterpoint by developing programs to play checkers, chess, backgammon, go, nim, and other delightful games. Many of the classic AI techniques such as tree generation and pruning were developed as a result of such programs, although the programs themselves were not intended to fulfill any special pragmatic demands. Simulations such as these suggested the possibility of exploring human cognitive processes but, by and large, they were more concerned with exhibiting humanlike behaviour than they were with capturing human thought. The point of developing such simulations was, in most cases, simply to demonstrate the capacity for computer intelligence. We may identify these as *demonstrative simulations*.

Researchers like Reitman (1965), Loehlin (1968), and Feigenbaum (1961), also constructed computer simulations, but with a different emphasis. Instead of simulating game-playing behaviour, they attempted to simulate broad cognitive abilities or personality traits, for the purpose of investigating human psychology. We may refer to such programs as *investigative simulations*. The earmark of an investigative simulation is that it moves from object to theory, rather than vice-versa. To produce such a simulation, one begins by observing the overt behaviour, the input and output, of a particular system. Once the gross input-output relations have been defined, the researcher sets out to create a system of structures and processes which will reproduce the behaviour. After suitable testing and modifications a simulation may be reached. The researcher then hypothesizes that the internal structures of the simulation are the same as, or similar to, the internal structures of the object modelled. A second investigative function involves the extension of the simulation to cover novel inputs for the purpose of predicting as-yet-unrealised behaviour.

Investigative simulations are quite common in scientific inquiry and existed long before the advent of artificial intelligence. Many of us are familiar with three-dimensional simulations of geostrata, micro-particles, and the like. The computerized investigative simulation is essentially the same as other such simulations, with the sole difference that it is uniquely applicable to the simulation of cognitive or intelligent behaviour.

(c) In contrast to the investigative simulation, we have the AI model, which moves primarily from theory to object. While both forms of simulation involve the construction of internal data structures and routines, neither places primary emphasis on these components. By its very nature, a simulation is concerned with similarity of appearance, i.e. of finished product or overt behaviour. The more closely the behaviour of the computer and the person match, the better the simulation. Within the narrow parameters of behaviour definition, Feigenbaum's EPAM and Newell and Simon's GPS (1963) were excellent simulations because they did indeed exhibit human like, intelligent behaviour.

A computer AI model, on the other hand, is primarily concerned with internal components, rather than overt behaviour. The finished product need resemble human behaviour, in none but the most abstract ways, so long as the data structures, internal states, and information processes provide a coherent and plausible model of the way people think. Such modelling has been extensively undertaken by researchers like Neisser (1967; 1976), Norman (1969), Colby (1973), Hunt (1973) and many others.

AI modelling is frequently identified with cognitive psychology, or as a branch of cognitive psychology, for obvious reasons. Many, if not most of the scientists who indulge in AI modelling are cognitive psychologists rather than computer scientists. The idiom, in both cases, is the same; that is, the terms used to frame theoretical statements belong to the vocabulary of information-processing. We may, however, draw a distinction between them: Since AI modelling moves from theory to object, there is no conceptual necessity which demands the use of the computer. As far as the cognitive idiom is concerned, as Neisser points out (1976: 103) even Freud's psychoanalytic theory includes 'flow charts on which the locations of Conscious, Unconscious, and Pre-Conscious are clearly marked'. In principle, at least, cognitive psychology could proceed without any appeal to AI models. In fact, many cognitivist theories are presented without mention of computers.

For many problems in cognitive psychology, however, the computer is an indispensable methodological tool. In order to adequately represent, manipulate, and explore the numerous factors pertinent to a particular facet of intelligent behaviour, the researcher must utilize the power of the computer. A mathematical, verbal, or visual model is simply incapable of handling the complexity of cognitive processing in a manner which is at all useful to the researcher. Thus, although we may distinguish between the study of cognitive psychology and AI modelling, we can see that the two are intimately related.

(d) The fourth area of research may be termed *AI theory*. Consider the definition of artificial intelligence which was recently given by Patrick Winston of MIT (Wilson, 1977: 1):

> The central goals of Artificial Intelligence are to make computers more useful and to understand the principles which make intelligence possible.

Note that there is no mention whatever of human psychology, cognitive models, or the like. Although, Winston later suggests that the study of artificial intelligence may supply important contributions to philosophy, psychology, and linguistics, he does not include the goals of those disciplines within the scope of AI proper. The only goals which are explicitly stated are: (a) the goal already identified as that of AI technology, viz., making computers more useful; and (b) the goal of understanding the principles which make intelligence possible.

The latter half of Winston's definition sounds remarkably similar to the definition of epistemology, especially as conceived by philosophers such as Whitehead and Kant. In epistemology, the study of the 'pure principles of knowledge' frequently results in some categorical scheme of analysis. Is AI theory after the same sort of thing? Not exactly.

The fundamental principles sought by AI theorists, though general in comparison to the programming principles of computer science *per se,* are somewhat less abstract than the principles traditionally sought by philosophers. The difference may arise from the fact that philosophers are concerned with a static representation of knowledge, whereas AI researchers are concerned with a dynamic one. This distinction may raise a few eyebrows since, it can be argued, *all* representations are, by definition, static. What I wish to emphasize, by using the terms 'static' and 'dynamic' is the fact that AI theorists are interested in principles of knowlege and intelligence which may be used to account for concrete, physically-instantiated, time- and perspective-dependent, cognition. Typically, philosophers have eschewed such elements in their quest for an epistemology which was 'ideal' in an almost Platonic sort of way. Despite this difference, the two studies are mutually informative and clearly share a number of theoretical interests.

The development of AI theory does not, of course, proceed in a vacuum; in fact, it is firmly embedded within the fabric of AI technology, AI simulation, and AI modelling. The distinguishing characteristic of AI theory, however, is its tendency towards conceptualization rather than implementation. An example of such theorizing would be Arbib's account of the 'slide-box metaphor' (Arbib, 1972) or Schank's 'conceptual dependency relations' (Schank, 1972), or Winograd's approach to natural language (Winograd, 1972), or best of all, Minsky's theory of 'frames' (Minsky, 1975). Although each of these examples has been given expression in a working computer system, they each represent a step towards an explicit theory of intelligence, rather than a contribution to programming techniques. They serve, as it were, to *guide* the development of such techniques in much the same way that a principle of physics guides the selection of a methodology for controlling atomic reactions.

The question may be raised, of course, as to the validity of calling this a theory of intelligence rather than a theory of human intelligence. Can a framework such as Schank's conceptual dependency relations (Cf. Schank's paper, this volume) give us any insight into other than human behaviour? This is a deceptively difficult question to answer for it demands that we extend our theory to domains where there are clearly no prima-facie grounds for empirical testing. Insofar as human beings are the only creatures we know of who possess complex natural languages, any theory of language comprehension which we construct will, *ipso facto*, pertain exclusively to humans. To argue in this way, however, is to confuse the grounds of theoretical plausibility with the grounds for verification. Given the definition of 'intelligence' as the capacity of a system or organism to successfully adapt its behaviour to attain its goals, we may apply the principles established by AI to any system, real or imagined, which we would, *a priori*, identify as intelligent and/or language using. The question then turns on whether or not we can ascribe intrinsic goals to systems other than ourselves since, after all, we tend to perceive the behaviour of all systems through the rigid perspective of human desires and purposes.

This problem is one which has already drawn a considerable amount of attention in philosophy (Cf. Dennett, 1971 for an incisive treatment of the matter). The most promising way of handling the question is to note the difference between ascription and discovery. To claim that we have discovered the intrinsic goals of a system is to say that we are somehow privy to that system's cognitive and motivational perspective. When we speak in terms of ascriptions, however, we are making the weaker claim that, for the purposes of explanation, we have assessed the motives and desires of a system according to the criteria of consistency, coherence, and observational accuracy. The problem of discovery may be avoided with a courteous tip of the hat to the metaphysician. Opting for ascriptions, however, does not totally eliminate our worries; we are still faced with a very pressing methodological demand to establish criteria for distinguishing appropriate ascriptions from inappropriate ones. Ascriptions based wholly on coarse, behavioural analogues could easily result in absurdities reminiscent of childhood misconceptions or the worst science fiction films. (One sparkling example of misguided goal descriptions was recently suggested to me by my niece, who observed that aeroplanes land at airports in order to rest and have a bite to eat.)

The investigation of the criteria for appropriate goal descriptions is a problem for the philosophy of science and I shall have more to say about it shortly. Assuming that we can give a satisfactory answer to the question of goal ascriptions, we may conclude that it is plausible to speak in terms of a theory of pure intelligence, rather than a theory of human intelligence. Notions such as Schank's 'scripts' and 'plans', Minsky's 'frames' or Newell's 'productions' (Newell, 1973(a)) may be legitimately construed as components of a pure theory of intelligent and linguistic behaviour which, when mature, will *subsume* the theory of human intelligence.

It should also be evident that the quest for these notions indicates an interest in concepts rather than techniques and marks the transition of AI from a technology to a science. While future work in AI will no doubt include the entire spectrum of demonstrative simulations, investigative simulations, cognitive models, and practical implementations, the long-term scientific impact will be the result chiefly of AI theory.

INTERACTIONS OF PHILOSOPHY AND ARTIFICIAL INTELLIGENCE

Though co-operation between philosophy and artificial intelligence has already yielded interesting offspring, the marriage of the two is barely past the honeymoon. Much remains to be done. Dennett's paper, in this volume, provides an excellent 'travel guide to philosophers' who are interested in AI. I shall therefore limit my remarks to a general outline of the philosophy/artificial intelligence interface. The issues which are of interdisciplinary concern may be categorized as (a) methodological, (b) logical, and (c) epistemological.

(a) A methodological problem which I have already touched on pertains to the explanatory status of investigative simulations. In dealing with cognitive processes, we are faced with a 'black-box' situation, i.e., we have no direct-observation access to the internal states, structures, and processes of cognition. Typically, in a black-box situation, a theory which is derived from a simulation must be verified indirectly by means of inference-testing, predictive power, consistency, economy, versatility, and coherence with other theories.

As Fodor (1968) points out, however, the validation of a cognitive simulation is extremely tricky since it presupposes that we have the means to identify and compare individual cognitive processes in people and computers. It is in no way clear that we have, or may expect to have in the near future, the capacity to isolate individual cognitive processes at any but the coarsest level of analysis. Once we begin to explore detailed areas of complex intelligent behaviour, we begin to lose touch with the behavioural barometers which are available to us at a lower level of resolution. This is precisely the sort of problem confronted by Ernst and Newell (1969) when they attempted to verify the data structures of GPS by appealing to verbal protocols of human subjects. Except for sketchy and dubious introspective statements by students performing GPS-type tasks, Ernst and Newell could assemble little empirical evidence to support the thesis that the structures and processes of GPS were representative of human structures and processes.

While the lack of evidence does not automatically disqualify a simulation like GPS, it does make verification extremely difficult, if not actually impossible. The difficulty with a GPS-type simulation is that it deals with high-resolution analysis in what amounts to virgin territory; we have no way of anchoring the resultant theory to a theory which has been previously established. This problem attends all simulations which focus on high-resolution analyses of isolated cognitive processes. It is as if we were trying to discover the proper orientation of a single piece of a jig-saw puzzle without being able to associate it with the other pieces. Thus far, we are barely able to construct the outside border; isolated tasks such as problem solving or letter recognition lie somewhere in the centre of the puzzle.

A second problem, closely related to the first, is frequently referred to as the 'grain problem.' By their very nature, both simulations and models must be simpler than the objects which they seek to represent. The requirement of simplicity, however, must be met with a criterion for determining the relative explanatory power of the representation. If we increase the simplicity of a model beyond a certain point we begin to lose sight of vital elements of the target object which we are seeking to explain. This is what happens, for example, when we attempt to model complex human emotions such as love, hate, and fear by means of rigid algebraic transformation rules (Cf. Loehlin, 1968).

Leaving the grain of a cognitive model unspecified may result in the sort of objection raised by Dreyfus (1972: see also his paper, this volume) concerning the distinction between analogue and digital computation. Since nearly all cognitive simulations and models are generated on digital computers, the processes which are involved utilize discrete information states and sequential programming. Dreyfus points out, however, that there is evidence, from both psychology and neurophysiology, that the human brain acts as an analogue computer, utilizing continuous operations and parallel programming structures. He argues, therefore, that the simulations and models of artificial intelligence must necessarily be off-target. Dreyfus is misled in his belief that a digital computer cannot produce a model of an analogue device (Cf. Pylyshyn, 1974), but his criticism is effective in drawing attention to the fact that no guidelines have been set to distinguish between those features of a model which are essential and those which are accidental. (For a closer look at this and related problems, Cf. Pylyshyn's paper, this volume).

A third methodological problem pertains to the status and expression of AI principles. It has now become commonplace for AI researchers to point to computer programs as statements of theory (Cf. Weizenbaum, 1976; T. Simon's paper, this volume). Two questions which we may ask are: (i) In what sense is a program a theory? and (ii) What are the logical relations which connect the elements of such a theory to one another? To construe a program as a theory is to classify it with symbolic structures such as mathematical formulae in phsyics. Typically, however, mathematical formulae are thought to express laws or other nomic generalizations; it can be debated whether or not the instructions of a computer program are, in this important sense, general enough to constitute the statement of a theory.

We may also wonder about the logic of theories stated as computer programs. While formulae in physics represent entities having causal connections and intentional 'rules' represent entities having rational relations, the entities of artificial intelligence, viz., data structures, semantic nets, frames, and so forth, do not clearly relate to each other in either of these ways. Assessing the validity of inferences based on such constructs requires a better understanding of the logical status of AI principles.

(b) A second area of mutual interest has to do with the formal representation of knowledge. Although logicians have traditionally concerned themselves with the problem of evaluating the validity of arguments form and axiomatic reasoning, their efforts have produced a sophisticated network of formal symbolisms. As I mentioned earlier, the representation of knowledge, as pursued by the philosopher, generally ignores the problems associated with physical instantiation, degradation through time, and individual perspective; nevertheless, it provides a rich source of ideas about how to formalize objects and events in the world.

To a large extent, the task of the AI technologist is to discover strategies for creating economical yet versatile information structures. Thus far, philosophers of logic have paid little attention to this aspect of artificial intelligence; the reverse, however, is not true. AI workers have long been aware of the work done in formal logic and have freely exploited this material in the development of AI languages, representational schemes and inference techniques. (Cf. McCarthy's paper, this volume). Presumably a joint effort of logicians and AI researchers would lead to powerful new methods of symbolic representation.

(c) The third junction of philosophy and artificial intelligence is the interface of epistemology and AI as pure theory. In order to give coherence to the science of artificial intelligence we must map out a set of reasonable objectives and relate them to each other in a useful way. While it may be accurate to say that the overriding goal of AI is to create an artificial system which will equal or surpass a human being in intelligence (Weizenbaum, 1976: 202), such a definition gives us little insight into the steps which must be taken in order to reach this goal. If we are to make any headway in this direction it is vital that we first identify the signs which point the way. What are these signs? Nearly three decades ago, John Von Neumann responded to a claim made about the limitations of machine intelligence by saying that the only real limitation to machine intelligence rested with man's ability (or inability) to precisely specify the mental processes that he wished to duplicate. Once we have a definite idea of what we are looking for, the task of replicating it with a computer is relatively easy.

The signs we need are precise specifications of the meaning of terms relating to intelligence. If a machine is built to simulate recognition, for example, we must first have a clear idea of what recognition is, and be able to distinguish it from 'classification' and 'identification' (Sayre, 1965). If we wish to build a system capable of natural language use, we must be sensitive to distinctions such as that of language *production* versus language *comprehension* (Cf. Straight, 1976).

The analysis of the meaning of these terms is the task of

epistemology. (See the papers by McCarthy and Sayre, this volume). Philosophers come heavily armed to the problem of semantic analysis, having trained to do battle with words for two and a half millenia. Among the most interesting problems which present themselves are the analyses of so-called 'intentional terms.' (Cf. Ringle, 1977).

When we analyze the behaviour of an intelligent machine we frequently employ the logic of intentional explanation and speak in terms of the machine's goals, its cognitions, and so forth (Dennett, 1971). Occasionally, we lapse into the full-blown intentional usage of purposes, beliefs, wants, and desires. While it now seems plausible to speak of the goals and cognitions of AI systems, there is a lingering uneasiness about using words like 'purpose,' 'belief,' 'hope,' 'aspiration,' 'fear,' 'desire,' and the like. Though familiarity with an operating AI system may reduce one's trepidation for mentalistic ascriptions, there are still substantial doubts as to the appropriateness of such examples as describing a computer's behaviour as the result of its 'hatred' for a particular learning task.

If we admit that it is legitimate to describe certain computer systems in the intentional idiom, we may sensibly ask: What additional requirements (*vis-a-vis* system capacities) would need to be added in order for us to consent to the use of the full-blown intentional vocabulary? To say, as Gunderson (1971) and Dreyfus (1972) have, that certain mental traits are program resistant, depending as they do on a protoplasmic body, avoids rather than answers the question. If bodies, indeed, are essential to certain mental attributes, what aspects of bodies are relevant and how may we conceptualize these aspects? Thus far, no hard argumentation has spelled out what it is about bodies (or for that matter, humans in general) that supplies the essential ingredients accountable for program resistant mental traits. To say, for example, that *purpose* depends on the existence of *desire*, which in turn depends on *sentience*, which in turn requires a protoplasmic body is merely to postpone the critical analysis. An investigation of this sort of chain, in the context of AI systems, may at last shed some light on the privileged character of (human) intentional descriptions. In the long run, we may anticipate a radical integration of analyses and AI models which will yield a coherent picture of intelligence and perhaps point the way to a comprehensive theory of consciousness as well.

REFERENCES

Arbib, M. *The Metaphorical Brain*, New York (Wiley-Interscience 1972)

Boden, M. *Artificial Intelligence and Natural Man*, New York (Basic Bks. 1977)

Buchanan, B., Sutherland, G., Feigenbaum, E. 'Heuristic DENDRAL: A program for generating explanatory hypotheses in organic chemistry'. *Machine Intelligence*, V. 4. New York (American Elsevier 1969).

Colby, K. 'Simulation of belief systems'. In R. Schank (ed) *Computer Models of Thought and Language*, San Francisco (Freeman & Co. 1973) 251-286.

Davis, R. King. J. 'An overview of production systems', Stanford University Artificial Intelligence Laboratory Memo 271 (1975)

Dennett, D. 'Intentional systems', *Journal of Philosophy*, 68 (1971) 87-106.

Dennett, D. *Content and consciousness*, New York (Humanities Press 1969).

Dreyfus, H. *What Computers Can't Do*, New York (Harper and Row, 1972).

Dreyfus, H. 'Why computers must have bodies in order to be intelligent', *Review of Metaphysics* 21 (1967) 13-32

Dreyfus, H. 'Alchemy and Artificial Intelligence', Rand Paper, P-3244 (1965).

Ernst, G., Newell, A. *GPS: A case study in generality and problem solving*, New York (Academic Press 1969).

Feigenbaum, E. 'The simulation of verbal learning behavior', Proceedings of the Western Joint Computer Conference, 19 (1961) 121-132.

Fodor, J. *Psychological Explanation*, New York (Random House 1968).

Gunderson, K. *Mentality and Machines*, New York (Doubleday, 1971).

Hamlyn, D. *The Psychology of Perception*, New York (Humanities Press 1957).

Hunt, E. 'The memory we must have', in R. Schank (ed) *Computer Models of Thought and Language*, San Francisco (Freeman 1973), 343-371.

Lehnert, W. *The process of question answering*, Ph. D. Thesis, Department of Computer Science, Yale University (1977).

Loehlin, J. *Computer models of personality*, New York (Random House, 1968).

MacKay, D. 'From mechanism to mind', in J.R. Smythies (ed) *Brain and mind*, New York (Humanities Press 1965) 163-200.

McCarthy, J., Hayes, P. (1969) 'Some philosophical problems from the standpoint of artificial intelligence', *Machine Intelligence*, V. 4, New York (Elsevier, 1969).

Minsky, M. 'A framework for representing knowledge', In P. Winston (ed) *The psychology of computer vision*, New York (McGraw Hill, 1975).

Minsky, M. 'Matter, mind and models', In M. Minsky (ed) *Semantic information processing*, Cambridge, Mass. (MIT Press, 1968).

Mischel, T. (1963) 'Psychology and explanations of human behavior'. In N. Care and C. Landesman (eds) *Readings in the theory of action* (Indiana University Press, 1963).

Neisser, U. *Cognition and reality*, San Francisco (Freeman, 1976).

Neisser, U. *Cognitive psychology*, New Jersey (Prentice-Hall, 1965).

Newell, A. 'Artificial intelligence and the concept of mind'. In R. Schank (ed) *Computer models of thought and language*, San Francisco (Freeman 1973) 1-60.

Newell, A. 'Production systems: models of control structures'. In W. Chase (ed) *Visual information processing*, New York (Academic Press, 1973)

Newell, A., Simon, H. 'GPS: A program that simulates human thought'. In E. Feigenbaum and J. Feldman (eds) *Computers and thought*, New York (McGraw-Hill, 1963).

Norman, D. *Memory and Attention*, New Jersey (Wiley-Interscience, 1969).

Putnam, H. 'Minds and machines'. In S. Hook (ed) *Dimensions of mind* (1960) 138-164.

Pylyshyn, Z. 'Minds, machines and phenomenology', *Cognition*, 3 (1974) 57-77.

Raphael, B. *The thinking computer*, San Francisco (Freeman, 1976).

Reitman, W. *Cognition and thought*, New York (Wiley-Interscience, 1965).

Ringle, M. 'Intentionality and seld-modelling'. (Forthcoming) Proceedings of the Society for the Interdisciplinary Study of the Mind, V.2. (1978).

Sayre, K. *Cybernetics and the Philosophy of Mind*, New York, (Humanities Press, 1976).

Sayre, K. *Consciousness*, Mass. (Peter Smith Publ., 1969).

Sayre, K. *Recognition*, Indiana (University of Notre Dame Press, 1965).

Schank, R. 'Conceptual dependency: a theory of natural language understanding', *Cognitive Psychology*, 3 (1972) 552-631.

Scriven, M. The mechanical concept of mind'. Reprinted in A. Anderson (ed) *Minds and machines*, New Jersey, (Prentice-Hall (1953) 31-42.

Straight, S. 'Comprehension vs. production in linguistic theory', *Foundations of Language*, 14 (1976) 525-540.

Taylor, R. *Action and purpose*, New Jersey (Prentice-Hall, 1966).

Turing, A. 'Computing machinery and Intelligence'. Reprinted in A. Anderson (ed) *Minds and machines*, New Jersey (Prentice-Hall, (1950) 4-30.

Weizenbaum, J. *Computer power and human reason*, San Francisco

(Freeman, 1976).

Winograd, T. 'Frame representations and the declarative-procedural controversy'. In D. Bobrow and A. Collins (eds) *Representation and understanding.* New York, (Academic Press, 1975).

Winograd, T. *Understanding natural language,* New York (Academic Press, 1972).

Winston, P. *Artificial Intelligence,* Mass. (Addison-Wesley, 1977).

Ziff, P. 'The feelings of robots'. In A. Anderson, (ed) *Minds and machines*, New Jersey (Prentice-Hall (1964) 98-103.

PART II
THE DEVELOPMENT OF AI THEORY

CHAPTER 2

COMPLEXITY AND THE STUDY OF ARTIFICIAL AND HUMAN INTELLIGENCE
Zenon W. Pylyshyn

The process of understanding and expressing our understanding is analagous to the process of creating a work of art such as a sculpture. In both cases there are three major elements that play an important role: the imagination and the tension in the creator, the nature of the tools he uses (which includes his skill in using them), and the resistance offered by the materials he has chosen. A sharp knife on soft wood will result in a very different process and a very different product than a massive chisel on a granite block. The materials have a grain and a texture which results in different tools yielding quite different effects.

So it is also in intellectual pursuits. A brilliant man tackling the world with only his eyes and ears and the concepts which his native tongue has given him will proceed to carve up his experiences in a very different way from a person equipped with the tools of a technological culture even though the world may in some sense be the same in both cases.

Conceptual tools dominate periods of progress. Susanne Langer (1962) puts it this way:

> In every age, philosophical thinking exploits some dominant concepts and makes its greatest headway in solving problems conceived in terms of them. The seventeenth- and eighteenth-century philosophers construed knowledge, knower, and known in terms of sense data and their association. Descartes' self-examination gave classical psychology *the mind and its contents* as a starting point. Locke set up sensory immediacy as the new criterion of the real. . . Hobbes provided the genetic method of building up complex ideas from simple ones. . . and, in another quarter, still true to the Hobbesian method, Pavlov built intellect out of conditioned reflexes and Loeb built life out of tropisms. (p 54)

History may well record that towards the middle of the twentieth century many classical problems of philosophy and psychology took on renewed interest and vigour with the emergence of a new (and not yet well understood) notion of *mechanism*. While the development of this notion has many roots within philosophy (especially in studies of the foundations of mathematics by Alonzo Church and others) the major milestone was probably the formalization of the idea of *computation* by Alan Turing in 1936. This work, in a sense, marked the beginning of the study of cognitive activity from an abstract point of view, divorced in principle from both biological and phenomenological foundations. It provided a reference point for the scientific ideal of a mechanistic process which could be understood without raising the spectre of vital forces or elusive homunculi, but which at the same time was sufficiently rich to cover every conceivable informal notion of mechanism. (That the Turing formulation does cover all such notions is, of course, not provable but it has withstood all attempts to find exceptions. The belief that it does cover all possible cases of mechanism has become known as the Church-Turing thesis.) It would be difficult to overestimate the importance of this development for psychology. It represents the emergence of a new level of analysis, which is independent of physics, yet is mechanistic in spirit. It makes possible a science of structure and function divorced from material substance, while at the same time avoids the retreat to behaviouristic peripheralism. It speaks the language of mental structures and of internal processes, thus lending itself to answering questions traditionally posed by psychologists.

While Turing and other mathematicians, logicians and philosophers laid the foundations for the abstract study of cognition in the 30s and 40s it was only in the last twenty or so years that this idea began to be articulated in a much more specific and detailed form: A form which lends itself more directly to attacking certain basic questions of cognitive psychology. This newer direction has grown with the continuing development of our understanding of the nature of computational processes and of the digital computer as a general, symbol-processing system. It has lead to the formation of a new intellectual discipline known as artificial intelligence, which attempts to understand the nature of intelligence by designing computational systems which exhibit it.

In spite of its apparent preoccupation with the engineering task of building intelligent systems, I believe that the field of AI is co-extensive with the field of cognitive psychology. What I mean by this is that as intellectual disciplines (not applied technologies) they both are concerned with the same problems and will stand or fall together because the same criteria of success must ultimately adjudicate them both. The final judgement which both must face is the extent to which they lead to a better understanding of the nature of intelligence, and the trial rules are those which govern any scientific enterprise. In both cases the meaning of the term intelligence and the rules of evidence will invariably drift as the science progresses. Nevertheless 'intelligence' will continue to have meaning only with reference to human goals and purposes and 'evidence' will continue to refer to that delicate balance between the rationally conceivable and the empirically demonstrable which characterizes evidence elsewhere in science.

Yet in spite of the almost complete overlap in their ultimate goals there are significant differences between the two disciplines which I will examine later. They derive from the priorities which the disciplines attach to different constraints on systems and to differences in their tolerance for various kinds of gaps and incompleteness. In other words they differ largely in the way in which they judge partial solutions to the problems of intelligence. In spite of these differences, however, I believe that AI is just the medicine that cognitive psychology needs at this stage in its development. My faith that artificial intelligence research will provide the fruitful conceptual approach to cognitive psychology is based on the following general observations:

(1) The delicate balance between rational systems and empirical observations which is the hallmark of mature science has been absent in much of psychology. I will not stop to speculate on why this is so since it is a matter of history. But among the consequences of this is that psychology is splintered with micro-models for phenomena which are so narrow that in many cases they are confined to a single experimental procedure. The discipline is largely paradigm-driven, rather than being guided

by major theoretical systems. Without such larger, formally structured systems the local puzzle-solving activities lack a convergent direction and may in fact degenerate into what in AI terms could be characterized as a hill climbing task dominated by local maxima. A piece-meal approach is hazardous because, as Allen Newell (1973(a)) has pointed out with characteristic insight 'You can't play twenty questions with nature and win'.

(2) My second point is related. As a poor cousin to physics, psychology is very much concerned with rigour, lest it be entrapped by the tyranny of words which often besets pre-scientific enterprises. But just as there are two sources of understanding, the empirical and the rational, so there are two corresponding *loci* of rigour. One can be rigorous by operationally defining one's constructs and sticking close to the experimental data. One can also be rigorous by ensuring that one's theoretical ideas are complete, consistent and logically sound. One can then try to capture one's intuitions and bring everyday knowledge to bear on the development of theoretical ideas with some confidence that they are neither incoherent nor contradictory, and furthermore with some way of exploring what they entail. The point is that there are better and worse places for introducing rigour into an evolving discipline. My own feeling is that we already know such a tremendous amount about human cognition which we cannot begin to account for by our mini-theories that a more top-down strategy, such as that which is characteristic of AI, is more appropriate at the present stage. One of the benefits of such an approach may be that we may then be in a position to ask better *empirical* questions.

(3) My third observation is that there is a growing feeling, not only among those working in AI but also among more enlightened experimental psychologists, that the study of intelligence cannot be decomposed along such traditional lines as those which, say, mark off typical elementary textbook chapter headings, e.g. sensation, perception, learning, memory, comprehension, reasoning, motivation, and so on. This is not to imply that we cannot usefully study problems which fall into these traditional areas. What I mean is that the way in which phenomena are described in these subdisciplines gives no indication of (and indeed often impedes the understanding of) the way in which such phenomena contribute to producing

intelligent behaviour. There is a growing suspicion that to understand the integration of cognitive acitivity we shall have to redraw the boundaries around such notions as, say, learning, comprehension and memory.

What I propose to do is to examine some of the ways in which the complexity associated with problems of intelligence can be carved up. I am going to be very sketchy because I want to try and paint a picture of the larger territory, bringing in some of the insights and problems of AI to suggest some alternative ways of casting questions about intelligence. I will consider three general categories of problems dealing with the nature of complexity. I refer to these as (1) the problem of the allocation of complexity—or the *organization* issue, (2) the problem of the allocation of responsibility—or the *control* issue, and (3) the problem of the allocation of constraints—or the *validation* issue.

ALLOCATION OF COMPLEXITY

Consider an obvious way of carving up the domain of study in AI and psychology depicted in Figure 1. In this scheme we can choose to attribute the complexity associated with problems of cognition in various ways at each level of the partitioning. Thus, for example, J.J. Gibson has devoted many years of study to showing that it is possible to conceptualize the problems of perception so that most of the complexity is associated not with the organism but with the organization of the environment. In particular he has argued that there are principles of what he calls 'ecological optics' which provide the organism with all the information it needs to apprehend the world as a three dimensional 'layout' without the need to postulate powerful inference processes taking place in the organism. This information is to be found in what Gibson (1966) refers to as 'timeless formless invariants' which the active organism is atuned to pick up from the patterns of covariation in the proximal stimulus. His is a theory of the preconditions for perception and I believe has been quite effective in disturbing the traditional partitioning of complexity between organism and environment. The problem with his theory is that it leaves too many unbound variables or place-holders for mechanisms about

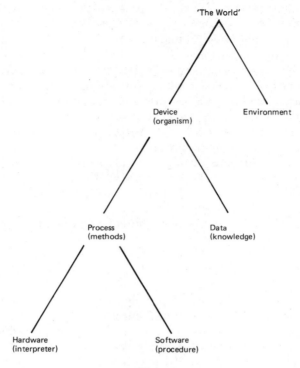

Fig. 1

which he has little to say, such as the nature of the all important 'information pickup' function.[2]

Simon's Compton lectures (1969) as well as Newell and Simon's (1972) book on human problem solving have also made an important contribution towards clarifying the issue of the assignment of complexity between organism and environment. They have argued that much of the complexity may be associated with the demands of the environment and that even a simple device might exhibit what appears to be complex behaviour by reacting in a simple manner to a complex environment.

There are other examples to illustrate that apparent complexity can often be shifted from organism to environment and we shall return to these in discussing the 'responsibility issue'.

On the next level down in Figure 1, the process-data distinction is really a very old one. It is related to the universal noun-verb distinction in language and to the function-argument distinction in mathematics and logic. It is not a distinction concerned with the intrinsic nature of a symbol but with the manner in which it functions at some particular instant. It is well known among computer scientists that there is a tradeoff between complexity of data structures and complexity of processes which access them. The precise nature of this tradeoff is not understood in general but the history of artificial intelligence shows that advances (especially in problem solving, computer graphics and information retrieval) have frequently been associated with new data structure organizations. In some cases the goal has been to build into the data structure, in an explicit manner, all the relevant aspects and to separate out those aspects which are invariant over typical transformations of the data from those which indicate changes. The concrete example of application of this principle is the use of ring structures to represent graphic information. The major structures in a ring are invariant over rotation, translation, change of scale, and attachment to other structures.

In other cases, such as in problem solving, a major task is to find a representation of the problem domain—or to discover a problem space—in which a simple procedure can be used to solve the problem. In this case 'simple' means available, familiar, or readily constructable from existing primitive operations.

In still other cases, such as in language comprehension systems, the problem may be one of elaborating a data structure which, in effect, anticipates the most likely uses to which the comprehension might be put, thus obviating the need for much deductive machinery which would otherwise need to be brought to bear at a later stage. This is the approach adopted by Roger Schank (this volume). It illustrates a principle which Newell refers to as 'natural intelligence' which, roughly speaking, goes something like this. In natural intelligence the dimension of problem difficulty is not uniform. The way in which the original problem is represented plus the primitive operations available define a class of problems which are trivial to the system: the solution can be read off the representation by the primitives.

Problems which are not in this class, however, require more powerful and specialized methods. As Moore and Newell (1974) put it, 'natural intelligence carries just a little way. To go further requires deliberate application of methods under the control of disciplined intention'. Thus, especially for the psychologist, the way in which one partitions the organism portion of the intelligence problem into data and process is critical. It should separate out a broad class of 'trivial' problems solvable by 'natural intelligence' from a class of more difficult problems which must be approached by generating more specialized and more deliberately 'problem solving' methods.[3]

Before turning to a discussion of the next dimension of complexity, that of control, I want to add a brief comment about the remaining distinction at the bottom of the tree in Figure 1. The belief that there is a clear distinction between hardware and software in computers has caused needless confusion— especially among psychologists but also among computer people. Because the mapping between algorithms and one physical device (a computer) is rather different from that between algorithms and another physical device (a brain) people are often reluctant to extend the same ontological status to the algorithms in the two cases. I believe the difficulty is a cultural one and stems in large part from too concrete a view of computers. In the regress of procedures to interpret procedures to interpret procedures etc., there is a point in the machine case where we invariably switch our descriptive vocabulary from the language of procedures to the language of electronics. But, except for the person designing hardware or operating systems, the point at which we stop talking about interpreters and talk about machines is dictated by convenience. It is much more appropriate to stop at the point below which the structures are not accessible to the programmer (which may be at the level of LISP) and call the rest the 'virtual machine'. This is good computer science practice. If we did this routinely the parallels between human and machine case would be more apparent. In both cases we should have a device whose construction was unknown but whose behaviour could be exhibited and modified in rather similar ways.

If we take this approach it becomes appropriate to ask about the nature of the human 'virtual machine': What processes can be considered primitive? How can the machine be programmed? and so on. It is still an open question whether there can be a single 'virtual machine' level useful for all aspects of human behaviour or whether for global behaviour (say social interactions) a different virtual machine should be postulated than when we are dealing with more elementary processes such as short-term memory. There are those who believe that there is indeed a unique virtual machine which can be programmed for a wide range of behaviour and that describing this machine in terms of a 'psychological programming language' is one of the tasks of cognitive psychology. This view is developed at length in Pylyshyn (in preparation).

ALLOCATION OF RESPONSIBILITY: THE CONTROL ISSUE

There is another closely related aspect of the organization of complex systems which has become a focus of study in computer science, yet has had very little impact in psychology. Let us start by introducing it in historical perspective.

A major breakthrough in understanding the nature of control was the articulation of the idea of feedback through the environment. Thus a certain relational balance was restored between a device or organism and its environment. Although only the device is credited with having a goal, the responsibility for its behaviour is shared. At times when the environment is passive the initiative appears to come primarily from the device, while at other times the environment appears to intervene and the initiative seems to go in the opposite direction. However, the idea of control flowing or changing its locus did not become commonplace until the advent of computers. Here the sequencing of instructions made the notion of flow of control quite natural, while branch instructions made it equally natural to think of passing control. By combining control-passing with a primitive message-passing (the message might be nothing more than the identity of the former locus of control) the idea of subroutines and hence of hierarchy of control was born. It soon became one of the most powerful conceptual tools for organizing complex processes. The subroutine notion was distilled by

Miller, Galanter, and Pribram (1960) who called it a TOTE unit and offered it to the psychological community as a new unit of analysis to replace the ubiquitous reflex arc. This idea has been influencial in shaping psychologists' thinking about cognition.

There are several good reasons why a hierarchical system of control is such a powerful concept (many of these are discussed by Simon, 1969). One of the main advantages of hierarchical organization of control is partial decomposability of the total system. By limiting the interactions between routine and subroutine—both in terms of messages exchanged and conditions for passing control—it becomes easier to add, modify, and understand the tasks being done. Furthermore, each subtree in the hierachy can be thought of as defining some subgoal so that we can descriibe the entire system as goal-directed. Passing control to a subroutine is equated with activating a subgoal and returning control becomes consumating a goal. So powerful an idea was this that its shortcomings were largely overlooked for many years.

However, as early as 1962, Newell recognised some of the sources of rigidity in such an organization (Newell, 1962). It encouraged minimal and rigidly prescribed communication between routine and subroutine. So long as the subroutine was a narrow specialist this worked well: if it was the subroutine whose job it was to compute square roots you could hand it control, give it a number and tell it 'come back here when you've done your thing with that number'. If the subroutine is not such a narrow specialist you might want to communicate the nature of the problem to it in more flexible terms. Furthermore you might want it to check back before committing the system to further major undertakings, to co-operate with other processes which may also be relevant to the task, to report its findings in a more flexible manner, especially if it failed to successfully consummate its goal, and you might even wish that the higher level routine could monitor what the subroutine was doing in some general manner to make sure it was not going astray. How to convert these anthropomorphically stated *desiderata* into mechanical form without bogging the system down in a bureaucracy of encoding and decoding of messages is one of the tasks to which the new generation of programming languages (PLANNER, CONNIVER, POPLER 1.5, QA4,

KRL) is addressed (see, for example, Bobrow and Raphael, 1974). From a psychological point of view, however, it is important to keep as much as possible of the process explicit (including the message-sending and control transfers) since these may have psychological implications. Although technical questions pertaining to how one could realize particular control structures are paramount for both AI and psychology, the psychologist has an additional responsibility to be wary of the way in which particular implementations tend to mould his perception of the problem. For this reason I wish to expose some general characteristics of the control problem. In doing this it is useful to make distinctions in terms of the locus of responsibility for such actions as transferring control and passing messages. In particular I wish to distinguish between giving away control—where the initiative is with the original locus or source, and capturing control, where the initiative is with the subsequent locus or consumer. Similarly, I want to distinguish between the case in which a message is sent specifically to one routine (or as I shall call it, 'module') and that in which it is sent simultaneously to all modules. I refer to the latter as broadcasting a message. A variety of different control structures may be distinguished on the basis of these two characteristics. For example, in the standard hierarchical sub-routine case, control is always given to a module and a message, containing parameters and a return address, sent to it. At the termination of that module control is again given back. In PLANNER-type languages a message, giving the goal or task requiring attention, is broadcast, then control is captured at the initiative of some module and subsequently sent to a prescribed point which depends on how the module terminates. In production systems a message is also broadcast, and control captured. But after the production is completed a message is again broadcast, control is usually not sent to a specific locus. I shall return to some of the implications of such control structures later. For now let us consider what these distinctions mean in terms of our more general analysis of complexity.

Remembering often consists of arranging the environment to trigger the appropriate processes at the appropriate times. We tie a knot in a handkerchief or set up unusual situations to act as very general reminders (really meta-reminders). While mnenomic cues such as those used to improve one's memory are usually content-oriented access keys, memories are often evoked by less specific signals from the environment. Such signals are more like interrupts in that the initiative for a capture of control originates outside of the currently active process—in fact outside of the organism. It might be useful to think of this allocation of responsibility to aspects of the environment as an even broader concept. There is a close parallel here with the allocation of complexity issue discussed earlier.

Consider a simple example. Suppose someone learns a set of household skills such as cooking, setting the table, cleaning up, and so on. Supposing, also, that in quite a different context he learns that a certain plate in his home is a delicate and valued hierloom. How does he bring these two types of knowledge together so that all his usual actions on kitchenware are moderated by a 'special case' warning where that dish is concerned? A possible, but impractical, answer is that when the person learns about the delicate dish, he modifies all his procedures which handle dishes (e.g. moving, washing, stacking) to test for whether that particular dish is about to be handled and branch accordingly. A slightly better way is to capitalize on the hierarchical structure of procedures and to identify a relevant primitive operation, such as grasping, and insert the test at that one point. There are several problems with this solution. The organization is rarely strictly hierarchical: Even if one could identify a single primitive module this module may not always be accessible for modification. It may have become compiled into some larger module which is not decomposable, such as a MACROPS in the STRIPS system. This is extremely common in human skill learning where larger units of skill become increasingly automated with practice. Furthermore, such an approach can result in complex primitive modules which spend most of their time testing. Even in the simple blocks world of Winograd's SHRDLU, (Winograd, 1972), the robot spends a very large proportion of its effort checking to see if it is holding something. Since modules like 'grasp' or 'move' can be called in any situation, the system cannot be sure that SHRDLU is not holding something at the time and hence the more primitive modules must keep checking.

A further improvement on these proposals might be achieved

by declaring a special object type, and putting all objects which could require special treatment into that type category. In that case only a single initial test is needed—to determine if the object is special. If it is, special processing would be done on it, otherwise the normal procedure would continue. But even this is not satisfactory in general since a single type will not suffice to determine where the tests ought to be inserted. On the other hand, increasing the number of types (e.g. delicate, hot, toxic) leads to either a proliferation of type-tests again or to the problem of adding new types. In fact, there are ways of dealing with the latter problem which are adopted by so-called extensible systems which we shall breifly mention below. For the present let me speak rather loosely and offer the following suggestion. Perhaps one ought to consider the responsibility for the special handling of the delicate dish to reside not with the organism but rather with the dish itself. In other words some partial recognition of that object (which must in any case precede an action upon it) would have the status of an interrupt rather than a test. The fundamental difference here is not in how these are implemented but rather in where the responsibility lies—whether control is given or captured.

Such anthropomorphic talk can be dangerous unless the details are filled out. In particular there is no point in interrupting a process unless the system knows (a) what qualifies as a legitimate interrupt (a system which does not know this will be too distractable to complete any task) and (b) what to do after it has been interrupted. We shall return to consider several approaches to distributed responsibility. But first let me point out that although notion of allocating responsibility to objects in the environment the same issue is at stake at the next level down in fig. 1. Here there is a question about the allocation of responsibility to data rather than process. This means loosening the hierarchical authority relation common to most programs, and distributing authority in a more democratic manner, allowing for 'local initiative'. Attempts to work out a balance between process-directed and data-directed procedure invocation is a major concern in the design of control structures for computational systems.

The distinction between data and procedures has been a flexible one since the development of symbol processing languages where a symbol can designate either a datum or an operation (or a structure of other symbols). Even in the early days of IPL systems such as EPAM, pieces of program code were linked into networks of data to be executed at the appropriate time. More recently, systems such as those of Winograd have carried the idea much further so that 'definitions' of some words and grammatical units are programs which are executed when those words are being processed. In Schank's conceptual dependency analysis for natural language the hierarchical control is even further eroded. Here a partial semantic analysis of such key elements as verbs and function words releases a network of information-seeking processes which attempt to fill vacant slots in the conceptual dependency scheme. These systems—as well as recent work on vision reported by Winston (1972)—show a trend away from strict hierarchical control. Responsibility for initiating a process can come from various 'levels'.

Another aspect of the distribution of responsibility arises in attempts to design ways of representing knowledge which are modular—i.e. consist of a collection of independent units. Modularity at some level is important to the orderly growth of complex systems. Goal-directed systems like the PLANNER-like languages represent one approach to this issue, we have already briefly alluded to this approach. By broadcasting the task description (in a very constrained form) and leaving the responsibility of capturing control to individual modules, a uniform scheme for extendability is built in.

Another approach to extendability—the so-called extensible algebraic languages—take a different approach, still retaining the distribution of responsibility idea. One of the problems to which such systems are addressed is that of adding new data types in a uniform manner. For example, suppose we had an algebraic language in which we had defined primitive arithmetic operations on real numbers and later wished to add a new data type, say complex numbers. To go back and redefine all arithmetic operations to check for this new data type and apply the appropriate operations is, in general, impractical. Furthermore it may involve some very difficult problems in cases where many already-compiled functions (say the trigonometric functions) were constructed on the basis of the old arithmetic operations.

One solution is to associate with the data type, rather than with the arithmetic operators themselves, the responsibility of specifying how certain operators are to be interpreted for that data type. Thus the attempt to add something to X would in effect first find out what data type it was (which information might be on X's property list), then check the data type identifier for the procedural definition of addition for that data type. Thus the procedure corresponding to the symbol "+" would be associated with X's data type and not with "+" itself. This decentralization of responsibility makes it an easy matter to add new and unanticipated data types and of course has implications for a broad class of problems—such as, for example, our 'delicate dish' problem.

A natural extension of this diffusion of responsibility is found in the language ABSET (Elcock, McGregor and Murray, 1971) where all responsibility for initiating procedures rests with the data. Data directed or decentralized control schemes have been incorporated in many systems including SMALL TALK, MERLIN, (Moore and Newell, 1974) PLASMA (Hewitt, 1977) and KRL (Bobrow and Winograd, 1977).

I shall discuss one additional system which follows this idea because it is especially relevant to psychological modelling. It is the production system formalism of Newell (1973(b)). (See also McDermott's paper, this volume.)

A production system consists of a communication area called the workspace (or sometimes, misleadingly, the Short-Term-Memory) which is capable of storing a number of symbols, and a set of condition-action pairs called productions. If the condition side of a production is satisfied by the current contents of the workspace (WS) then the production is said to be evoked and the actions of that production are carried out. The effect of an action may be to modify the contents of WS or to perform an I/0 operation. There are no control transfer operations (i.e. go-to's) nor subroutines in the strict sense. The system is completely homogeneous, distributed and modular. All messages are broadcast since the contents of WS are visible to all productions, and control is always captured by the production whose conditions are satisfied by the current WS contents. We shall not consider here such questions as when conditions are satisfied and what to do when more than one condition is satisfied at one time. Even without giving further details (most of which depend on which particular production system formalism one is talking about) one might note certain attractive properties of production systems from the psychologists' point of view. (See Newell and Simon, 1972, for more on this.)

(1) The system is responsive to a limited number of symbols which may be thought of as being in its focal attention. It is completely data-directed insofar as nothing happens unless the presence of symbols in WS initiates processing by evoking a production.

(2) It combines data-directed and environment-directed effects such as those we discussed earlier. Since symbols in WS can originate from an interrupt from the environment or from the execution of an action there is a uniform treatment of what psychologists have called stimulus-bound and stimulus-independent activity.

(3) The primitive operation is one of recognizing that some condition holds of the symbols to which the system is currently attending. This recognition can be made as elementary or as complex as we wish but choosing a recognition scheme is tantamount to selecting the primitive operations of the 'virtual machine'. For a psychologist this is at least partially an empirical question.

(4) Because it is data-directed a production system model incorporates an explicit model of the control structure of the process. Since there is no hidden control apparatus (e.g. a pushdown stack of return addresses) flow of control must be handled by placing appropriate symbols in WS to evoke relevant actions. These symbols then identify goals. A typical production system contains many goal-setting and goal-consummating productions. This has the interesting consequence that the contents of WS at any instant may be thought of as containing all those items which occupy the system's attention—including all active goals as well as the debris of recent processing.

(5) Production systems are highly modular and therefore are readily extendable. (Readily extendable does not mean it is *easy* for a programmer to extend it. It means that there is a uniform way of doing so without making distributed alterations to the existing system. In fact it is difficult to program production

systems because the conventions of communicating between productions have to be kept in mind and the actions of related productions taken into account.) An additional benefit of this modularity is that individual productions tend to represent meaningful components of the entire system so that the psychological interpretation of production systems may be facilitated.

(6) Since WS is conceived as the dynamic working memory to which the system is responsive at each moment, the capacity of WS is assumed to be small (although perhaps somewhat larger than Miller's magic number seven since it contains goals and 'bookkeeping' symbols as well as the usual memory items Miller was concerned with). In order to attend to more aspects then, it is necessary to tradeoff space for time. A natural way to do this is to group together a set of symbols and assign a single symbol as the name of this structure. At some future time the new symbol can be used to reconstruct the structure in WS. This procedure, which emerges quite naturally in production systems fits well with a great deal of psychological evidence for the existence of a mnemonic process called 'chunking' (see Johnson, 1972). Recently Newell (1973b) has developed a model to account for Sternberg's high speed memory scan results using this decoding concept.

I have been examining various ways in which the strictly hierarchical organization of control is being challenged by recent systems as the notion of dispersion of responsibility is developed. It is not yet clear whether a complete decentralization of authority is possible or desirable. The way in which distributed and centralized authority should interact is one of the challenging design issues. Perhaps we might get an idea of some of the unresolved issues by considering some methods available in human organizations for which we do not have counterparts in computer systems.

One important feature of human organizations is that control is never given over completely to a local expert. When responsibility is delegated, the superior authority retains the right to monitor progress (via progress reports), to reformulate goals in the light of changing conditions, and even to terminate the work of the expert before it is completed. There is no good counterpart to monitoring in the computer case. The main difficulty lies not in the parallel processing present in the human organization but in the problem of communicating enough relevant information for the higher routine to make a wise decision. The human boss has much in common with his expert worker. In fact, he could almost, but not quite, do the job himself. He is at least capable of understanding a more general or sketchy account of progress being made and to relate this to other things he knows in order to estimate the likelihood of success and the cost of completion.

In the human organization there are other devices to prevent a complete relinquishing of authority, or at least to prevent an indefinite loss of control. One is to obtain some advance committment of the time and cost associated with attempting a subgoal. We can, in other words call for tenders before contracting a task. This involves a rather sophisticated meta-evaluation capacity: the expert must decide whether the task is within his competence and how difficult it would be. I know of no general approaches to such meta-evaluation, although all tree-pruning techniques involve something of this kind. Another technique is to delegate limited authority. The expert may have authority to do anything that does not, for example, involve subcontracting or expending a maximum amount of resources. This approach has some of the difficulties that monitoring has. For example, does the executive have either the competence or the relevant information about the local context to decide what to do when the expert comes to him for a decision? And what happens if the required decision exceeds *his* authority and control cascades up through many levels of the hierarchy?

Many of these difficulties reduce to the following three questions: How to enable flexible and effective communication among modules, how to ensure that decisions are made in the context of all relevant information, and how to withhold and release the making of decisions (including meta-decisions) at appropriate times. In fact these three questions are central to the whole control problem. The communication question raises the problem of appropriate ways of describing situations and plans. One way might perhaps be to frame the description in a more abstract space as suggested by Sacerdoti (1973). The context question raises a host of problems that many people are actively working on. The context mechanisms of CONNIVER, and POPLER are directed at providing means for rendering various contexts visible to different processes. The more general problem is reminiscent of the model theoretic notion of 'possible worlds'. The third question, that of timing decisions, has also been the concern of a number of studies. The PLANNER/CONNIVER distinction between if-added and if-needed procedures (sometimes called 'demon' and 'servant' procedures), ABSET's sequencer mechanism, and MERLIN's compile-when-used mechanisms are all efforts to deal with some aspect of this problem. The issue is of special concern to psychologists (e.g. Bransford and Johnson, 1972) who have experimentally demonstrated that many inferences are carried out in advance of being required for some particular task (e.g. at the time utterances are heard). Making decisions or executing procedures must sometimes be withheld until the appropriate context is available. Several proposals for dealing with such linguistic problems as referential opacity rely on this notion of withholding execution pending the appropriate context. For instance, Davies and Isard's (1972) discussion of language comprehension places considerable emphasis on the importance of withholding the evaluation of procedures which attempt to identify the referents of various parts of an utterance until the appropriate time. Thus there is a growing recognition among investigators interested in problems of cognitive psychology that a variety of questions related to control must play a more prominent role.

ALLOCATION OF CONSTRAINTS: THE VALIDATION ISSUE

The most frequent question that psychologists working in the computer simulation (or AI) tradition get asked goes something like this: 'Maybe your program can perform the same task as poeple can (in some domain). But how do you know whether it does it the same way that people do? In this section I would like to discuss this question and contrast the psychological and the AI approach. Before I do, however, I would like to point out that the question itself is not as well-defined as is generally believed.

The question rests on the assumption that there is a clear

distinction between process and product—between *what* an organism or a device does and how it does it. But to say that a computer performed the same task as a person, though perhaps in a different way, is not to claim that the machine actually behaved outwardly as some person did on some particular occasion. The claim is about a rather more abstract relation between the capabilities of the person and the machine in respect to some class of problems. It is not about some particular behaviour but rather about a class of potential behaviours—those which can be characterized as 'doing a certain task', such as solving some problem. Now the point is that in characterizing this class of potential behaviour—in saying *what* people can or will do—we are also saying something about how they do it. If 'what people do', say, in playing chess, could be satisfactorily described by listing their observed behaviours, then perhaps the distinction between their behaviour and the process underlying it would be simple. But this is surely an unsatisfactory description of what they do. We would at least have to characterize the contingencies under which they did one thing rather than another and extrapolate to what they might do in related circumstances. But *this* kind of a description must in effect take the form of a *procedure* since it must characterize an extremely large class of moves. We can still ask whether there are not other procedural descriptions which better capture the behavioural regularities we observe but we should recognize that such a description of *what* people do is at some level also a description of how people do it.

As a consequence, any AI system is at some level a psychological theory simply because the description of the intelligent task to which it is addressed already is essentially a description of some psychological process. We would not call something a 'description of intelligent behaviour' if all it consisted of was a chronicle of what people did, for example, if it were a summary of the regularities of some corpus of observed behaviour. For a description to be referred to as a 'description of intelligent behaviour' it would have to go beyond mere reporting. It would, in Chomsky's (1964) terms have to meet criteris of 'descriptive adequacy' and not simply criteria of 'observational adequacy'. Such a description already incorporates theoretical committments in the sense that it necessarily involves interpretations. It asserts for example, that a person does such-and-such in order to accomplish some goal, that certain conditions result in the person taking a certain action etc. Such a description is not theoretically neutral.

Now, if this is so, then the statement that a person and machine do the same task (say, solve the same class of problems) but do it in different ways, is to some extent self-contradictory. What the statement must mean is that there are differences between the processes in the human and in the machine which can be revealed by some types of observation, even though the two are indistinguishable with respect to some other types of observation. This is an important point which I shall try to elaborate on below.

Whenever a class of evidence is admitted as relevant, constraints are placed on the processes which are considered adequate. In other words the range of admissible devices or systems is reduced every time an additional constraint is applied. Thus if the only constraint we place on the process is that it solve the problem in finite time then the Church-Turing thesis states that if the problem is mechanically solvable there exists a Turing machine (in fact infinitely many) which will fit the requirements. But this is clearly not a strong enough constraint to be of interest. There is a wide choice of additional constraints, ranging all the way from efficiency and elegance to realizeability in brain tissue. It is in the application of these additional constraints and in the designers' tolerance for various kinds of partial solutions that psychologists and AI people tend to diverge. This divergence is often simply one of personal preference or research strategy but occasionally it appears to be deeper. In the remaining pages I will examine some of the constraints that are or can be imposed on systems.

As with complexity, constraints on systems can be either intrinsic or extrinsic. Moore and Newell (1974) list a number of intrinsic constraints in their discussion of what they call 'the design issues which arise in the construction of understanding systems'. These are broken down into constraints on how knowledge is assimilated from the environment, how it is represented (including how partial knowledge and multiple representations are handled), how new internal structures are developed to accommodate environmental structures; how the system attempts to access all its represented knowledge, to use it appropriately and to convert it to action; how it deals with the need for both efficiency and breadth, i.e. how it trades off between efficient rigid methods and inefficient flexible methods (e.g. between interpretation and compilation, input-time elaboration and retrieval-time inferences, data-specific method or uniform formalisms); and finally how the system handles errors, ie. is it 'brittle' in that it either works or fails completely on some input, or are there degrees of how intelligently it handles all problems. This is not the place to elaborate on such questions. I wish simply to point out that there is a wide range of primarily rational constraints which can be brought to bear in the design of intelligent systems. The more of these constraints a system meets the better a psychological model it will be, even though it is true that one can sometimes design an 'idiot-savant' system which is superb on some of these criteria yet fails to be a reasonable psychological model. This is invariably because it fails miserably in meeting other intrinsic or extrinsic constraints.

Sources of extrinsic constraints are limited only by the imagination of the psychologist. Apart from such obvious sources as known limitations of human information processing and the standard experimental techniques of hypothesis-testing there are three major sources of empirical constraints on computer models. I refer to these three sources for convenience as intermediate state evidence, relative complexity evidence, and component analysis evidence.

In order to introduce the idea behind these sources of constraint I shall begin by posing the following question. Suppose I appeared here with a standard, production model, mechanical calculator and claimed that it constituted a model of human arithmetic skill. What grounds might you offer to counter my claim? Before I suggest several typical arguments I should point out that a lot depends on exactly how I present the original claim. An object sitting on the table is not in itself a model. As Sellars (1963) has pointed out, a model is always accompanied by a 'commentary' describing how the object is to be interpreted *qua* model. My commentary would have to specify, for example, that such physical properties as colour, weight, size and the like are not meant to be part of the modelling function. On the other hand the numbers entered into the machine and the numbers appearing in the display window are relevant. In addition there is in any model a substantial grey region where it is not obvious, *a priori*, whether certain aspects, such as the time taken to calculate an answer in our example, are relevant or not. Assuming then that we have our calculator and some reasonable commentary, what are some grounds for thinking that this is not an adequate model? Let me suggest a few.

(1) If we give the device two numbers to add and examine it closely as it goes through its calculation, for example by slowing it down or stopping it periodically, we find that there are intermediate states in the computation in which all digits have undergone some change but none are yet at their final value. Subsequently there are intermediate states where the register contains some correct digits but these are scattered throughout the sum. And finally a number of positions, again apparently scattered through the sum, arrive at their final value at the same time at the end of the calculation. Now we have at least three general characteristics of what might be called 'states of knowledge', intermediate between the initial and final states, which appear to be quite different from the intermediate states which people go through (although what these are is an empirical question). Methods for studying intermediate states in human tasks are very few and rather crude compared with more conventional experimental methods. They consist mostly of the analysis of thinking-out-loud protocols, supplemented by some inferences about missing states. However, such evidence does represent a unique source of constraint on models which cannot be dismissed out of hand. The authoritative source on this methodology is the recent book by Newell and Simon (1972). I will consider some counter-arguments to these criteria after mentioning examples of other sources of constraints.

(2) We could attempt to rank various arithmetic problems in order of their complexity for the model. Various complexity measures might be sought but two simple ones are the time taken to complete the task or the number of elementary operations, such as machine cycles, which they required. More complex measures might include some more abstract notion of elementary operation which applied not only to this one machine but to a class of such machines. Sticking to the simple measures, however, we find that complexity in the model is independent of

how many digits are involved in the addition and of which specific digits are used. Similarly with multiplication we obtain some function between number of digits and complexity and ascertain that the latter does not depend critically on which digits are involved.

We can now do the same for human subjects. The scale of complexity here can depend on such measurements as the time taken to complete the task or the frequency of errors. Again we can examine the empirical complexity as a function of variations in the task. We might observe that this complexity measure increases with the number of digits to be added, increases even more rapidly with the number of digits to be multiplied, and depends critically on the presence of zeros, on the magnitude of individual digits, and perhaps on how many columns required 'carries' in adding. Clearly on such measures the two complexity orderings would not correspond very well.

(3) If we examine the model in finer detail we can identify various subtasks which contribute to the total computational process. We might then be able to evaluate these subtasks independently. For example, it could be that individual columns are processed 'in the same way that people do it' but that the overall performance differences arise from the way in which these are combined (e.g. from the fact that in the model they are done in parallel). If this were so it should be possible to show similar intermediate state or complexity effects on single column addition tasks. Data on human addition of pairs of digits shows that the amount of time it takes is not constant (as might seem subjectively to be the case) but depends on the smaller of the two digits (see Groen and Parkman, 1972). This is not likely to be the case in the model, even if we keep in mind that 'time' may map into a more complex dimension in the model.

Component analysis of the task provides a powerful method of validating models. The nature of errors people make often helps to pinpoint *loci* of processing difficulty. Such bottlenecks can also be revealed frequently by deliberately stressing certain aspects of the system, for example by examining what happens on progressively larger problems when external memory aids are forbidden compared with when they are permitted. Young (1973) has tuned his model of seriation in children by examining what specific differences occur when certain types of information is selectively provided or blocked during the task, e.g. by letting the child see all the blocks, or only two at a time. By letting him see all the blocks he has seriated or only letting him see, for example, the last one or the largest one. Simon has argued that we might obtain the most discriminating evidence concerning human information processing by observing the human at the limits of his performance. If we could apply the stress to his performance in a selective manner, governed by the model we are constructing, we might be in an even better position to make direct use of the observations.

Let me offer an example of selective stressing. I have already mentioned a phenomenon discovered by Sternberg (1967). If we teach a subject a short list of items, say the digits 3, 7, 8 and then flash on a probe digit, say 7, the amount of time it takes to say whether the probe digit was in the memorized set is a linear function of the number of items in the set. Because the slope of the line is usually less than 40 milliseconds per item—certainly not enough time to say the digits to oneself—the question arises whether the search for a matching item is done on the basis of physical features of the presented probe. One way to test this is to present a degraded image of the probe, or one using a different script from the original memory set presentation. If the search is on physical features, each individual comparison should take longer (we know this from independent studies) and so the slope should be greater. If, on the other hand the probe is first converted to some internal symbolic form the intercept should be higher but the slope the same for the degraded probe. Sternberg showed that the latter was clearly the case, thus neatly eliminating one possible mechanism. Newell (1970) gives a number of such examples to show that there are ways not only to apply global constraints to possible processes but in fact to carry out a detailed analysis of subprocesses allowing one to empirically constrain even the fine structure of models.

These examples will suffice to give you an idea of how general empiracal constraints can be applied to validate processes as psychological models. Such constraints are applied routinely by investigators, like Newell and Simon, who are determined that not only the gross behaviour but also the detailed structures of computer systems must be taken seriously as psychological mechanisms.

In addition to the types of empirical constraints discussed above there are a number of other general categories worth mentioning. One is evidence regarding the malleability of behaviour, which includes the ability of a system to assimilate new information, to accommodate to new environmental demands, and to learn by doing, as well as by being told or shown how. Part of this problem, notably that related to the ability of an oganism to change its behaviour in response to the consequences of different behaviours, has been studied at great length by psychologists. The other sources of change on the other hand, have seen very little investigation outside a few islands of study such as the work done by Piaget or more recently by Papert.

A second source of constraint which we have ignored is related to the *development* of intelligence—particularly ontogenetic, but also to some extent phylogenetic development. Suppose we have a number of systems which accurately model the intelligence of a human at various states in his development from infancy to adulthood. One of the questions we might be inclined to ask is how the transitions from one system to the next occur. What is it that is changing and what general principles govern the changes? More importantly, should we try to understand the systems at each stage first and then inquire about the changes? Or is it the case, as Piaget would argue, that we can only understand the intelligence at each stage by attending to the way in which the changes come about? Many people appear to have implicit faith that if we understand intelligent functioning at several stages then a comparison of the function at these stages will make it clear what it is that is changing and how. But this is not necessarily true. We might conceivably be able to give an account of both childhood and adult intelligence while neglecting completely a variety of factors, such as perceptual-motor experience, which are essential to account for the developmental sequence. Furthermore, development is not merely a process of incrementally adding new skills, but involves also radical reorganization of intellectual structures. The mechanism for such reorganization may never be discovered unless the evidence of developmental sequences is introduced as part of the empirical constraint on systems.

A third source of empirical constraint comes from the

evidence of neurophysiology and allied disciplines. While the information processing approach deliberately sets a level of analysis independent of material forms it cannot ignore physiological evidence entirely. For example a variety of interesting evidence is available which bears on the problem of decomposing intelligence into partially independent functions. Evidence from pathologies such as aphasias, agnosias, and apraxias as well as evidence of localization of certain functions are all relevent to the question of how the total function might be decomposed. For example, it is not irrelevant to our understanding of language comprehension that certain local brain injuries resulted in a condition (described by Geschwind, 1972) in which a patient could repeat utterances fluently and memorize verses and songs but could not understand what she was saying. Data of this kind, along with more detailed analyses of such neural subsystems as the visual system, are all potential sources of constraint on theories of intelligence. In fact evidence of the type collected by Sperry and his colleagues on split-brain patients promises to shed new light even on such deep philosophical problems as the nature of conscious experience.

Ultimately the question of the nature of human intelligence may even involve us in a consideration of such *strong* constraints as how a mechanism could realize such functions within the real-time and real-space confines of the brain, how it can do this subject to such principles as captured roughly in Lashley's notions of 'equipotential' and 'mass action', and ultimately how subjective experience itself is mapped on to these mechanisms.

Even if you accept that the sorts of constraints on intelligent systems which we have been discussing are all potentially valid, there still remain very important question of priority. If we apply minimal constraints we will have a Turing machine. If we apply all the constraints there may be no place to stop short of producing a human. Thus a system through which we are to understand intelligence must necessarily be partial—though perhaps it should be no more so than is necessary at any point in the development of the science. The question of which sequence of approximations or of application of constraints one ought to adopt as a matter of principle, and consequently of what type of incompleteness one prefers to tolerate along the way, is one on which there is a wide spectrum of opinion. For example Newell (1972) states his position on this question as follows:

> I will, on balance, prefer to start with a grossly imperfect but complete model, hoping to improve it eventually, rather than start with an abstract but experimentally verified characterization, hoping to specify it further eventually. These may be looked at simply as different approximating sequences toward the same scientific end. But they do dictate quite different approaches. . .
> (p 375)

This position might be taken to characterize the AI or information processing approach generally, were it not for different ways of interpreting such phrases as 'imperfect but complete' and 'abstract but experimentally verified'. In stating his position Newell was contrasting his approach with the more conventional theorizing on short term memory and learning, where abstract constructs like 'imaginal mediators', 'chunks' or 'strategies' are operationally defined within an experimental paradigm. In such studies little attention is paid to the details of a mechanism capable of carrying out the required operations. The interest is not so much with processes, although this term is frequently used, but with what are called 'functional relations' among variables. This approach essentially attempts to exhibit empirical regularities by something more akin to curve-fitting than by design of mechanisms to do the task. However, Newell was concerned in this case with completeness over the domain of what he called 'stimulus encoding', not over the domain of, say, perception or comprehension. Therein lies one of the dimensions which distinguish AI endeavours from typical psychological models. The kind of 'grossly imperfect' mechanisms necessary to achieve some degree of completeness over a very broad domain may be more than the empirically-minded psychologist would be willing to tolerate. On the other hand to develop a model which has close ties with experimental data in a large domain such as that of human memory, as Anderson and Bower (1973) have attempted in their HAM system, currently requires that the model be incomplete in fundamental ways. For example, HAM itself is extremely restricted in what it can understand and in what it can do with the things it does understand. Furthermore it is not clear how the principles in its design would suggest that one proceed to extend HAM into a more general type of comprehension and reasoning system. In other words it contains no suggestion of an interface. I don't intend these remarks merely to run down HAM which is a major effort at developing some experimentally-based ideas about semantic memory. But it does illustrate, I believe, one of the dimensions of tension between the AI and psychological approaches.

As a further illustration of the differences in approach between psychology and AI let us return to our earlier example of the calculator, proposed as a psychological model. One could offer a variety of rebuttals to the criticisms of the model which we discussed. Recall that we found that the model went through different intermediate states than people do in solving arithmetic problems, that the model induced different complexity relations among tasks than people did when we examined latency and error data, and that an analysis of component subtasks revealed inadequacies in the fine structure of the model.

One might object to the intermediate state criteria on several grounds. For example it might be that we have been attending to the wrong aspects of the calculator in singling out intermediate states. This may be one of the grey regions where the commentary does not explicitly state whether the visible contents of the registers or some other aspects of the device are to count as true intermediate states. A similar objection might be directed against the states of knowledge inferred from protocol analyses. Here the case for the reality of intermediate states of knowledge is somewhat stronger. After all, a subject can produce the answer to part of the problem before he can solve the entire problem, and can provide a rationale for the transitions in terms of subgoals. But there is still a 'grain' problem. It is not obvious *a priori* at what 'level of aggregation', to use Newell and Simon's (1972) phrase, one ought to be comparing the protocol and a trace of the model's behaviour. Should 'states of knowledge' in the mental arithmetic example cited earlier correspond to individual integers, as they would appear if the problem were done by writing down intermediate steps, or to finer states—perhaps even corresponding to the steps involved in accessing a stored addition table? In the latter case, how do we obtain evidence of these states?

Similar questions can be raised regarding the other sources of constraint. What are to count as primitive operations in determining complexity of computation in the model? What reasons do we have for expecting complexity scaled in this manner to correlate with latencies? Such an expectation only follows if one makes additional simplifying assumptions about what contributes to human response latencies. But perhaps these are not due to extra computations but simply to some operations being faster than others in the 'virtual machine'.

The list of such objections can grow long and tedious. I have sketched a few only to point out that the validation of models involves meta-theoretical assumptions. I personally do not believe that these present fundamental difficulties. Indeed the problems here are no different from those in any scientific discipline. The validation of theories always rests on meta-theoretical assumptions. What is unique in information-processing theories is that we have not lived with them long enough for these background assumptions to become part of the general, scientific culture.

But the story does not end here, for there are arguments against the application of such empirical constraints as sketched above, which I believe are more serious. Consider the calculator model again. Another type of argument against such a model is the following. What is wrong with the calculator as a model is that it is simply too narrow. There is no reason to believe that mechanisms of the type found in the calculator would be of any use whatever to a system which understood English, perceived scenes, solved crossword puzzles, or did any other intellectual tasks. Indeed, in the light of our earlier discussions regarding the organization of complexity and the problems of control, there are good reasons to believe that such a model is fundamentally and irreparably limited. In particular there is no suggestion in it of an incrementally expandable knowledge base. Without some hint, however, 'grossly imperfect', of an approach to the epistemological problem, the model is at the outset prevented from growing towards an intelligent mechanism. As Donald Michie (1971) has put it, in speaking of recent developments in AI, '. . . we now have as a touchstone the realization that the central operations of the intelligence are . . . transactions on a knowledge base'. In view of this it would be of little comfort even if our model met all the empirical constraints we examined. It might in some sense provide a model of arithmetic performance which summarized experimental findings in this area but it would not serve as a step towards understanding the broader problems of cognition. And this is the kind of incompleteness for which the AI community has developed a pronounced intolerance.

Basically the problem is this: a system which is able to encompass some domain of evidence A may bear very little resemblance to a system which is able to encompass both some domain of evidence A and some domain of evidence B. It is the part-whole problem again. If we have learned anything from the last decade or more of research on artificial intelligence (for example, from work on pattern recognition) it is that continued progress is extremely sensitive to the way in which we attempt to decompose the overall problem into strategic parcels. And, as I suggested at the beginning of this essay, psychologists have opted for a type and size of parcel which many people, particularly in AI, are beginning to feel is fundamentally wrong-headed.

In closing let me simply reiterate that there are many ways of approaching an understanding of intelligence. The experimental psychologist has traditionally preferred to take small steps while standing on solid data. The rationalist and the more formally inclined scholar (the logician, the linguist) also prefers to take small steps, while perched on a more abstract and intuitive foundation. There have also been grand theoreticians, in the tradition of Freud, James, or Piaget, who have enjoyed varying degrees of success, but who have ultimately run up against the limits of the conceptual technical tools available to them— which, in most cases, have been some sort of metaphor. What is needed is not only a dialectical relation among these approaches but also a technical language with which to discipline one's imagination. As I said at the beginning I believe that the notion of mechanism, as it is being developed in the study of artificial intelligence is the most promising idea yet to be enunciated for the exploration of these problems and for bringing some convergence to the multiple strands of cognitive psychology.

NOTES

1. It will be apparent to the reader acquainted with the literature in artificial intelligence and psychology that the ideas in this paper derive primarily from the work of Allen Newell and Herb Simon and that it has been influenced by the recent MIT approach to artificial intelligence. (An earlier version of this paper was presented at a conference on Objectives and Methodologies for Artificial Intelligence, Canberra, Australia, May 1974.)

2. In fairness to J.J. Gibson a word of caution is in order here. The distinction between a description of a visual scene in terms of the invariant characteristics of the proximal stimuli to which it gives rise, and a description of a device which can perceive the scene, may not be as sharp as might, at first, appear. In particular, the former might be viewed as the function computed by the latter, or, even more to the point, both might be viewed as alternative ways of characterizing the same function. See the related point concerning the distinction between process and product discussed in the section on allocation of constraints. The difficulties with the Gibson approach are discussed at length in Pylyshyn (in preparation).

3. The problem of devising a system which can generate appropriate representations, transform them into new ones and deal with multiple representations is one of the major unsolved problems in AI. In particular there is reason to believe that it has been one of the stumbling blocks in the development of machine perception. In the latter case an attempt is made to compensate for the weakness in representation-generating/transforming power by the application of more powerful problem-solving methods—an approach at variance with Newell's 'natural intelligence' principle.

REFERENCES

Anderson, J.R. and Bower, G.H. *Human Associative Memory*. Washington, D.C. (Winston, 1973).

Bobrow, D. and Raphael, B. 'New programming languages for artificial intelligence research', *Computer Survey*, 6 (1974) 153-174.

Bobrow, D.G. and Winograd, T. 'An overview of KRL, a knowledge representation language', *Cognitive Science*, 1 (1977).

Bransford, J.D. and Johnson M.K. 'Considerations of some problems of comprehension'. In W. Chase (ed), *Visual information processing*, New York (Academic Press, 1973).

Chomsky, N. *Current issues in linguistic theory*. The Hague (Mouton, 1964).

Davies, D.J.M. and Isard, S.D. 'Utterances as programs'. In B. Meltzer and D. Michie (eds) *Machine Intelligence, 7* (1972) 325-339.

Elcock, E.W., McGregor, J.J. and Murray, A.M. 'Data directed control and operating systems'. *The Computer Journal*, 15(1972) 125-129.

Geschwind, N. 'Language and brain'. *Scientific American*, 226 (1972) 76-83.

Gibson, J.J. *The Senses considered as perceptual systems*. Boston (Houghton-Mifflin, 1966).

Groen, G.J. and Parkman, J.M. 'A chronometric analysis of simple addition'. *Psychological Review*, 79 (1972) 329-343.

Hewitt, C.E. 'Viewing control structures as patterns of passing messages', *Artificial Intelligence* (1977).

Johnson, N.F. 'Organization and the concept of a memory code'. In A.W. Melton and E. Martin (eds.) *Coding Processes in Human Memory*. New York (Winston, 1972).

Langer S. *Philosophical sketches*. Baltimore (Johns Hopkins Press, 1962).

Michie, D. *'On not seeing things'*. School of Artificial Intelligence, University of Ediburgh. EPR (1971) 22.

Miller, G.A. Galanter, E. and Pribram, K.H. *Plans and the structure of behavior*. New York (Holt, Rinehart and Winston, 1960).

Moore J. and Newell, A. 'How can Merlin understand' (CCMU report). In L. Gregg (ed.), *Knowledge and Cognition*, Potomac, Md. (Erlbaum Associates, 1974).

Newell, A. 'You can't play 20 questions with nature and win'. In W. Chase (ed) *Visual information processing*. New York (Academic Press, 1973).

Newell, A. 'Production systems: models of control structures', in W. Chase (ed) *Visual information processing*. New York (Academic Press, 1973).

Newell, A. 'A theoretical exploration of mechanisms for coding the stimulus'. In A. W. Melton and E. Martin (eds) *Coding processes in human memory,* New York (Winston, 1972).

Newell, A. 'Remarks on the relationship between artificial intelligence and cognitive psychology'. In R. Banerji and M.D. Mesarovic (eds) *Theoretical approaches to non-numerical problem solving*. New York (Springer-Verlag, 1970).

Newell, A. 'Some problems of basic organization in problem solving programs'. In M.C. Yovits, G.T. Jacobi and G.D. Goldstein (eds) *Self organizing systems,* Washington, D.C. (Sparton, 1962).

Newell, A. and Simon, H.A. *Human problem solving*. Engelwood Clifts, New Jersey (Prentice-Hall, 1972).

Pylyshyn, Z.W. 'Foundations of Cognitive Science'. Book Ms. *(in preparation)*.

Sacerdoti, E.D. 'Planning in a hierarchy of abstraction spaces'. *Proceedings of the Third International Joint Congress on Artifiical Intelligence* (Stanford 1973) 412-422.

Sellars, W.F. *Science, Perception and Reality.* New York (The Humanities Press, 1963).

Simon, H.A. *The Sciences of The Artificial.* Cambridge, Mass. (M.I.T. Press, 1969).

Sternberg, S. 'Two operations in character recognition'. *Perception and Psychophysics, 2, (1967),* 43-53.

Wilkes, Y. 'Understanding without proofs'. *Proceedings of the Third International Joint Congress on Artificial Intelligence* (Stanford, 1973).

Winston, P.H. The M.I.T. Robot. In B. Meltzer and D. Michie (eds) *Machine Intelligence 7* (Edinburgh University Press, 1972).

Young, R.M. Children's seriation behaviour: A production system analysis. *Unpublished doctoral dissertation,* (Carnegie-Mellon University, 1973).

CHAPTER 3
ARTIFICIAL INTELLIGENCE AS PHILOSOPHY AND AS PSYCHOLOGY
Daniel C. Dennett

Philosophers of mind have been interested in computers since their arrival a generation ago, but for the most part they have been interested only in the most abstract questions of principle, and have kept actual machines at arm's length and actual programs in soft focus. Had they chosen to take a closer look at the details I do not think they would have found much of philosophic interest until fairly recently. But recent work in Artificial Intelligence, or AI, promises to have a much more variegated impact on philosophy, and so, quite appropriately, philosophers have begun responding with interest to the bold manifestos of the Artificial Intelligentsia.[1] My goal in this paper is to provide a sort of travel guide to philosophers pursuing this interest. It is well known that amateur travellers in strange lands often ludicrously misconstrue what they see, and enthusiastically report wonders and monstrosities that later investigations prove never to have existed, while overlooking genuine novelties of the greatest importance. Having myself fallen prey to a variety of misconceptions about AI, and wasted a good deal of time and energy pursuing chimaeras, I would like to alert other philosophers to some of these pitfalls of interpretation. Since I am still acutely conscious of my own amateur status as an observer of AI, I must acknowledge at the outset that my vision of what is going on in AI, what is important and why, is almost certainly still somewhat untrustworthy. There is much in AI that I have not read, and much that I have read but not understood. So traveller beware; take along any other maps you can find, and listen critically to the natives.

The interest of philosophers of mind in Artificial Intelligence comes as no surprise to many tough-minded experimental psychologists, for from their point of view the two fields look very much alike: there are the same broad generalizations and bold extrapolations, the same blithe indifference to the hard-won data of the experimentalist, the same appeal to the deliverances of casual introspection and conceptual analysis, the aprioristic reasonings about what is impossible in principle or what must be the case in psychology. The only apparent difference between the two fields, such a psychologist might say, is that the AI worker pulls his armchair up to a console. I will argue that this observation is largely justified, but should not in most regards be viewed as a criticism. There is much work for the armchair psychologist to do, and a computer console has proven a useful tool in this work.

Psychology turns out to be very difficult. The task of psychology is to explain human perception, learning, cognition, and so forth in terms that ultimately will unite psychological theory to physiology in one way or another. And there are two broad strategies one could adopt: a 'bottom-up' strategy that starts with some basic and well-defined unit or theoretical atom for psychology and builds these atoms into molecules and larger aggregates that can account for the complex phenomena we all observe, or a 'top-down' strategy that begins with a more abstract decomposition of the highest levels of psychological organization, and hopes to analyse these into more and more detailed smaller systems or processes until finally one arrives at elements familiar to the biologists. It is a commonplace that both endeavours could and should proceed simultaneously, but there is now abundant evidence that the bottom-up strategy in psychology is unlikely to prove very fruitful. The two best developed attempts at bottom-up psychology are stimulus-response behaviourism and what we might call 'neuron signal physiological psychology', and both are now widely regarded as stymied, the former because stimuli and responses prove not to be perspicuously chosen atoms, the latter because even if synapses and impulse trains are perfectly good atoms, there are just too many of them, and their interactions are too complex to study once one abandons the afferent and efferent peripheries and tries to make sense of the crucial centre.[2] Bottom-up strategies have not proved notably fruitful in the early development of other sciences, in chemistry and biology for instance, and so psychologists are only following the lead of 'mature' sciences if they turn to the top-down approach. Within that broad strategy there are a variety of starting points that can be ordered in an array. Faced with the practical impossibility of answering the empirical questions of psychology by brute inspection (how *in fact* does the nervous system accomplish X or Y or Z?), psychologists ask themselves an easier preliminary question:

(1) How could any system (with features A, B, C,. . .) possibly accomplish X?[3]

This sort of question is easier because it is 'less empirical'; it is an *engineering* question, a quest for a solution (*any* solution) rather than a discovery. Seeking an answer to such a question can sometimes lead to the discovery of general constraints on all solutions (including of course nature's as yet unknown solution) and therein lies the value of this style of aprioristic theorizing. Once one decides to do psychology this way, one can choose a degree of empirical difficulty for one's question by filling in the blanks in the question schema (1).[4] The more empirical constraints one puts on the description of the system, or on the description of the requisite behaviour, the greater the claim to 'psychological reality' one's answer must make. For instance, one can ask how any neuronal network with such-and-such physical features could possibly accomplish human colour discriminations, or we can ask how any finite system could possibly subserve the acquisition of a natural language. Or, one can ask how human memory could possibly be so organized as to make it so relatively easy for us to answer questions like 'have you ever ridden an antelope?' and so relatively hard to answer 'what did you have for breakfast last Tuesday?' Or, one can ask, with Kant, how anything at all could possibly experience or know anything at all. Pure epistemology thus viewed, for instance, is simply the limiting case of the psychologists' quest, and is *prima facie* no less valuable *to psychology* for being so neutral with regard to empirical details. Some such questions are of course better designed to yield good answers than others, but properly carried out, any such investigation can yield constraints that bind all more-data-enriched investigations.

AI workers can pitch their investigations at any level of

empirical difficulty they wish; at Carnegie Mellon University, for instance, much is made of paying careful attention to experimental data on human performance and attempting to model human performance closely. Other workers in AI are less concerned with that degree of psychological reality and have engaged in a more abstract version of AI. There is much that is of value and interest to psychology at the empirical end of the spectrum but I want to claim that AI is better viewed as sharing with traditional epistemology the status of being a most general, most abstract asking of the top-down question: how is knowledge possible?[5] It has seemed to some philosophers that AI cannot be plausibly so construed because it takes on an additional burden: it restricts itself to *mechanistic* solutions, and hence its domain is not the Kantian domain of all possible modes of intelligence, but just all possible mechanistically realizable modes of intelligence. This, it is claimed, would beg the question against vitalists, dualists and other anti-mechanists. But as I have argued elsewhere, the mechanism requirement of AI is not an additional constraint of any moment. For, if psychology is possible at all, and if Church's thesis is true, the constraint of mechanism is no more severe than the constraint against begging the question in psychology, and who would wish to evade that?[6]

So I am claiming that AI shares with philosophy (in particular, with epistemology and philosophy of mind) the status of most abstract investigation of the principles of psychology. But it shares with psychology in distinction from philosophy a typical tactic in answering its questions. In AI or cognitive psychology the typical attempt to answer a *general* top-down question consists in designing a *particular* system that does, or appears to do, the relevant job, and then considering which of its features are necessary not just to one's particular system but to any such system. Philosophers have generally shunned such elaborate system-designing in favour of more doggedly general inquiry. This is perhaps the major difference between AI and 'pure' philosophical approaches to the same questions, and it is one of my purposes here to exhibit some of the relative strengths and weaknesses of the two approaches.

The system-design approach that is common to AI and other styles of top-down psychology is beset by a variety of dangers of which these four are perhaps the chief:

(A) designing a system with component subsystems whose stipulated capacities are miraculous given the constraints one is accepting. (e.g., positing more information-processing in a component than the relevant time and matter will allow, or, at a more abstract level of engineering incoherence, positing a subsystem whose duties would require it to be more 'intelligent' or 'knowledgeable' than the supersystem of which it is to be a part.

(B) mistaking conditional necessities of one's particular solution for completely general constraints: a trivial example would be proclaiming that brains use LISP; less trivial examples require careful elucidation.

(C) restricting oneself artificially to the design of a subsystem, such as a depth perceiver or sentence parser, and concocting a solution that is systematically incapable of being grafted on to the other subsystems of a whole cognitive creature.

(D) restricting the performance of one's system to an artificially small part of the 'natural' domain of that system and providing no efficient or plausible way for the system to be enlarged.

These dangers are altogether familiar to AI, but are just as common, *if harder to diagnose conclusively,* in other approaches to psychology. Consider danger (A): both Freud's ego subsystem and J.J. Gibson's invariance-sensitive perceptual 'tuning forks' have been *charged* with miraculous capacities. Danger (B): behaviourists have *been charged* with illicitly extrapolating from pigeon-necessities to people-necessities, and it is often claimed that what the frog's eye tells the frog's brain is not at all what the person's eye tells the person's brain. Danger (C): it is notoriously hard to see how Chomsky's early syntax-driven system could interact with semantical components to produce or comprehend purposeful speech. Danger (D): it is hard to see how some models of nonsense-syllable rote memorization could be enlarged to handle similar but more sophisticated memory tasks. It is one of the great strengths of AI that when one of its products succumbs to any of these dangers this can usually be quite conclusively demonstrated.

I now have triangulated AI with respect to both philosophy and psychology, as my title suggested I would: AI can be, and should often be taken to be, as abstract and 'unempirical' as philosophy in the questions it attempts to answer. But at the same time, it should be as explicit and particularistic in its models as psychology at its best. Thus one might learn as much of value to psychology or epistemology from a particular but highly unrealistic AI model as one could learn from a detailed psychology of, say, Martians. A good psychology of Martians, however unlike us they might be, would certainly yield general principles of psychology or epistemology applicable to human beings. Now, before turning to the all important question: 'What, so conceived, has AI accomplished?' I want to consider briefly some misinterpretations of AI that my sketch of it so far does not protect us from.

Since we are viewing AI as a species of top-down cognitive psychology, it is tempting to suppose that the decomposition of function in a computer is intended by AI to be somehow isomorphic to the decomposition of function in a brain. One learns of vast programs made up of literally billions of basic computer events and somehow so organized as to produce a simulacrum of human intelligence, and it is altogether natural to suppose that since the brain is known to be composed of billions of tiny functioning parts, and since there is a gap of ignorance between our understanding of intelligent human behaviour and our understanding of those tiny parts, the ultimate, millenial goal of AI must be to provide a hierarchical breakdown of parts in the computer that will mirror or be isomorphic to some hard-to-discover hierarchical breakdown of brain-event parts. The familiar theme of 'organs made of tissues made of cells made of molecules made of atoms' is to be matched, one might suppose, in electronic hardware terms. In the thrall of this picture one might be discouraged to learn that some functional parts of the nervous system do not seem to function in the digital way the atomic functioning parts in computers do. The standard response to this worry would be that one had looked too deep in the computer. This is sometimes called the 'grain problem'. The computer is a digital device at bottom, but a digital device can simulate an 'analogue' device to any degree of continuity you desire, and at a higher level of aggregation in the computer one may find the analogue elements that are mapable onto the non-digital brain parts. As many writers have observed,[7] we cannot gauge the psychological reality of a model until we are given the commentary on the model that tells us which features of the model are intended to mirror real saliencies in nature and which are either backstage expediters of the modelling or sheer inadvertent detail. In the eighteenth century, scientists built beautiful brass clockwork models of the solar system called orreries. The *gears* of an orrery are not intended to represent anything real in the firmament, nor are the reflections of one brass globe in another. When one looks at AI programs in detail one sees mountains of digital calculation or 'number crunching'; if this looks disappointingly unbiological, this is to be excused, since that part of the model's structure is to be viewed as backstage, not part of the model we are supposed to compare with nature.

This story is fine in principle, I think, and the day may come when this imagined isomorphism down to the neuronal level (but not backstage) is proclaimed. But in fact we see nothing remotely like this in current AI work. We see instead models that diverge from nature very early on the downward path. AI programs typically model relatively high-level cognitive features, such as concept learning or revision of goals or beliefs, and it does indeed often take millions of basic computer events to simulate just a handful of these intended model features. But no one really knows or cares what these basic events are, for no one supposes that any of the saliencies in the mass of activity that subserves the intended features are to be taken seriously as psychology or physiology. The psychological reality of an AI program is thus usually only intended to be skin deep; only the highest levels of program description and commentary are to be counted as the model.

The thinness of the psychological reality of AI models is obscured for the uninitiated by a particularly misleading feature of most of the AI programs that get into the limelight. What especially attracts audiences and evokes wonder is the marvelous verisimilitude of some of the programs. Consider this excerpt of conversation, minus the programmer's excellent commentary, between Terry Winograd's SHRDLU and its interlocutor. (SHRDLU is a program that lives in an imaginary 'block world' where it can manipulate coloured blocks on a table in response to commands and answer questions about its life in this world). Computer responses are capitalized.

Had you touched any pyramid before you put the
green one on the little cube?
YES, THE GREEN ONE.
When did you pick it up?
WHILE I WAS STACKING UP THE RED
CUBE, A LARGE RED BLOCK AND A
LARGE GREEN CUBE.
Why?
TO GET RID OF IT.
Why did you do that?
TO CLEAR OFF THE RED CUBE.
Why did you clear off that cube?
TO PUT IT ON A LARGE GREEN CUBE.
Why did you do that?
BECAUSE YOU ASKED ME TO.[8]

When SHRDLU replies to the last question with 'Because you
asked me to', one can hardly help being struck by the apparent
humanity of the response—'SHRDLU is *one of us!*' it is
tempting to exclaim. If one is naive, one will be awestruck; if
one is not, one will still be titillated by the illusion, for that is
largely what it is. SHRDLU's response, though perfectly
appropriate to the occasion, and not by coincidence, is 'canned'.
Winograd has simply given SHRDLU this whole sentence to
print at times like these. If a child gave SHRDLU's response
we would naturally expect its behaviour to manifest a general
capacity which might also reveal itself by producing the
response: 'because you told me to', or 'because that's what I
was asked to do' or, on another occasion, 'because I felt like it'
or 'because your assistant told me to'. But these are dimensions
of subtlety beyond SHRDLU.[9] Its behaviour is remarkably
versatile, but it does not reveal a rich knowledge of inter-
personal relations, of the difference between requests and
orders, of being co-operative with other people under appropriate circumstances. It should be added that Winograd's paper
makes it very explicit where and to what extent he is canning
SHRDLU's responses, so anyone who feels cheated by
SHRDLU has simply not read Winograd. Other natural
language programs do not rely on canned responses, or rely on
them to a minimal extent.

The fact remains, however, that much of the antagonism to AI is due to resentment and distrust engendered by such legerdemain. Why do AI people use these tricks? For many reasons. First, they need to get some tell-tale response back from the program and it is as easy to can a mnemonically vivid and 'natural' response as something more sober, technical and understated, such as, 'REASON: PRIOR COMMAND TO DO THAT'. Second, in Winograd's case he was attempting to reveal the minimal conditions for correct analysis of certain linguistic forms (note all the 'problems' of pronominal antecedents in the sentences displayed), so 'natural' language output to reveal correct analysis of natural language input was entirely appropriate. Third, AI people put canned responses in their programs because it is fun. It is fun to amuse one's colleagues, who are not fooled of course, and it is especially fun to bamboozle the outsiders. As an outsider one must learn to be properly unimpressed by AI verisimilitude, as one is of the chemist's dazzling forest of glass tubing, or the angry mouths full of teeth painted on World War II fighter planes. Joseph Weizenbaum's famous ELIZA program,[10] the computer 'psychotherapist' who apparently listens so wisely and sympathetically to one's problems, is intended in part as an antidote to the enthusiasm generated by AI verisimilitude. It is almost all clever canning, and is not a psychologically realistic model of anything, but rather a demonstration of how easily one can be gulled into attributing too much to a program. It exploits syntactic landmarks in one's input with nothing approaching genuine understanding, but it makes a good show of comprehension nevertheless. One might say it was a plausible model of a Wernicke's aphasic, who can babble on with well-formed and even semantically appropriate responses to his interlocutor, sometimes sustaining the illusion of comprehension for quite a while.

The AI community pays a price for this misleading if fascinating fun, not only by contributing to the image of AI people as tricksters and hackers, but by fueling more serious misconceptions of the point of AI research. For instance, Winograd's real contribution in SHRDLU is not that he has produced an English speaker and understander that is psychologically realistic at many different levels of analysis, though that is what the verisimilitude strongly suggests, and what a lot of the fanfare—for which Winograd is not responsible—has assumed, but that he has explored some of the deepest demands on any system that can take direction, in a natural language, plan, change the world, and keep track of the changes wrought or contemplated. And in the course of this exploration he has clarified the problems and proposed ingenious and plausible partial solutions to them. The real contribution in Winograd's work stands quite unimpeached by the perfectly true but irrelevant charge that SHRDLU doesn't have a rich or human understanding of most of the words in its very restricted vocabulary, or is extremely slow.

In fact, paying so much attention to the performance of SHRDLU, and similar systems, reveals a failure to recognize that AI programs are not *empirical* experiments, but *thought*-experiments, prosthetically regulated by computers. Some AI people have recently become fond of describing their discipline as 'experimental epistemology'. This unfortunate term should make a philosopher's blood boil, but if AI called itself thought-experimental epistemology (or even better: *Gedanken*-experimental epistemology) philosophers ought to be reassured. The questions asked and answered by the thought experiments of AI are about whether or not one can obtain certain sorts of information processing, recognition, inference, control of various sorts, for instance, from certain sorts of designs. Often the answer is no. The process of elimination looms large in AI. Relatively plausible schemes are explored far enough to make it clear that they are utterly incapable of delivering the requisite behaviour, and learning this is important progress even if it doesn't result in a mind-boggling robot.

The hardware realizations of AI are almost gratuitous. Like dropping the cannonballs off the Leaning Tower of Pisa, they are demonstrations that are superfluous to those who have understood the argument, however persuasive they are to the rest. Are computers then irrelevant to AI? 'In principle' they are irrelevant, in the same sense as diagrams on the blackboard are 'in principle' unnecessary to teaching geometry, but in practice they are not. I described them earlier as 'prosthetic regulators' of thought-experiments. What I mean is this: it is notoriously difficult to keep wishful thinking out of one's thought-experiments; computer simulation forces one to recognize all the costs of one's imagined design. As Pylyshyn observes, 'What is needed is . . . a technical language with which to discipline one's imagination.'[11] The discipline provided by computers is undeniable, and especially palpable to the beginning programmer. It is both a good thing—for the reasons just stated—and a bad thing. Perhaps you have known a person so steeped in, say, playing bridge, that his entire life becomes, in his eyes, a series of finesses, end-plays and cross-ruffs. Every morning he draws life's trumps and whenever he can see the end of a project he views it as a lay-down. Computer languages seem to have a similar effect on people who become fluent in them. Although I won't try to prove it by citing examples, I think it is quite obvious that the 'technical language' Pylyshyn speaks of can cripple an imagination in the process of disciplining it.[12]

It has been said so often that computers have huge effects on their users' imaginations that one can easily lose sight of one of the most obvious, but still underrated, ways in which computers achieve this effect, and that is the sheer speed of computers. Before computers came along the theoretician was strongly constrained to ignore the possibility of truly massive and complex processes in psychology because it was hard to see how such processes could fail to *appear* at worst mechanical and cumbersome, at best vegetatively slow, and of course a hallmark of mentality is its swiftness. One might say that the speed of thought defines the upper bound of subjective 'fast', the way the speed of light defines the upper bound of objective 'fast'. Now suppose there had never been any computers but that somehow (by magic, presumably) Kenneth Colby had managed to dream up these flow charts as a proposed model of a part of human organization in paranoia. The flow charts are from his book, *Artificial Paranoia*. (Pergamon, 1975). Figure 1 represents the main program; Figures 2 and 3 are blow-ups of details of the main program.

It is obvious to everyone, even Colby I think, that this is a vastly over-simplified model of paranoia, but had there not been computers to show us how all this processing, and much, much more, can occur in a twinkling, we would be inclined to dismiss the proposal immediately as altogether too clanking and inorganic, a Rube Goldberg machine. Most programs look like that in slow motion (hand simulation) but speeded up they often reveal a dexterity and grace that appears natural. This grace is entirely undetectable via a slow analysis of the program (Cf. time lapse photography of plants growing and buds opening). The grace in operation of AI programs may be mere illusion. Perhaps nature is graceful *all the way down*, but for better or for worse, computer speed has liberated the imagination of theoreticians by opening up the possibility and plausibility of very complex interactive information processes playing a role in the production of cognitive events so swift as to be atomic to introspection.

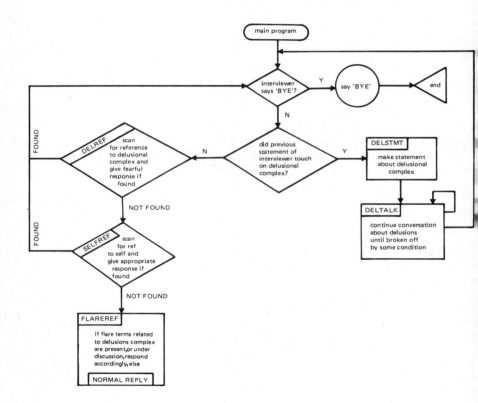

Fig. 1

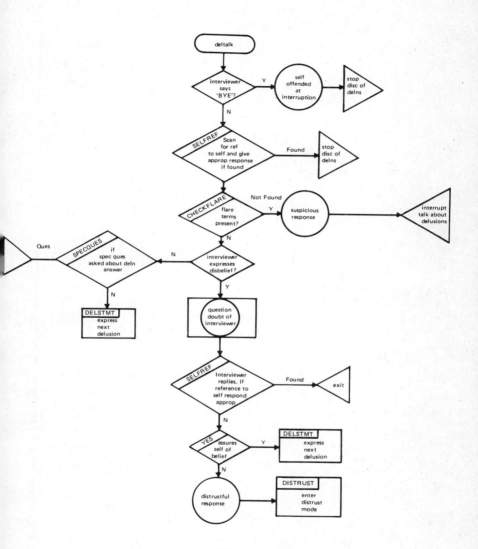

Fig. 2

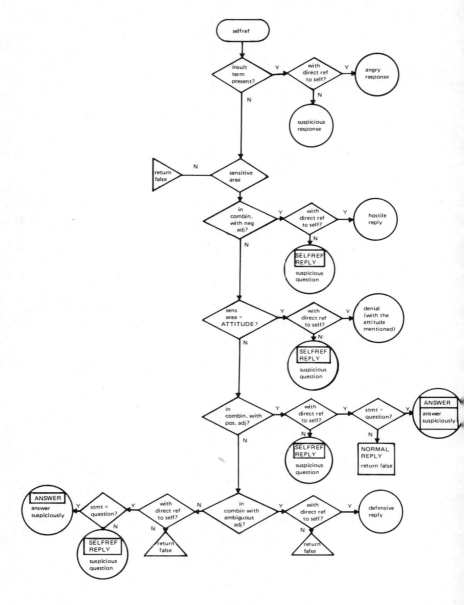

Fig. 3

At last I turn to the important question. Suppose that AI is viewed as I recommend, as a most abstract inquiry into the possibility of intelligence or knowledge. Has it solved any very general problems or discovered any very important constraints or principles? I think the answer is a qualified yes. In particular, I think AI has broken the back of an argument that has bedeviled philosophers and psychologists for over two hundred years. Here is a skeletal version of it: First, the only psychology that could possibly succeed in explaining the complexities of human activity must posit internal representations. This premise has been deemed obvious by just about everyone except the radical behaviourists (both in psychology and philosophy—both Watson and Skinner, and Ryle and Malcolm). Descartes doubted almost everything but this. For the British Empiricists, the internal representations were called ideas, sensations, impressions; more recently psychologists have talked of hypotheses, maps, schemas, images, propositions, engrams, neural signals, even holograms and whole innate theories. So the first premise is quite invulnerable, or at any rate it has an impressive mandate.[13] But, second, nothing is intrinsically a representation of anything; something is a representation only *for* or *to* someone; any representation or system of representations thus requires at least one user or interpreter of the representation who is external to it. Any such interpreter must have a variety of psychological or intentional traits[14]: it must be capable of a variety of *comprehension,* and must have beliefs and goals, so that it can use the representation to inform itself and thus assist it in achieving its goals. Such an interpreter is then a sort of homunculus.

Therefore, psychology *without* homunculi is impossible. But psychology *with* homunculi is doomed to circularity or infinite regress, so psychology is impossible.

The argument given is a relatively abstract version of a familiar group of problems. For instance, it seems to many that we cannot account for perception unless we suppose it provides us with an internal image or model or map of the external world. And yet what good would that image do us unless we have an inner eye to perceive it, and how are we to explain *its* capacity of perception? It also seems to many that understanding a heard sentence must be somehow translating it into some internal message. But how will this message in turn be understood, by translating it into something else? The problem is an old one. Let's call it Hume's Problem, for while he did not state it explicitly, he appreciated its force and strove mightily to escape its clutches. Hume's internal representations were impressions and ideas, and he wisely shunned the notion of an inner self that would intelligently manipulate these items. But this left him with the necessity of getting the ideas and impressions to 'think for themselves'. The result was his theory of the self as a 'bundle' of nothing but impressions and ideas. He attempted to set these impressions and ideas into dynamic interaction by positing various associationistic links, so that each succeeding idea in the stream of consciousness dragged its successor onto the stage according to one or another principle, all without benefit of intelligent *supervision*. It didn't work, of course. It couldn't conceivably work, and Hume's failure is plausibly viewed as the harbinger of doom for any remotely analogous enterprise. On the one hand how could any theory of psychology make sense of representations that understand themselves, and on the other how could any theory of psychology avoid regress or circularity if it posits at least one representation-understander in addition to the representations?

Now no doubt some philosophers and psychologists who have appealed to internal representations over the years have believed in their hearts that somehow the force of this argument could be blunted, that Hume's problem could be solved. But I am sure no one had the slightest idea how to do this until AI and the notion of data-structures came along. Data-structures may or may not be biologically or psychologically realistic representations, but they are, if not living, breathing examples, at least clanking, functioning examples of representations that can be said in the requisite sense to understand themselves.[15]

How this is accomplished can be metaphorically described (and any talk about internal representations is bound to have a large element of metaphor in it) by elaborating our description of AI as a top-down theoretical inquiry.[16] One starts, in AI, with a specification of a whole person or cognitive organism – what I call, more neutrally, an intentional system[17] – or some artificial segment of that person's abilities, such as chess-playing, or answering questions about baseball, and then breaks that largest intentional system into an organization of subsystems, each of which could itself be viewed as an intentional system, with its own specialized beliefs and desires, and hence as formally a homunculus. In fact homunculus talk is ubiquitous in AI, and is almost always illuminating. AI homunculi talk to each other, wrest control from each other, volunteer, sub-contract, supervise and even kill. There seems no better way of describing what is going on.[18] Homunculi are bogeymen only if they duplicate entire the talents they are rung in to explain, a special case of danger (A). If one can get a team or committee of relatively ignorant, narrow-minded, blind homunculi to produce the intelligent behaviour of the whole, this is progress. A flow chart is typically the organizational chart of a committee of homunculi (investigators, librarians, accountants, executives); each box specifies a homunculus by prescribing a function without saying how it is to be accomplished. One says, in effect, put a little man in there to do the job. If we then look closer at the individual boxes, we see that the function of each is accomplished by subdividing it, via another flow chart, into still smaller, more stupid homunculi. Eventually this nesting of boxes within boxes lands you with homunculi so stupid (all they have to do is remember whether to say yes or no when asked) that they can be, as one says, 'replaced by a machine'. One discharges fancy homunculi from one's scheme by organizing armies of such idiots to do the work.

When homunculi at a level interact, they do so by sending messages, and each homunculus has representations which it uses to execute its functions. Thus typical AI discussions do draw a distinction between representation and representation-user.[19] They take the first step of the threatened infinite regress. But as many writers in AI have observed[20], it has gradually emerged from the tinkerings of AI that there is a trade-off between sophistication in the representation and sophistication in the user. The more raw and uninterpreted the representation – like the mosaic of retinal stimulation at an instant – the more sophisticated the interpreter or user of the representation. The more interpreted a representation – the more procedural information is embodied in it, for instance – the less fancy the interpreter need be. It is this fact that permits one to get away with lesser homunculi at high levels, by getting their earlier or lower brethren to do some of the work. One never quite gets completely self-understanding representations, unless one stands back and views all representation in the system from a global vantage point, but all homunculi are ultimately discharged. One gets the advantage of the tradeoff only by sacrificing versatility and universality in one's subsystems and their representations[21], so one's homunculi cannot be too versatile nor can the messages they send and receive have the full flavor of normal human linguistic interaction. We've seen an example of how homuncular communications may fall short in SHRDLU's remark 'because you asked me to'. The context of production and the function of the utterance makes clear that this is a sophisticated communication and the product of a sophisticated representation, but it is not a fully-fledged Gricean speech act. If it were, it would require too fancy a homunculus to use it.

There are two ways a philosopher might view AI data structures. One could grant that they are indeed self-understanding representations or one could cite the various disanalogies between them and prototypical or real representations, such as human statements, paintings, or maps, and conclude that data-structures are not really internal representations at all. But if one takes the latter line, the modest successes of AI simply serve to undercut our first premise: it is no longer obvious that psychology needs internal representations; internal pseudo-representations may do just as well.

It is certainly tempting to argue that since AI has provided us with the only known way of solving Hume's Problem, albeit for very restrictive systems, it must be on the right track, and its categories must be psychologically real, but one might well be falling into danger (B) if one did. We can all be relieved and encouraged to learn that there is a way of solving Hume's Problem, but it has yet to be shown that AI's way is the only way it can be done.

AI has made a major contribution to philosophy and psychology by revealing a particular way in which simple cases of Hume's Problem can be solved. What else has it accomplished of interest to philosophers? I will close by drawing attention to the two main areas where I think the AI approach is of particular relevance to philosophy.

For many years philosophers and psychologists have debated, with scant interdisciplinary communication, about the existence and nature of mental images. These discussions have been relatively fruitless, largely, I think, because neither side had any idea of how to come to grips with Hume's Problem. Recent work in AI, however, has recast the issues in a more perspicuous and powerful framework, and anyone hoping to resolve this ancient issue will find help in the AI discussions.[22]

The second main area of philosophical interest, in my view, is the so-called frame problem.[23] The frame problem is an abstract epistemological problem that was in effect discovered by AI thought-experimentation. When a cognitive creature, an entity with many beliefs about the world, performs an act, the world changes and many of the creatures beliefs must be revised or updated. How? It cannot be that we perceive and notice all the changes. For one thing, many of the changes we know to occur do not occur in our perceptual fields, and hence it cannot be that we rely entirely on perceptual input to revise our beliefs. So we must have internal ways of up-dating our beliefs that will fill in the gaps and keep our internal model, the totality of our beliefs, roughly faithful to the world.

If one supposes, as philosophers traditionally have, that one's beliefs are a set or propositions, and reasoning is inference or deduction from members of the set, one is in for trouble, for it is quite clear, though still controversial, that systems relying only on such processes get swamped by combinatorial explosions in the updating effort. It seems that our entire conception of belief and reasoning must be radically revised if we are to explain the undeniable capacity of human beings to keep their beliefs roughly consonant with the reality they live in.

I think one can find an appreciation of the frame problem in Kant (we might call the frame problem Kant's Problem) but unless one disciplines one's thought-experiments in the AI manner, philosophical proposals of solutions to the problem, including Kant's of course, can be viewed as at best suggestive, at worst mere wishful thinking.

I do not want to suggest that philosophers abandon traditional philosophical method and retrain themselves as AI workers. There is plenty of work to do through thought-experimentation and argumentation disciplined by the canons of philosophical method and informed by the philosophical tradition. Some of the most influential recent work in AI – Minsky's papers on 'Frames' is a good example – is loaded with recognizably philosophical speculations of a relatively unsophisticated nature. Philosophers, I have said, should study AI. Should AI workers study philosophy? Yes, unless they are content to reinvent the wheel every few days. When AI reinvents a wheel, it is typically square, or at best hexagonal, and can only make a few hundred revolutions before it stops. Philosopher's wheels, on the other hand, are perfect circles, require in principle no lubrication, and can go in at least two directions at once. Clearly a meeting of minds is in order.[24]

NOTES AND REFERENCES

1. J. Weizenbaum, *Computer power and human reason* (1976) p. 179, credits Louis Fein with this term.
2. Cf. My *Content and consciousness* (1969) ch. IV and 'Why the law of effect will not go away', *Journal of the Theory of Social Behavior* (Oct. 1975).
3. George Smith and Barbara Klein have pointed out to me that this question can be viewed as several ways ambiguous, and hence a variety of quite different responses might be held to answer such a question. Much of what I say below about different tactics for answering a question of this form can be construed to be about tactics for answering different, but related, questions. Philosophers who intend a question of this sort rhetorically can occasionally be embarrassed to receive in a reply a detailed answer of one variety or another.
4. Cf. Zenon Pylyshyn, 'Complexity and the study of artificial and human intelligence', elsewhere in this volume, for a particularly good elaboration of the top-down strategy, a familiar theme in AI and Cognitive Psychology. Moore and Newell's 'How Can MERLIN Understand?' in Lee W. Gregg, *Knowledge and Cognition*, NY (1974), is the most clear and self-conscious employment of this strategy I have found. Cf. also my 'Why the law of effect will not go away'.
5. This question, and attempts to answer it, constitutes one main branch of epistemology; the other main branch has dealt with the problem of skepticism, and its constitutive question might be 'is knowledge possible?'
6. 'Why the law of effect will not go away'. In summary, the argument is that psychology is impossible if it cannot discharge all its homunculi, but, if it can, then its ultimate non-homuncular constituents will have

capacities requiring no intelligence and hence these constituents can be viewed as computing functions that are intuitively 'effective', hence mechanistically realizable if Church's thesis is true, as there seems no reason to doubt. See also Judson Webb, 'Gödel's theorem and Church's thesis: A prologue to mechanism', *Boston Studies in the Philosophy of Science*, Vol. 31 (1976) Reidel.

7. See esp. Wilfrid Sellars, *Science, Perception and Reality*, (1963) 182 ff.

8. Terry Winograd, *Understanding natural language*, NY (Academic Press, 1972) 12 ff.

9. Cf. Correspondence between Weizenbaum, *et al*. in *Communications of the Association for Computing Machinery;* Weizenbaum, CACM, Vol. 17, no. 7 (July, 1974) 425; Arbib, CACM 17:9 (Sept, 1974) 543; McLeod, CACM 18:9 (Sept, 1975) 546; Wilks, CACM, 19:2 (Feb, 1976) 108; Weizenbaum and McLeod CACM 19:6 (June, 1976) 362.

10. J. Weizenbaum, 'Contextual understanding by computers', CACM 10:8 (1967) 474-480; also *Computer power and human reason*.

11. Cf. Pylyshyn, op cit.

12. Cf. Weizenbaum, *Computer power and human reason*, for a detailed support of this claim.

13. Cf. Jerry Fodor, *The language of thought* (1975) and my Critical Notice, *Mind* (April, 1977).

14. Cf. my 'Intentional systems', *Journal of Philosophy* (1971).

15. Joseph Weizenbaum has pointed out to me that Turing saw from the very beginning that computers could, in principle, break the threatened regress of Hume's Problem, and George Smith has drawn my attention to similar early wisdom in Von Neumann. It has taken a generation of development for their profound insights to be, after a fashion, confirmed by detailed models. It is one thing—far from negligible—to proclaim a possibility in principle, and another to reveal how the possibility might be made actual in detail. Before the relatively recent inventions of AI, the belief that Hume's Problem could be dissolved somehow by the conceptual advances of computer science provided encouragement but scant guidance to psychologists and philosophers.

16. What follows is an elaboration of my discussion in 'Why the law of effect will not go away'.

17. Cf. 'Intentional systems', loc. cit.

18. Cf. Jerry Fodor, 'The appeal to tacit knowledge in psychological explanation', *J. Phil* (1968); F. Attneave, 'In defense of homunculi', in W. Rosenblith, (ed) *Sensory communication*, Cambridge, Mass (MIT Press, 1960); R. deSousa, 'Rational Homunculi', in A. Rorty, (ed) *The Identities of Persons* (1976); Elliot Sober, 'Mental representations', *Synthese, 33* (1976).

19. See e.g. Daniel Bobrow, 'Dimensions of representation', in D. Bobrow and A. Collins (eds) *Representation and understanding*, (Academic Press, 1975).

20. W.A. Woods, 'What's in a link?' in Bobrow and Collins, op. cit.; Z.

Pylyshyn, 'Imagery and artificial intelligence', in C. Wade Savage (ed) *Minnesota Studies in the Philosophy of Science*, Vol. IX (forthcoming); and Pylyshyn, 'Complexity and the study of human and artificial intelligence', in this volume; M. Minsky, 'A framework for representing knowledge', in P. Winston (ed) *The Psychology of Computer Vision*, New York (Prentice-Hall, 1975).
21. Cf. Winograd on the costs and benefits of declarative representations in Bobrow and Collins, op. cit. p. 188.
22. See, e.g. Winston, op. cit. and Pylyshyn, 'Imagery and artificial intelligence', op. cit., 'What the mind's eye tells the mind's brain', *Psychological Bulletin*, (1972) and the literature referenced in these papers.
23. See, e.g. Pylyshyn's paper in this volume; Winograd in Bobrow and Collins, op. cit., Moore and Newell, op. cit., Minsky, op. cit.
24. I am indebted to Margaret Boden for valuable advice on an early draft of this paper. Her book, *Artificial Intelligence and Natural Man*, (Harvester, 1978), provides an excellent introduction to the field of AI for philosophers.

PART III
THE REPRESENTATION OF KNOWLEDGE

CHAPTER 4
REPRESENTING PHYSICAL OBJECTS IN MEMORY
Wendy Lehnert

Many people who have watched artificial intelligence research over the years perceive some irony in the general direction the field has taken. In its early years artificial intelligence was dominated by an interest in behaviours that were ostensibly intelligent: theorem proving, chess playing and general problem solving were strong areas of research activity. These tasks are no longer in the mainstream of artificial intelligence. Research in artificial intelligence is currently dominated by 'fundamental' problems like visual scene analysis and natural language processing. It looks as if we have regressed from activities that are impressively 'adult' to activities that are mastered by three-year-olds. Today, it would be considered a tremendous step forward if we could produce a computer program that conversed on the level of a three-year-old child.

Those processes which are most basic and fundamental for people tend to be the processes that are most challenging for a computer. This is largely due to the fact that the more fundamental a process is, the less we know about the cognition behind it. When an activity requires conscious thought, like playing chess or proving theorems, we are able to say something about the cognition involved, at least insofar as we can be conscious of such things. We can study the process by introspection and protocol analysis. But when a process is so low level, like recognizing the letter 'A' or remembering your middle name, that there is no conscious awareness of how it is achieved, it is very hard to know where to begin our study.

Natural language understanding is one such low level process that cannot be consciously monitored to any significant degree. We cannot introspect about the form of information in memory or the processes which facilitate recognition and generate expectations. Yet these are precisely the problems we must address in developing a theory of information processing. Current research in natural language is centred around problems in semantic processing, the generation of memory representations, and the use of conceptual knowledge.

Understanding language is largely a process of inference generation. If one hears, 'John filled the ice cube tray' it is natural to infer that John filled it with water. This inference can be suppressed if information to the contrary is given. But normally, people comprehend by making inferences to fill in implicit information. Researchers in natural language processing are in general agreement that a system must be able to access knowledge about the world in order to make inferences. However, we do not yet have a comprehensive theory of inference generation that explains exactly what inferences are made, when they are made, and precisely how they are made.

Before we can arrive at a viable theory of inference, we must first establish a theory of memory representation. Inference processes are manipulations of information in memory. It is therefore necessary to have a theory of memory representation in order to specify inference processes. We need to know how information is encoded in memory before we can seriously tackle the processes that manipulate that information.

A few representational systems have been implemented for computer models of natural language processing. Quillian (1968), Winograd (1972), Wilks (1973), and Schank (1975) have all implemented some version of a semantic memory representation. Each of these systems has been motivated by a different task orientation. Quillian was concerned with word disambiguation, Winograd with the execution of procedures, Wilks with translation. Schank developed a representational system that was motivated primarily by problems in inference. His system of 'conceptual dependency' mainly represents verbs by decomposing them into a small set of primitive acts.

In this paper we will describe another representational system that is motivated by problems of inference generation. A set of seven 'object primitives' will be presented which are used primarily for the representation of nouns. These object primitives are intended to augment Schank's set of primitive acts in computer programs which simulate human language processing.

SOME PROBLEMS IN INFERENCE GENERATION

Before describing the seven object primitives, we will look at a few of the problems that motivated them. The problems outlined here do not constitute a comprehensive view of problems in inference. They are merely representative of a class of inferences that benefit from the use of object primitives.

Recognizing appropriate objects

Consider the following sentences:

(1) John went into the grocery store and put a chocolate bar in his shopping basket.

(2) John went into the grocery store and put a chocolate bar in his coat pocket.

In the first instance, we expect John will buy the chocolate bar; he is acting according to the usual rules for shopping in a grocery store. In the second case, we suspect John may intend to steal the chocolate bar; he is not behaving like a normal shopper. These inferences are made on the basis of knowledge we have about normal behaviour in a grocery store, and objects associated with normal behaviour. Had we heard that John put the chocolate bar in a shopping cart or a plastic bag, we would infer that he intended to buy it. But if we hear that he slipped it into his pocket, we infer that he intends to steal it. In addition to these distinctions we can also recognize events that are contextually aberrant. Had we heard that John went into the grocery store and put a chocolate bar into his filing cabinet, we would be confused: what filing cabinet?

Each of these inferences relies on recognizing the intentionality behind human behaviour. In this particular problem, recognition centres around the use of a physical object. We must be able to recognize that a plastic bag may be an acceptable substitute for a shopping basket, but a coat pocket is not.

Context-sensitive associations

Consider the following:

(1) John went to the store and got some milk.

(2) John went into a fancy restaurant and got some milk.

In understanding (1) it is important to infer that the milk is in a milk carton or a milk bottle. No one hearing this sentence imagines John cupping a small quantity of milk in his hands. But (2) should be understood to mean that John ordered some milk and received it in a glass. If these inferences were not made, then the following stories would sound perfectly reasonable:

(3) John went to the store and got some milk. But the glass was very full and he spilled it on the floor.

(4) John went into a fancy restaurant and got some milk. But the container was partially open so he asked for another one.

In (3) the reference to a very full glass which spills doesn't make sense. Stores don't supply milk in glasses. In (4) the same sort of confusion arises. We expect John to be served milk in a glass. When we hear that it came in a container we are forced to conclude that the restaurant must be more like a cafeteria than the term 'fancy restaurant' suggests.

Implicit information

Information is often present only implicitly. Consider the following:

(1) The pen was leaking.

(2) The refrigerator was full.

(3) The car radiator had been drained.

It is natural for people to fill in missing information for each of these statements: the pen was leaking ink, the refrigerator was full of food, water was drained from the car radiator. Inferences of this sort often depend on more than a simple notion of default containment. For example, if John fills an ice cube tray, it is reasonable to assume that he filled it with water. But if John empties the ice cube tray, it is likely that he got ice out of it. Knowledge about objects must be organised so that inferences of this sort can be made easily.

State descriptions

States can often be understood in terms of the actions they enable or disenable.

(1) It was raining so John opened his umbrella.

(2) John opened the bottle and poured a glass of wine.

(3) John opened the folding chair and sat down.

In each of the above examples the verb 'opened' describes a state change that enables specific activities. An open umbrella can keep John from getting wet in the rain. An open bottle can be poured. An open folding chair can be sat upon. These sentences make sense because we understand the enabling causality between specific states and actions. If we substitute the word 'closed' for 'opened' in each of the above, the sentences demand a very different interpretation:

(1) It was raining so John closed his umbrella.

(2) John closed the bottle and poured a glass of wine.

(3) John closed the folding chair and sat down.

In (1) it is difficult to understand why anyone would close an umbrella because it was raining (he didn't want it to get wet?). (2) forces us to assume that John poured wine from some other bottle. Similarly, (3) suggests that John sat elsewhere. Words like 'open' and 'closed' describe different states when used in reference to different objects. The representation acts of an object should include information about these object-specific states.

Associations underlying descriptions

Consider the following story:

> John was sitting in a dining car. When the train stopped the soup spilled.

Suppose we now ask:

> Q: Where was the soup before the train stopped?

It is natural for people to answer:

> A1: In a bowl.

> A2: On the table.

But one answer that seems very unnatural would be:

> A3: On a plate.

Yet a natural description of this scene would include a bowl of soup resting on a plate on a table in a dining car. Acceptable and unacceptable answers indicate that locational specifications must take into account associative structures in memory. Somehow the plate is grouped together with the bowl and is subordinate to the bowl as a descriptive device. Yet the table is independent of this grouping and can be used as an appropriate locational reference. Objects must be organized in memory according to an associative structure which allows us to account for phenomena of this sort.

OBJECT PRIMITIVES

In the same way that a set of 'primitive acts' have been

developed in conceptual dependency for the conceptual representation of acts, a set of 'primitive objects' are used to represent physical objects. Seven primitives will be proposed for representing physical objects. Just as a verb is conceptually represented in conceptual dependency by a decomposition into primitive acts, a noun is conceptually represented by a decomposition into object primitives. When two objects are conceptually similar in some ways and different in others, their object primitive decomposition should reflect those similarities and differences.

The primitives proposed here are designed to encode prototypical information about objects. They reflect normal expectations that people have about familiar objects. But 'normality' is a property which changes as context changes. While milk is normally found in a milk container in a shop, it is normally found in a glass when being served at a restaurant. Object primitives therefore rely to some extent on contingent descriptions. That is, part of the information in an object primitive decomposition may be applicable at some times and not at others. An object primitive description of milk will encode the expectation that milk in a grocery store will be found in a milk container, but milk served in a restaurant will be in a glass.

Setting

When an object is big enough to hold a person it is often called a place. From a conceptual viewpoint, what is important about a place are the activities that are predictably associated with that place. Places like dining cars and grocery stores are characterized by the scripts (Schank and Abelson 1977) associated with them.

A script is a knowledge structure that encodes information about stereotypic event sequences. Scripts describe the normal routines that occur in places, like restaurants, grocery stores, and movie theatres. People engaging in scriptal activities exhibit highly predictable behaviour. These script-based predictions are used in natural language processing in order to generate inferences. The process by which inferences are generated from scriptal knowledge structures is called script application (Cullingford, 1978). For example, suppose a script-based system hears that John went to a restaurant and ate lasagna. Using the restaurant script, the system will be able to infer that John ordered lasagna, a cook prepared it, it was served to him, and he paid for it.

The object primitive SETTING is used to represent places and instrumental objects which have scripts associated with them. When a SETTING is a place, such as a dining car or classroom, the associated scripts describe activities which take place within those SETTINGS. But when a SETTING is not a place in the sense of being occupied by people, but something like a washing machine or pen, then the associated scripts describe the instrumental or functional aspects of that object. Since the normal use of an object can be described in terms of a script, this information is encoded under the primitive SETTING by specifying an associated script.

SETTINGS can be associated with other SETTINGS as well as scripts. For example, a dining car is a SETTING which invokes the related SETTING of a passenger train. Once we hear that John is in a dining car, we immediately infer that John is in a passenger train. If we hear a subsequent reference to 'the train' there is no confusion about what train:

John was sitting in a dining car. The train pulled out.

When the second sentence references a train, there is no ambiguity about what kind of train. We do not wonder if it is a freight train, a toy train, a subway train, or a train of thought. We have already been told, by implicit inference, that John is on a passenger train. The object primitive SETTING describes objects in terms of their associated scripts and other SETTINGS.

There are also cases where an object has a single event strongly associated with it rather than, or in addition to a scriptal event sequence. For example, a pill is something which is normally swallowed. This event is encoded as a simple 'ingest' act. Such events are organized within the SETTING primitive under the description 'Acts'.

[Washing Machine
  (a SETTING with
  <Scripts = $Washing Machine>
  <Settings = Home, Laundromat >)]

[Dining Car
  (a SETTING with
  <Scripts = $Restaurant, $Preparefood>
  <Settings = Passenger Train>)]

[Pill
  (a SETTING with
  <Acts = HUMO <=> INGEST <- pill>)]

[Pen
  (a SETTING with
  <Scripts = $Pen>)]

SETTINGS do not distinguish between places where scripts take place and objects that are the primary prop of a script. The scripts themselves make this distinction. A situational script describes an activity which commonly occurs in a fixed situation, while an instrumental script describes an activity which can occur in various situations but which requires a specific prop for its execution. Hence the restaurant script depends on a restaurant locale, but the pen script relies only on the presence of a pen.

Gestalt

Many objects are characterized as being something greater than the sum of their parts. Trains, stereos, universities, kitchens, all evoke images of many components that interrelate and interact in any number of ways. The object primitive which is designed to capture these clustering effects is a GESTALT. All GESTALT objects are described by their Parts. A place setting is a GESTALT object whose parts include a plate, knife, fork, spoon, glass, napkin, placemat, and so forth. But a place setting is more than just the set of those elements. It is a particular configuration of those elements. A plate balanced on an upside-down glass, is not recognized as a place setting. Similarly, a train is thought to be a linear configuration of cars usually headed by the engine; it is not a set of cars piled up on top of each other.

[Freight Train
    (a GESTALT with
    <Parts = Engine, freight cars, Caboose)
    <Configuration = Linear string of Engine,
    Freight cars, and Caboose>)]

[Place Setting
    (a GESTALT with
    <Parts = Plate, glass, bowl, silverware, napkin>
    <Configuration = Radial configuration with plate
    at center, silverware placed vertically at
    three o'clock, glass upright at one o'clock,
    bowl at eleven o'clock>)]

While GESTALT objects all have configurations in theory, we do not yet have a system for encoding the information that belongs under configurations. The configuration descriptions given in the examples above are intended to convey what sort of information should be encoded under configurations. In order to encode this information in a useful way we need to develop a representational system for spatial relationships. We do not claim to have a theory of spatial representation at this time. But we are offering an organizational framework which specifies where such information should be found in an overall memory structure.

Relational

In addition to objects that can be described in terms of their components or parts, many objects are distinguished by the relationships they normally assume with other objects. Containers such as rooms, bottles, shopping carts, etc., are described by a capacity for containment. Supporting objects, like tables, chairs, and plates, are described by their ability to support other things. Hinges support doors, bulletin boards hold papers, and chalk adheres to blackboards. The object primitive which encodes prototypical relationships between objects is a 'RELATIONAL' object.

All RELATIONAL objects have a 'relationlink' which specifies the relation the object normally assumes. The relationlink value for a table will be 'on-top-of' while a bottle takes the relationlink value 'inside-of'. Each RELATIONAL object includes constraints for the relations specified under its relationlink. For example, a piano stool, of the variety which opens up, has two relationlinks: on-top-of and inside-of. But different constraints operate on the objects that assume these relations. Something that goes inside the piano stool must not exceed certain dimensional constraints. A final aspect to RELATIONAL objects is the possibility of instrumental objects which enable certain relationships. For example, a bulletin board maintains a 'stuck-to' relationship with papers but only if a thumb tack is utilized:

[Table
    (a RELATIONAL with
    <Relationlink = on-top-of>)]

[Blackboard
    (a RELATIONAL with
    <Relationlink = stuck-to>
    <Constraints = chalk>)]

[Bulletin board
    (a RELATIONAL with
    <Relationlink = stuck-to>
    <Constraints = paper>
    <Instruments = thumb tack>)]

One aspect of RELATIONAL objects that may seem to be a natural part of these descriptions is the notion of specific defaults. For example, an egg carton is a RELATIONAL object with a very strong tendency to harbour eggs. The idea of default objects of this sort is a very strong one which enables a large class of inferences. If John fills his lighter, it is standard to infer that the lighter is filled with lighter fluid. If a pen leaks, it is expected to leak ink. When the tank of a car is full, it should be full of gasoline. This characteristic is not restricted to RELA-TIONAL objects, however. A faucet is expected to produce water and a radio commonly emits music or verbal communication. The ideas of production and consumption among objects motivate the next two object primitives.

Source and Consumer

A 'SOURCE' is an object which is characterized by its tendency to produce other things. Sugar bowls are SOURCES of sugar, egg boxes are SOURCES of eggs, and faucets are SOURCES of water. A 'CONSUMER' is an object which tends to consume other things. A drain consumes liquids and a slot machine consumes coins. Of course a slot machine can also be a SOURCE of coins but it tends on the average to be more of a CONSUMER.

A SOURCE is related to the objects it produces by an 'output' link while CONSUMERS have corresponding 'input' links. In addition to these descriptors, some SOURCES and CONSUMERS require 'activation' scripts and/or 'deactivation' scripts. For example, a sponge and a pipe are both SOURCES that need to be activated and deactivated.

[Wine Bottle
    (a SOURCE with
    <Output = Wine>
    <Activation = $Pour>)]

[Book
    (a SOURCE with
    <Output = MObject>
    <Activation = $Read>)]

[Mailbox
    (a CONSUMER with
    <Input = Letters>)]

[Ice Cube Tray
  (a SOURCE with
  <Output = Ice Cubes>)
  (a CONSUMER with
  <Input = Water>)]

[Sponge
  (a SOURCE with
  <Output = Liquids>
  <Activation = $Squeeze>)
  (a CONSUMER with
  <Input = Liquids>
  <Activation = $Wipe>)]

[Pipe
  (a SOURCE with
  <Ouput = Smoke>
  <Activate = $Smoke>)
  (a CONSUMER with
  <Input = Tobacco>
  <Activation = $Smoke>)]

Object primitives can be used to encode conceptual senses of some verbs and adjectives as well as nouns. 'To empty' an object means to do something which results in an 'inoperative' flag on that object's SOURCE description. If John empties an ice cube tray, we can infer from the SOURCE description of an ice cube tray that he got ice from it. If John fills an ice cube tray, we infer from the CONSUMER description of an ice cube tray that he put water in it.

When objects are described as SOURCES and CON-SUMERS their descriptions are necessarily based on egocentric experience. That is, the most common experience of these objects must dominate their conceptual description. For example, most people experience a wine bottle as a source of wine. But someone who works in a winery, who fills the bottles but never drinks the stuff, will conceptualize a wine bottle as more of a CONSUMER than a SOURCE. Most people share a tremendous amount of episodic knowledge. Since the inferences made in natural language processing are derived from this realm of generally shared and common experience, the knowledge representations used in natural language processing must reflect this body of common episodic knowledge.

This egocentric bias in conceptual perception has a significant impact on all of our inferencing mechanisms. Environmentalists try to convince people that the earth is not an endless SOURCE of resources and that it may not be very bright to think of the ocean as a CONSUMER of all our wastes. People conceptualize the world according to their immediate experience of it and therefore operate with something less than a global view of things. A garbage can is a CONSUMER of garbage since objects which are in the garbage can do not have to be dealt with anymore. The fact that garbage does not mystically disappear from the cosmos is an intellectual awareness lacking the immediacy of episodic knowledge.

Separator and Connector

In causal chain theory, states and acts alternate; states very often enable acts and acts result in state changes (Schank, 1973). A state is often conceptually significant because of the acts it enables or disenables. The last two primitive objects are designed to represent objects in terms of states which enable and disenable conceptual acts.

A 'SEPARATOR' disconnects two regions or spatial locations with respect to a Primitive Act. For example, an opaque wall separates two regions with respect to visual MTRANS (information transfers achieved by sight). SEPARATORS disenable specific acts. A 'CONNECTOR' joins two regions or spatial locations with respect to a Primitive Act. A road connects two locations with respect to PTRANS (physical transfers of location). CONNECTORS enable specific acts. Objects must assume a fixed state when being described in terms of SEPARATORS and CONNECTORS. For example, an open window is a CONNECTOR with respect to MTRANS and PTRANS between the inner and outer regions bounded by the window. A closed window is still a CONNECTOR with respect to visual MTRANSing but it is a SEPARATOR with respect to auditory MTRANSing and all PTRANSing. An open window and a closed window are two conceptually distinct objects. It must be understood that an open window can be transformed into a closed window, and vice-versa, but the conceptual representation of a window is ambigious unless we know whether the window is open or closed. If a window is open we want to infer that air passes through it and that physical objects (of appropriate dimensions) can be PTRANSed through the window. But if a window is closed, none of this should be assumed. Conceptual descriptions of objects must distinguish objects in terms of valid inferences about those objects.

[Window (closed)
   (a SEPARATOR with
   <Disenabled = PTRANS,
   MTRANS ← SPEAK>)
   (a CONNECTOR with
   <Enabled = MTRANS ← ATTEND ← Eyes>)]

[Window (open)
   (a CONNECTOR with
   <Enabled = MTRANS, PTRANS>)]

[Road
   (a CONNECTOR with
   <Enabled = $Drive, $Bicycle, $Walk>)]

[Cut (open)
   (a CONNECTOR with

                            ┌→ outside (Hum0)
   <Enabled = PTRANS ← Blood ←┤
                            └⤚inside (Hum0)
                            ┌→ inside (Hum0)
           PTRANS ← Germs ←┤
                             └⤚outside (Hum0)>)]

[Band-aid (on)
   (a SEPARATOR with

                                ┌→ inside (Hum0)
   <Disenabled = PTRANS ← Germs ←┤
                               └⤚outside (Hum0)>)]

[Umbrella (open)
　　(a SEPARATOR with

$$\text{<Disenabled = PTRANS} \leftarrow \text{Rain} \leftarrow \begin{cases} \rightarrow \text{Hum0} \\ \\ \rightarrow \text{<sky>)} \end{cases}$$

It is important to describe SEPARATORS and CON-
NECTORS in terms of enabled and disenabled acts. For
example, a dog leash might be thought of as a CONNECTOR
which fixes some locational proximity on the dog. But this is not
a very useful representation in terms of potential inferences. A
dog leash (when on the dog) is actually a SEPARATOR which
disenables the dog from PTRANSing itself outside a fixed
radius.

USING OBJECT PRIMITIVES

In section two we outlined a few problems in inference which
are related to representational issues for physical objects. Now
we will indicate how object primitives can be utilized to help
solve these problems.

Recognizing appropriate objects

Scripts very often predict events that involve physical objects.
In the restaurant script we expect the patron to sit in a chair and
eat from a table. Sometimes there is a lot of flexibility within a
script concerning precisely what object can be used. For
example, in the grocery store script we expect the customer to
use a shopping cart for collecting his purchases. But there is a
wide spectrum of appropriate substitutions for a shopping cart.
The customer could use a shopping basket, a plastic bag, a
wicker basket from home, a shopping trolley, a cardboard
carton, or any one of a large number of possibilities. Of course,
there are many substitutions that are not acceptable. A grocery

store customer who puts items in his pockets or in a hollowed-out book will arouse suspicion.

If the script applier is responsible for recognizing when the customer is using an acceptable substitution, the script must include some descriptive constraints that distinguish appropriate substitutions from inappropriate ones. It will not be sufficient to give the script a pre-assigned list of all the possible objects that could be used. No matter how exhaustive any such list is, there will always be something missing that qualifies as an acceptable substitution. The script needs some conceptual description of those features that must be present in all acceptable objects. Any object not meeting these conceptual constraints can then be recognized as inappropriate.

On an intuitive level, we might define acceptable substitutions for a shopping cart to be those containers which can be carried, pushed, or pulled, and which do not hide their contents. These conceptual constraints can be represented using the object primitives RELATIONAL, SETTING, and CONNECTOR. An object which can be appropriately substituted for a shopping cart in the grocery store script is one that satisfies the following conceptual constraints in its object primitive representation:

(a SETTING with   I
    <Acts = Hum0 <=> PTRANS <- OBJ ←— -
                                                    |
    ┌ — — — — — — — — — — — ┐
    | I |
    | Hum0 <=> GRASP ← OBJ ←HAND |
    └ — — — — — — — — — — — ┘

                                       I
    Hum0 <=> PTRANS ← OBJ ← - - -
                                            |
    ┌ — — — — — — — — —— — ┐
    | I |
    | Hum0 <=> PROPEL ← OBJ ←HAND |
    └ — — — — — — — — — — — ┘

(a RELATION with
    <Relationlink = Inside-of>)
(a CONNECTOR with   I
    <Enabled = Hum1 <=> MTRANS ← ¬
┌ — — — — — — — — ─┘ — — ─┐
│   I   │
│   Hum1 <=> ATTEND ← EYES>)   │
└ — — — — — — — — — — — — — ┘

These object primitive descriptions specify a container that can be carried, pushed, or pulled, and which does not obscure or hide its contents. Any appropriate substitute for a shopping basket, such as a trolley, box, carrier-bag, or plastic sack, will meet these specifications. Inappropriate objects like pockets, book shelves, dump trucks, plates, or hollowed-out books, will fail to meet these descriptive constraints.

OK THINGS:
    cart
    box (if open)
    crate
    carrier-bag
    plastic sack
    basket

NOT OK THINGS:
    pocket (fails the CONNECTOR specification)
    book shelf (fails the SETTING specification)
    dump truck (fails the SETTING specification)
    plate (fails the RELATIONAL specification)
    hollowed-out book (fails the CONNECTOR specification)

If a script encodes descriptions of objects in terms of object primitives and can check object primitive decompositions of the objects mentioned in input sentences, there will be no recognition problem when appropriate substitutions for prototypical objects can be made.

Context-sensitive associations

While many psychologists have concentrated on the concept of associative memory, little research has been conducted concerning the role of associative memory in natural language processing. Quillian (1968) proposed a semantic network for the task of word disambiguation which relied on intersection searches and node expansion within associative memory. One of the problems with these intersection searches was a lack of direction that resulted in an exponential increase of the number of concept nodes examined. For example, suppose the network tried to disambiguate 'log' in 'John consulted the ship's log'. Many of the search paths would begin with the concept for a ship and move into a related string of associations that could never lead to a ship's log. For example, a possible search path might look like 'ship-ocean-fish-scales-reptile-lizard-. . .' Since the number of doomed paths increases exponentially with each expansion, expansion searches in associative memory tend to blow up before they make the desired connection.

While we do not agree with Quillian's use of intersection searches for the task of word disambiguation, there do seem to be situations where an intersection search is needed (Lehnert, 1978). When an intersection search is required, it must be implemented with a search strategy that is smart enough to ignore hopeless paths. This could be done in one of two ways: (1) the system could have some evaluation mechanism that discerns when it is 'hot' or 'cold', or (2) the system could initiate fewer paths and thereby never consider all the paths which lead off in a wrong direction. It is possible to implement a search mechanism of the second sort using object primitives as the basis of an associative memory model. The critical key in eliminating bad paths is to introduce associative links that are sensitive to context.

Associative memory is more than a static structure of concepts and fixed links between concepts. The set of concepts in memory is static, but the associative links between concepts change as context shifts. For example, in the context of a dairy farm, there should be a strong link between the concept of a cow and the concept of milk. But in the context of a grocery store, the associative links of milk should lead to milk cartons or milk bottles instead of cows.

We have seen how slots within a primitive description of one object can be filled with another object. For example, the output slot within the source description of a wine bottle is filled with wine. This amounts to an associative link from wine bottles to wine; if we examine the conceptual description of a wine bottle, we get to wine. But there should also be a link which will allow us to get from wine to wine bottles; the conceptual description of wine should lead us to a wine bottle in most contexts. In the same way, the gestalt description of a table setting will take us to plates, but there should be an associative link from plates to table settings as well. And the relational description of a bulletin board will take us to thumb tacks, but another link is needed to get from thumb tacks to a bulletin board. Before inserting reciprocal links in memory, two restrictions must be observed.

(1) Some associative links should operate in one direction only. For example, it is reasonable that a link should exist from dining cars to restaurants since a dining car can be easily recognized to be a type of restaurant. But it is not so clear that a link should exist from restaurants to dining cars. If asked to enumerate all the different kinds of restaurants there are, dining cars may not get included as an example one thinks of when considering different kinds of restaurants.

(2) Associative links may be present in some contexts but not in others. For example, in the context of eating at a table, it is reasonable that there should be a link from plates to table settings. But in the context of washing dishes, it is less likely that a plate will be perceived as part of a table setting. The organization of associative memory should be sensitive to context.

The first restriction will prevent us from postulating associative links arbitrarily whenever a need for one seems to arise. The second restriction forces us to design contingencies in conceptual memory. By utilizing associative links between objects that are contingent upon context, the context of a story can control descriptions of objects in conceptual memory.

There are four kinds of contingent links which can exist between objects outside of their object primitive descriptions. The type of link which is used in any given case is determined by the object being pointed to. The four links are:

OUTPUTFROM (points to a SOURCE)
INPUTTO (points to a CONSUMER)

PARTOF (points to a GESTALT)
DEFAULTLOCATION (points to a RELATIONAL)

The conceptual definition of a prototypical object in memory may include one or more of these associative links along with default or contingent values. A contingency in these cases is always specified by either a setting or a script.

For example, the conceptual definition for soup describes an entity which is 'outputfrom' a bowl during the eating script, and 'outputfrom' a can while in the SETTING of a kitchen or supermarket. It also has a 'defaultlocation' inside a pot during the prepare-food script. A bowl is described as a RELATIONAL object with locationlink = inside-of and as a SOURCE object during the eating script with output = food. It is also 'partof' a place setting during the eating script and it has a defaultlocation inside a cabinet when in the SETTING of a kitchen.

[Soup
    <OUTPUTFROM = (a bowl during $Eat)
                          (a can during kitchen, supermarket)>
    <DEFAULTLOCATION = (a pot during $Preparefood>)]

[Bowl
    (a RELATIONAL with
       <Locationlink = Inside-of>)
    (a SOURCE with
       <Output = food during $Eat>)
    <PARTOF = (a placesetting during $Eat>)
    <DEFAULTLOCATION = (a cabinet during Kitchen>)]

By utilizing contingent descriptions, it is possible to make the desired associative connection without examining a host of irrelevant associations.

(1) John was cooking some soup when the pot cracked.

(2) John was cooking some soup when the vase cracked.

The reference to a pot in (1) seems reasonable because the conceptual description of soup predicted that soup is found inside a pot when the cooking script is being executed. We assume that the pot which cracked is the same pot John is using to prepare soup. This assumption is made on the basis of an associative link from soup to pots. Since the association needed for (1) could be made within the context of the prepare – food script, it was not necessary to consider irrelevant associations with cans and bowls before recognizing the connection with pots. The reference to a vase in (2) is more problematic since there is no associative link from soup to vases. Without more information, there is no connection between the two events other than their simultaneous occurrence.

Implicit information

Causal connections within text often rely on inferences that fill in missing information:

John's pen leaked on his shirt and the ink wouldn't wash out.

In order to understand this sentence it is necessary to know that ink leaked from the pen. Many inferences of this sort can be handled by examining the SOURCE or CONSUMER description of an object.

If John fills an ice cube tray, we can infer from the CONSUMER description of the ice cube tray that John probably filled it with water. Similarly, if John empties an ice cube tray, we can infer from the SOURCE description of an ice cube tray that John got ice cubes out of it. When an object does not have a SOURCE or CONSUMER description in its object primitive decomposition, we can make no inferences about a default object in events of filling and emptying that object. For example, if John fills a carton, we cannot make any assumptions about what he put in the carton without some additional information.

State descriptions

Many states can be represented in terms of object primitive decompositions. Often an object which assumes two states is best described in terms of two distinct conceptual objects. For example, a closed window and an open window are conceptually distinct because of the different acts they disenable and enable. Things can be PTRANSed through an open window, but not through a closed one, without breaking it.

A conceptual representation for states should make it easy to recognize causal relationships between states and acts. It is not enough to tag a memory token with the descriptor 'Open' or 'Closed' since these states descriptors mean different things for different objects. Open doors, open coats, open umbrellas, and open electrical switches all carry inferences which are specific to those objects. By using the object primitives CONNECTOR and SEPARATOR, many of the acts enabled and disenabled by these states are immediately apparent in the conceptual decomposition of these objects. An open door enables PTRANS (CONNECTOR) while a closed door disenables PTRANS (SEPARATOR). An open umbrella disenables the PTRANS of rain on to whatever is under the umbrella (SEPARATOR). An open electrical switch disenables the PTRANS of current (SEPARATOR) while a closed switch enables that same PTRANS (CONNECTOR).

CONNECTORS and SEPARATORS can be used to describe the states 'open' and 'closed'. SOURCES and CONSUMERS can be used to describe other states such as 'on', 'off', 'full', and 'empty'. When a radio is off it is not realizing its SOURCE description. When it's on, it is. When a wine bottle is empty, it is not realizing its SOURCE description. When it's full, it is. When a garbage disposal is on, it is realizing its CONSUMER description.

Other miscellaneous states can be described in terms of object primitive descriptions as well. When the sun is 'up' it is realizing its SOURCE description with Output = light and heat. When John has his sunglasses 'on' they are acting as a SEPARATOR which disenables the PTRANS of light from the sun to John's eyes. When the telephone is 'broken' it is not realizing its SETTING description with the associated telephone script.

These state descriptions are useful because they specify in what way the state of a particular object relates to potential actions. Any representation of states which does not lend itself to object-specific inferences is a weak representation. Object primitives provide a method for state representation when the conceptual meaning of a given state varies over different objects which can assume that state.

Associations Underlying Descriptions

Problems in inference arise in language generation as well as language comprehension. Even seemingly simple answers to questions can rely on a strong foundation of inference. For example, answers that describe a locational specification rely on assumptions about what the questioner knows and doesn't know. A similar but less obvious problem occurs when answers rely on common associations in memory. Suppose John is eating soup in a dining car. A conceptualization of that scene will include the fact that the soup must be in a bowl which is on a plate that probably rests on some sort of place mat or table cloth on top of a table on the floor of the dining car which is part of a passenger train.

But when asked to describe the location of the soup, not all of these objects are equally useful as locational specifications:

> in a bowl
> on a plate (bad answer)
> on a table cloth (bad answer)
> on a table
> on the floor (bad answer)
> in the dining car
> in the train

The distinction between a good answer and a bad answer can be attributed to associative structures in memory which serve to 'clump' certain objects together into conceptual entities. By using the four associative links described in 4.2 (outputfrom, inputto, partof, defaultlocation), it is possible to design a retrieval heuristic which returns only those locational specifications that seem natural. For example, the object primitive decomposition for soup includes a Defaultlocation link (inside-of) pointing to a bowl during the eating script. Similarly, a table setting also has a defaultlocation link (on-top-of) pointing to a table during the eating script. A bowl has a partof link pointing to a place setting during the eating script, and a place setting points to a table setting by way of a permanent partof link. Then, given the following path, a retrieval heuristic can produce appropriate answers like 'in a bowl', or 'on a table', by simply ignoring all objects in the path connected by a partof link:

> soup (Defaultlocation)
> bowl (Partof)
> place setting (Partof)
> table setting (Defaultlocation)
> table

The actual construction of this path is described in Lehnert (1978). The effectiveness of the heuristic relies on a model of associative memory that distinguishes different types of associations. Partof links connect objects which are clumped together under GESTALT descriptions. These links are more permanent than a Defaultlocation link which connects objects according to locational expectations. A table setting is not part of a table but it is often found on top of a table. Soup is not part of a bowl but it is often found inside a bowl. On the other hand, a bowl is part of a place setting and a place setting is part of a table setting according to the GESTALT decompositions of place setting and table setting. It is intuitively agreeable that a retrieval heuristic should prefer information which is contextually sensitive (expected locations) to information that is independent of context (GESTALT configurations). At the most general level, an answer to a question should provide the questioner with information he does not already have. Since people are more likely to have information that is independent of context, it makes sense to direct retrieval heuristics toward contextually-sensitive information.

COMPUTERS, HUMAN KNOWLEDGE AND LANGUAGE

There is a common belief that computers can only manipulate precise data in a ruthlessly predictable manner and they are therefore best suited for numerical operations. This idea is valid only insofar as computers are restricted to precisely stated algorithmic processes. But assumptions about what can or cannot be conveyed in an algorithm very often reflect a limited understanding of processes and the power of process models as descriptive devices.

Computers are still in the infancy of their evolution in terms of computational domains. Originally computers were designed to manipulate numbers and perform arithmetic computations. General research in computer science is still dominated by a view of computers as number crunchers. But a growing number of researchers (primarily in artificial intelligence) have come to think of computers in a larger context: a computer is a symbol manipulating machine. Numbers are merely one kind of symbol. If people are slow to grasp the power of general symbol manipulation, this reluctance is quite understandable. After all, human beings have been processing numbers for thousands of years according to rigorous rules of manipulation that readily lend themselves to algorithmic description. The only other widespread symbolic system people have developed is the communication device of language. But the comprehension and generation of language is not understood algorithmically in the way we understand processes for adding or multiplying numbers. If computers are 'good at' numerical manipulations and 'useless for' natural language processing, this does not reflect anything about computers, arithmetic or human language. It simply indicates two things: people understand arithmetic in terms of process models, and people have no analogous process model understanding of human language.

With this in mind, we must pursue the notion of computational process models for the cognitive processes which underly human language comprehension. These computational processes will manipulate knowledge representations according to precisely defined algorithms. But neither the information in these knowledge structures nor the functions which operate on that information have to conform to the laws or the notational appearance of mathematics as we know it. To assume that our current knowledge of formal mathematics has exhausted or even touched on all realms of possible symbol manipulation would be rather narrow minded and naive.

The knowledge a natural language system needs about the physical world should form the basis for a cognitive understanding of the world rather than a formal or scientific understanding. Within the framework of cognitive processes we can talk about different kinds of knowledge that people have about physical objects. To illustrate the wide range of knowledge which is associated with objects, consider what people know about balloons.

To begin with, there is perceptual knowledge about balloons. People have visual images of balloons which they can consult or refer to when they think about balloons. There is perhaps one image of a round balloon and another of an elongated balloon. There is an image for an inflated balloon and one for an uninflated balloon. People can visualize the knot tying a full balloon and the opening of an uninflated balloon. In addition to visual information about balloons, other perceptual information includes an auditory image of the noise a balloon makes when it's being blown up, the noise of air escaping from a full balloon, what happens when people rub balloons to make them squeak, or the popping noise when a balloon bursts. Further perceptual information might include a smell peculiar to balloons or a tactile sensation associated with them.

After perceptual information, we might next consider episodic information which people have about balloons. Episodic knowledge of an object is composed of the individualized experiences people accumulate either first hand or vicariously. For example, many people may share a first-hand traumatic balloon episode from an early age, in which a highly valued balloon was either lost or broken. Other people may harbour fond memories of water fights or balloon bombings, from a slightly later age. Most of us have seen animals created by someone twisting and tying balloons together. These episodic associations constitute another type of knowledge people have about objects.

Finally there is cultural knowledge about objects. Balloons are known to be relatively cheap and common objects in our culture. They are appropriate decorations for light, happy festivities and celebrations. And balloons are entertaining to small children.

In addition to all this, people have predictive knowledge about the behaviour of balloons. People know what happens if you blow one up and let it go. They know what is liable to cause a balloon to burst, and how a balloon filled with air is different from a balloon filled with helium. This sort of information is both perceptual and episodic.

The system of object primitives introduced here is not intended to capture all the different kinds of knowledge people have about objects. Perceptual and episodic knowledge is not found within an object primitive decomposition. Features such as shape, size, weight and composition are not dealt with. Therefore a flashlight and a penlight are indistinguishable according to their object primitive representations. But the decomposition of a black light would differentiate it from ordinary light fixtures because the inferences about visual enablement are different for a black light than for a flashlight or desk lamp.

When we develop a representational system to encode mundane knowledge about the world, we are engaging in what might be described as applied epistemology. We attempt to characterize and organize knowledge people have about the world. In evaluating artificial intelligence research it is essential to remember that our interest in human knowledge and our methodology for studying a problem is extremely task oriented. A sociologist or psychologist might be interested in whether or not a specific piece of knowledge is innate, acquired, culture-specific, or universal. But from the viewpoint of artificial intelligence, we will ask how a specific piece of knowledge is used by cognitive processes, in tasks like problem solving, visual scene analysis or natural language understanding.

While it is clear that people have lots of perceptual and episodic knowledge about objects, it is not clear that such information is needed for the task of natural language processing. Perceptual information is needed for other tasks, such as vision recognition, but is it necessary for language comprehension? We know that inference mechanisms are needed for understanding language, yet it is not clear exactly what kinds of knowledge are required for a complete inferencing system. As we can see from the representational system of object primitives, a great deal can be accomplished without accessing information from episodes or perceptual imagery. As we implement more computer programs to simulate human language understanding, we will learn more about categories of human knowledge and the application of that knowledge in natural language processing.

REFERENCES

Cullingford, R.E. *Script Application: Computer understanding of newspaper stories.* Computer Science Dept., Research Report #116, New Haven, Ct. (Yale University, 1977).

Lehnert, W. *The Process of question answering.* Hillsdale, New Jersey (Lawrence Erlbaum Assoc., 1978).

Quillian, M.R. 'Semantic memory'. In *Semantic information processing*, M. Minsky (ed) Cambridge, Mass. (MIT Press, 1968).

Schank, R.C. 'Causality and reasoning'. *Technical Report* 1. Istituto per gli Studi Semantici e Cognitivi, Castagnola, Switzerland, (1973).

Schank, R.C. *Conceptual information processing.* Amsterdam (North Holland, 1975).

Schank, R.C. and Abelson, R.P. *Scripts, plans, goals and understanding.* Hillsdale, New Jersey (Lawrence Erlbaum Assoc., 1977).

Wilks, Y. 'An artificial intelligence approach to machine translation'. In *Computer models of thought and language* R. Schank and K. Colby (eds). San Francisco (W.H. Freeman & Co., 1973).

Winograd, T. (1972). *Understanding natural language.* New York (Academic Press, 1972).

CHAPTER 5
REPRESENTING KNOWLEDGE IN INTELLIGENT SYSTEMS
John McDermott

One of the most difficult theoretical problems faced by epis-
temologists, psychologists, and artificial intelligence researchers
is the nature of knowledge representation in memory. All
intelligent behaviour depends upon the ability of a system to
access large amounts of information and to continuously refine
that information in the face of new data. In order to accomplish
these tasks effectively, a system, whether natural or artificial,
must have an efficient means of representing, retrieving, and
updating its knowledge.

Philosophers who have speculated upon the nature of memory
representations have done little to improve upon the Humean
notion of 'photographic' impressions. Epistemological constructs such as 'sense-data', 'propositions', or 'icons', fail to
provide the basis for a comprehensive and useful model of
thought processes. What is needed is a precise and detailed
description of suitable knowledge structures and their associated
operators. The importance of artificial intelligence (AI) research
is that it provides us with both a theoretical framework and a
methodological tool for exploring the low-level aspects of
knowledge representation. Whether or not humans utilize the
same, or even a similar, technique for representing knowledge is
irrelevant; the AI approach serves to demonstrate the minima
for a plausible, physically-realized, epistemic system.

Work in AI has as its goal the construction of programs
which, when run on a computer, will exhibit intelligent
behaviour of the same generality and power as that exhibited by
human beings. During the past two decades, many systems have
been built that are capable of doing a single task in a
well-defined and limited environment. Some of these systems

are quire powerful; the tasks that they are capable of are difficult ones by human standards. However, none of these powerful systems is general. The capabilities that each possesses cannot be exploited in tasks different from the one for which it was designed. Furthermore, the designers of each of these systems have placed rather severe restrictions on the complexity of the environments with which their systems are capable of interacting.

Unfortunately, building a system whose capabilities are general as well as powerful involves more than simply conjoining a number of powerful, single-task systems. Considerable effort has been directed toward solving the problems hindering the development of such systems. In this paper I will consider the two problems that seem to me to be the most serious:

> The problem of the *accessibility* of relevant knowledge. A general-problem solving system must be able to recognize the relevance of whatever knowledge it has in whatever situation it finds itself.

> The problem of the *refinement* of incomplete knowledge. A general problem solving system must be able to refine its knowledge so that it will not repeatedly make the same mistakes.

I will first discuss some of the weaknesses of two schemes for representing knowledge in a general-problem system and indicate some of the characteristics that any adequare scheme will have to possess. Secondly, I will show through a description of the production-system language, OPS, that these characteristics can be realized by making use of what is called the production-system control structure. Finally, I will describe a production-system, currently under construction, that is written in OPS, and will explain why we think this system can become a system capable of performing a wide range of tasks in a complex environment.

The Problems of Accessibility and Refinement

I have suggested that creating a system having generality as well as power involves more than conjoining a large number of distinct programs, each of which is highly capable in a single task. It is perhaps not obvious why this solution is inadequate since, clearly, if each of the programs were associated with a description of the task that it could perform, then a system containing these programs could simply select the one whose associated description matched the description of the task currently demanded. Part of the inadequacy of the multi-program approach is due to the fact that a general problem solving system is not just a system that can perform many tasks, but a system that can perform each of these tasks under a wide variety of conditions—that is, a system that can operate successfully in a complex environment. Since no existing AI program is capable of functioning in a complex environment, any system that was simply a collection of these programs would not be general. But again, this problem may not seem particularly hard to solve since a number of different programs could be written to perform the same task under different sets of conditions. Then, instead of simply associating each program with a description of the task it is capable of, one could associate each program with that description together with a description of the conditions under which that program could be expected to perform its task successfully.

This solution appears to have some plausibility until one considers the amount of effort that would be involved in building it. The number of programs that would be needed for such a system would be (at the very least) immense. Now surely there is nothing intrinsically wrong with immensity, but as anyone who has attempted to write a program capable of interesting behaviour knows, the job of fully testing the program and refining it to the point where its behaviour is adequate is a long and arduous one. Thus any attempt to attain generality that relied on a large number of independent programs, programs that shared no knowledge, could hardly be expected to succeed, since each program would have to be perfected independently.

If we consider for a moment why the multi-program approach to generality is inadequate, it should be clear that it is an attempt to solve the accessibility problem without taking the refinement problem into account. By representing knowledge in a way that brings together, and organizes, those pieces of knowledge that are relevant to each task, the problem of how the system is to find the knowledge it needs for a particular task is apparently solved. But by representing knowledge in this way, the problem of refinement becomes insurmountable.

A solution to the accessibility problem that takes the problem of refinement into account has been proposed by Newell and Simon and is made use of in their general problem solving system, GPS (Newell, Shaw, and Simon, 1960; Newell and Simon, 1972). In order to make it possible to refine the knowledge in their system in a way that makes repeatedly refining the same knowledge unnecessary, and avoids the need of storing a great deal of redundant knowledge, they represent the system's knowledge as a 'table-of-connections'. This table effectively associates goals that the system might have with the operators that may be of use in achieving those goals. More precisely, each entry in the table-of-connections associates a difference with a list of operators. A difference is the difference between some possible situation and a goal. Each of the associated operators may be useful in reducing this difference and thus in bringing the system closer to its goal.

In solving a problem, GPS first computes the difference between the situation it is in and its goal, which, initially, is simply to perform whatever task is demanded of it. It then selects one of the operators associated with that difference and tests to determine if the operator can be applied to the current situation. If the operator can be applied, a new situation will result that is less different from the goal than was the original situation; GPS will repeat the process using this new situation in place of the original one. If the operator selected cannot be applied, then GPS will generate, as a subgoal, the goal of reducing the difference between the current situation and the situation to which the operator can be applied.

This representational scheme makes it rather easy to refine a system's knowledge. If GPS encounters a situation that it does not know how to deal with, a new entry can be added to its table-of-connections specifying the appropriate operators in that situation given its current goal. If GPS makes a mistake, one of the operators associated with a particular difference has been applied in a situation in which it should not have been applied; this can be corrected by specifying that that operator is inapplicable in situations like the current one.

Although this approach to representing knowledge appears to provide an adequate solution to the refinement problem, its implementation in GPS does not provide an adequate solution to the accessibility problem. As GPS works on a task, the only knowledge that it has access to at any given time is the knowledge associated with the difference that it is currently attempting to reduce. This knowledge is simply inadequate for a system that is to function in a complex environment. There is much knowledge that might be relevant to many goals that cannot be associated with all of those goals without resurrecting the refinement problem.

The source of the difficulty is readily apparent. GPS employs a control structure that makes it incapable of entertaining more than one goal at a time and this makes it unresponsive to knowledge which, though relevant, has not been associated with its current goal. What seems desirable, then, is a control structure that could support a system that stored knowledge in a GPS-like fashion, thus preserving the obvious advantages for both refinement and the coordination of action that associating knowledge with differences provides, while at the same time, not hiding from the system any of its other, possibly relevant knowledge. Such a control structure would eliminate the inadequacies of the GPS solution to the accessibility problem. It is for this reason, as well as for some others, that many AI researchers have been experimenting during the past few years, with what are called production system languages (Waterman and Hayes-Roth). These languages appear to have the right sort of characteristics to realize a system that has both power and generality. In the following section, I will describe one such language, OPS, and point out how it provides an implicit solution to both the accessibility and the refinement problems.

OPS, A PRODUCTION SYSTEM LANGUAGE

OPS (Forgy and McDermott) has three major components.[1] It contains a production memory, a memory that can contain any number of conditional statements, called productions. Each production is a rule that can be used to associate the description of a situation with a description of the actions that are likely to be appropriate in that situation. A production has the form:

$$P_i (C_1 C_2 \cdots C_n \rightarrow A_1 A_2 \cdots A_m)$$

I will refer to the part of the production that contains the conditions (C's) under which it is applicable as the condition side of the production, and to the part that contains the associated actions (A's) as the action side. OPS also contains a 'working memory', a memory that can hold descriptions of situations that are currently of interest. The third component is an 'interpreter'. The interpreter is a program that has three functions which it performs repeatedly: (1) It matches, or compares, the conditions of each production in production memory with the descriptions in working memory to determine which productions are relevant. (2) It selects from that set of relevant productions one production to fire. (3) Then it fires the production selected. Firing a production simply means doing whatever actions are specified in the action side. Ordinarily this will result in changes to working memory: New elements, descriptions, will be added, or elements already there will be deleted.

Each condition is a partial description of some possible situation, it is a list containing constant terms and variables. An element matches a description in working memory if each of the constants in the condition corresponds to a constant in the memory element and if the variables in the condition can be bound to the remaining constant terms in the memory element. A variable that occurs in an action element has the value bound during the match. The use of variables allows the descriptions in productions to be patterns, and thus allows a single production to specify actions appropriate for a class of situations.

OPS presupposes that all of the permanent or long term knowledge represented in the system will be represented as productions. Each production describes a small piece of behaviour that is likely to be appropriate in situations having certain characteristics. A production is a self-contained unit, it needs no knowledge at all of the content of other productions. Whether it is to be fired or not is an affair that is completely between itself and the descriptions in working memory, and perhaps the interpreter's conflict resolution rules. If it is fired, then working memory will be changed in some way, and a new cycle will begin. The production that fires needs no knowledge of what productions fired before it or of what productions will fire after it. Because there is no necessary dependency among productions, new productions can be added to production memory at any time, without specifying how this new knowledge is related to knowledge that is already represented. Of course GPS, with its table-of-connections, provides the same kind of modularity. What OPS or any production system language provides that GPS does not is a more sensitive control structure. Because working memory can contain many descriptions, each of which may partially support a number of different productions, a system written in OPS has much knowledge available to it at each step in the problem solving process.

It should be clear now how the control structure provided by OPS supports solutions to both the accessibility and the refinement problems. Since the relevance of a particular production is determined by the actual situation that the system is encountering, the knowledge that is available to the system at any given time is not just the knowledge that is necessary for achieving its current goal, but all of the knowledge that is in any way relevant to the situation it is in. If the system encounters a situation that it cannot deal with effectively, then it can be given additional knowledge, a new production, that is sensitive to precisely those aspects of the situation that are causing the problem. If the system subsequently encounters a situation with those characteristics, even if it is working on a totally different task, it will have access to that knowledge.

Of course by making so much knowledge available to the system on each cycle, the problem arises of how to select from among all of the potentially relevant productions the one most likely to help in achieving the goal. OPS uses only a few simple rules in making the selection. For example, it prefers productions that are supported by the most current description, in order to promote continuity in its behaviour. And when given a choice between two productions making unequal informational demands, it prefers the one making the stronger demands, since that production is more specific and hence more likely to be relevant to the particular situation. Clearly, because these rules make use of limited information, they will sometimes make inappropriate selections. OPS could, of course, be modified in such a way that it would carefully consider the consequences of firing each of the relevant rules before making its selection. This modification would result in fewer inappropriate selections being made, but would at the same time make the system less responsive to changes in its environment, since the additional processing would take a great deal of time. After describing, in the next section, a production system written in OPS, I will return to this problem of selection and indicate one way in which it might be dealt with more adequately.

IPS, AN INSTRUCTABLE PRODUCTION SYSTEM

OPS is a production system langauge; its behaviour depends, of course, on what productions are contained in its production memory. What I will describe now is a particular production system that we are currently working with at Carnegie-Mellon University (Rychener and Newell). Our purpose is to explore the problems involved in building a system that can exhibit intelligent behaviour that is general as well as powerful. Because the system is to grow by being instructed, we call it the Instructable Production System (IPS). Before I describe in some detail the form that IPS productions take, I want to say a few things about the task environment within which IPS functions.

The task environment is an abstract job shop. Like a real job shop, it contains raw materials and machines. It differs from a real job shop in its simplicity. The objects, materials and machines, in the shop are simple descriptions; each description is a set of attribute-value pairs. A machine differs from other objects in that its description contains descriptions of the objects that it can input and descriptions of the objects that it outputs. The first object below is a piece of wood, the second is a saw.

```
(NAME        W6
 TYPE        WOOD
 LENGTH      72
```

```
WIDTH            4
THICKNESS        1
COST             16
LOCATION         L12
POSITION         3)


(NAME            M87
 TYPE            MACHINE
 INPUT
     (TYPE               WOOD
      LENGTH             =X
      LOCATION           L23)
     (TYPE               SPEC
      LENGTH             =Y
      LOCATION           L24)
 OUTPUT
     (TYPE               WOOD
      LENGTH             (SUB =X =Y)
      LOCATION           L32)
     (TYPE               WOOD
      LENGTH             =Y
      LOCATION           L32)
 POSITION        1
 LOCATION        L33)
```

Notice that the saw inputs two objects. One of the inputs is a piece of wood of any length (denoted by the '='); the other input is a specification of the length of the piece of wood desired. The saw outputs two pieces of wood, one of them is a piece of the desired length, the other is the piece left over.[2] Each object occupies one of eighteen locations in the shop; any number of objects may be stacked in each of the locations. There are four primitive operations that IPS can perform on the environment. It can *view* an object in the environment if it knows the object's name. It can *scan* for an object that has a particular set of attributes. The result of both view and scan is the same; a description of the object viewed or scanned is deposited in working memory. IPS can also *transfer* an object from one location to another. And it can *start* any of the machines in the shop. Although this environment is exceedingly simple, it can easily be made more complex. Moreover, as I will show, it is complex enough to enable us to explore the problems involved in building an intelligent system.

In addition to the job shop, the task environment includes a human instructor. The function of the instructor is, of course, to provide information to the system when it finds itself in a position where it does not know what to do or when its behaviour is inappropriate for the situation it is in. The instructions that the instructor gives the system are of two types. The instructor may tell the system how to achieve some goal (ie, how to reduce the difference between a current state and a goal state), or the instructor may give the system a goal to achieve. When IPS is told how to achieve a goal, it maps the instruction into one or more productions and then stores these productions in production memory. When IPS is given a goal, it simply deposits that goal in working memory. Initially IPS contains only a few hundred productions. These productions enable it to communicate with the instructor. As the system interacts with its environment, and the instructor provides it with knowledge of how to do things, the number of productions in production memory gradually increases.

The condition side of each production that IPS builds contains a goal and a description of those aspects of a situation that are relevant when determining how to reduce the differences between that goal and the current situation. The action side of the productions contains descriptions of the actions that, if performed, are likely to reduce the difference between the goal state and the current state. These descriptions are most frequently subgoals, that is, descriptions of states that must be realized in order for the goal to be realized. It is by using subgoals in this way that production autonomy can be achieved. The instructor need have no knowledge of what productions the system has. He can give the system rather elaborate instructions simply by appealing to knowledge that he thinks the system has already. If the system does not know how to achieve one or more of the subgoals, then this knowledge can be provided in the same fashion. Of course not all of the instructions that the instructor gives can be in terms of subgoals. At some point, the system must achieve its goals directly. Thus, the system also possesses a few primitive capabilities that enable it to operate on its environment and on the descriptions in its working memory. I have already described the four operations that it can perform on objects in the task environment: view, scan, transfer, and start. It also has a set of primitive operations that it can perform on the elements in working memory. These operations enable it to add descriptions to working memory and to modify the descriptions that are there. These primitive operations, given the goal-subgoal organization of knowledge, provide IPS with all that it needs to achieve rather complex goals.

I would like now to give you some idea of how IPS would behave given a specific goal to achieve. At the same time, I want to use this example to give an indication of the kinds of knowledge I had in mind when I claimed above that there is a great deal of knowledge not obviously related to achieving a particular goal that must be available to a system if it is to function in a complex environment. The particular task that I will use as an example is the following: Make a chair, model CH-3, by Wednesday. I selected this task because on the surface, at least, chair-building might seem to be a task that could be performed adequately by a system that has only knowledge directly related to building chairs. Since, in fact, this is not the case, the example should provide some indication of the pervasiveness of the accessibility and refinement problems.

If I were going to instruct IPS in how to achieve this task, I would first give it many chair-building instructions; that is, I would try to give the system all of the knowledge it would need to make a model CH-3 chair. I would tell IPS to find a piece of maple at least five feet long; then I would tell it to cut out of the maple board two pieces, one three feet long, the other two feet long, and so on. Many of my instructions would be quite specific. For example, I might say:

> Find an object whose type is wood, whose subtype is maple, and whose length is at least 5, if you have found an object whose type is wood and whose subtype is maple, then test to determine if the length of that object is at least 5.

Given this instruction, the production that IPS would build and then store in its production memory would look like this

P1006 ((WANT FIND OBJECT = I)
　　　　(DESCRIPTION = I = NM TYPE WOOD)
　　　　(DESCRIPTION = I = NM SUBTYPE MAPLE)
　　　　(DESTRUCTION = I = NM LENGTH (AT LEAST 5))
　　　　(TRUE =NM TYPE WOOD)
　　　　(TRUE =NM SUBTYPE MAPLE)
　　　　→
　　　　(WANT TEST OBJECT 2)
　　　　(DESCRIPTION 2 =NM LENGTH (AT LEAST 5)))

After giving all the instructions I could think of, I would give IPS the goal of making a model CH-3 chair. This would result in the following description being deposited in working memory.

　　　　(WANT MAKE OBJECT 1)
　　　　(DESCRIPTION 1 C1 MODEL CH-3)
　　　　(DESCRIPTION 1 C1 STATE
　　　　(FINISHED BY WEDNESDAY))

Let me now indicate a few of the problems that IPS might encounter in trying to achieve this goal if it had no knowledge other than that directly related to building chairs. First, of course, IPS might not be able to find a piece of maple at least five feet long; perhaps after discovering that all of the pieces of maple in the shop are either two feet long or three feet long, it would just give up. Or perhaps it would find a piece exactly five feet long, and would proceed to rip it out of the centre of the maple table that it had just finished building and saw it up. Or perhaps it would find several long pieces of maple smouldering in a corner of the shop and saw one of them up.

Avoiding any of these three problems requires that a system have access to knowledge not directly related to the goal of building a chair. To avoid the first problem, the system would have to be able to recognize that the goal it is currently trying to achieve is not really necessary. IPS can recognize this since it can entertain many goals at the same time. To avoid the second problem, the system would have to be able to recognize when its proposed means of achieving a goal are inappropriate. IPS can recognize this since it can be given general rules indicating that when it finds itself in certain kinds of situations (eg, when it is about to destroy something), it should carefully consider the implications of what it is about to do. To avoid the third problem, the system must be able to recognize when its current goal has become less important than some other goal. IPS can recognize this since it can respond to events in its environment that have no relationship to its current goal.

CONCLUDING REMARKS

Production systems appear to have at least some of the characteristics that must be possessed by any general problem solving system. Because a system's permanent knowledge is represented in production memory as a set of independent rules, each of which associates a small bit of knowledge with the context in which that knowledge is likely to be useful, and because the descriptions in working memory can each partially support many different productions, all of the knowledge that a system might need for a particular task is potentially accessible and easy to refine.

As I suggested above, however, the production system representation allows so much knowledge to be accessible on each cycle that the problem arises of how to determine quickly what knowledge it would be most useful to attend to. OPS selects the productions to be fired on the basis of a few simple criteria. The rules that OPS currently makes use of are strongly biased toward maintaining the system in whatever behaviour it is engaged in, that is, knowledge associated with the system's current goal is preferred to knowledge associated with other goals. To use radically different criteria would make maintaining continuity of behaviour difficult. To retain the present criteria, however, appears to make the knowledge associated with the other goals almost useless, just as it is in GPS. One possibility that seems worth exploring is to provide OPS with a mechanism for augmenting its selection rules with rules sensitive to the content of satisfied productions. This would allow OPS to make use of its simple rules in situations in which they provide adequate selection, but also to build more adequate rules for situations in which the simple rules are discovered to be inadequate.

NOTES

This work was supported in part by the Defense Advanced Research Projects Agency (F44620-73-C-0074) and is monitored by the Air Force Office of Scientific Research.
1. OPS was designed by C. Forgy, A. Newell, M. Rychener, and myself.
2. The symbol '=' preceding any name indicates that that name is to be treated as a variable. Any value can be bound to that name.

REFERENCES

Forgy, C. and McDermott, J. 'OPS, A domain-independent production system language'. Proceedings of the Fifth Intl. Jt. Conf. on Artificial Intelligence (1977) 933-939.

Newell, A., Shaw, J.C., and Simon H.A., 'A variety of intelligent learning in a general problem solver'. In M.C. Yovits and S. Cameron (eds) Self-organizing systems. (Pergamon Press, 1960) 153-189.

Newell, A. and Simon H. Human problem solving, New Jersey (Prentice Hall, 1972).

Rychener, M. and Newell, A. 'An instructable production system: initial design issues'. In Waterman, D. and Hayes-roth, F. (eds) Pattern-directed inference systems. New York (Academic Press, 1978) 135-153.

Waterman, D.A., and Hayes-Roth, F. (eds) Pattern-directed inference systems. New York (Academic Press, 1978).

CHAPTER 6

A FRAMEWORK FOR MISREPRESENTING KNOWLEDGE

Hubert L. Dreyfus

ARTIFICIAL INTELLIGENCE AND PERCEPTION THEORY

When *What Computers Can't Do* appeared in 1972, accusing workers in artificial intelligence of covering up stagnation with *ad hoc* 'successes', the response of many workers in the AI field was that the book had gone to press just at the time of a new breakthrough at MIT which made its criticisms *passé*. This new work in scene analysis, concept learning, and so on, is summarized and placed in epistemological perspective by Marvin Minsky and Seymour Papert in their latest book, a series of lectures entitled *Artificial Intelligence*[1]. Some of the papers on which these lectures were based, as well as Minsky's famous 'frame' paper (1975), subsequently appeared in Patrick Winston's book, *The Psychology of Computer Vision* (1975). To determine whether or not this work constitutes real progress and calls into question the thesis of my book, we must examine some of the most interesting contributions in some detail, bearing in mind especially how they deal with my objections that digital computer programs, because they must process whatever they deal with in terms of elementary facts and operations, cannot deal with the gestalt character of perception and the related role of concrete exemplars in intelligent behaviour.

Both the above books reveal that an interesting change has, indeed, taken place at the MIT AI Laboratory. In previous works (Minsky, 1968) Minsky and his co-workers sharply distinguished themselves from workers in cognitive simulation, who presented their programs as psychological theories, insisting that the MIT programs were 'an attempt to build intelligent machines without any prejudice toward making the system. . .humanoid'.[2] Now the preface to *Artificial Intelligence* states 'the primary use of computers for research into the nature of intelligence is that of simulation',[3] and Minsky and Papert attempt to argue for the role of symbolic representations in intelligent behaviour by a constant polemic against behaviorism and gestalt theory. Likewise Winston claims, in support of his collection of papers on computer vision that 'making machines see is an important way to understand how we animals see'.[4]

Underlying this change, one can detect the effect of growing success in the sixties with the manipulation of fixed micro-worlds, accompanied by the failure to produce a system which even begins to approach the adaptibility to changing contexts shown by a dog, a cat, or a six-months-old child. Instead of concluding from this frustrating situation that the machine techniques which work in context-free, game-like, micro-worlds, may in no way resemble human and animal intelligence, the AI workers have taken the less embarrassing, if less plausible, tack of suggesting that even if they cannot succeed in building intelligent systems, the *ad hoc* techniques successful in micro-world ' analysis can be justified as a valuable contribution to psychology.

Such a pitch, however, since it involves a stronger claim than the old slogan that as long as the machine was intelligent it did not matter at all whether it performed in a humanoid way, runs the obvious risk of refutation by empirical evidence. The risk is especially great at this moment when recent work in cognitive psychology on the role of rotation of images in pattern recognition,[5] the discovery of the use of prototypical images in categorization (Rosch), and of examplars in the history of science (Kuhn), bring into question the explanatory power of a formal model of perception and cognition.

A computer model must, however, be a symbolic structure, so Minsky and Papert are compelled to take a polemical stand in favour of abstract representations, and against concrete exemplars and underlying neurological processes. Thus making a virtue of necessity, they revive the intellectualist position of Kant's *Critique of Pure Reason*, according to which concrete perception is assimilated to the symbolic descriptions used in abstract thought.

The Gestaltists look for simple and fundamental principles about how perception is organized, and then attempt to show how symbolic reasoning can be seen as following the same principles, while we construct a complex theory of how knowledge is applied to solve intellectual problems, and then attempt to show how symbolic description, that is what one 'sees', is constructed according to similar such processes.[6]

But this attempt to invert the *prima facie* priority of perception to thinking, gets Minsky and Papert into the same sort of trouble that eventually led Kant, in the *Critique of Judgement*, to give up his earlier view. Before one can begin to select primitives to use in a symbolic description of a scene, the scene must be segregated into local units and salient features. Minsky recognizes this as the Gestaltists' argument for the priority of the figure-ground distinction but, on the basis of A. Guzman's success in the analysis of scenes involving rectilinear objects, he retorts that:

> In complex scenes, the features belonging to different objects have to be correctly segregated to be meaningful; but solving this problem—which is equivalent to the traditional Gestalt 'figure-ground' problem—presupposes solutions for so many visual problems that the possibility and perhaps even the desirability of a separate recognition technique falls into question.[7]

This, however, presupposes that the top-down technique of looking for edges and corners, which works in segmenting rectilinear objects, can somehow be generalized to curved surfaces. In the absence of any such techniques, the question remains how to account for the organization of the primitive wholes which form the basis of higher-order recognition processes.

Recently, Goldmeier's (1972) extension of early Gestalt work on the perception of similarity of simple perceptual figures— arising in part as a response to 'the frustrating efforts to teach pattern recognition to (computers)'—has revealed sophisticated distinctions between figure and ground, matter and form, essential and accidental aspects, norms and distortions, and so on, which are already apparent at the perceptual level even when no recognizable objects are present. Goldmeier has painstakingly shown that these perceptual functions cannot be accounted for in terms of any known formal features of the phenomenal figures. They can, however, perhaps be explained on the neurological level, where the importance of Pragnanz, or singularity suggests physical phenomena such as 'regions of resonance'.

Minsky is aware that there are theorists who claim that the organization of perception can only be explained in terms of physical processes such as resonance and holograms, but he rejects this view with the remark that:

> The output of a quantitive mechanism, be it numerical, statistical, analog, or physical (non-symbolic), is too structureless and uninformative to permit further analysis.[8]

But this thrice begs the question. First, if the Gestaltists are right, perception is not a symbolic activity like thinking, and even thinking does not necessarily involve analysis. Thus the stable patterns of perceptual organization need not provide the sort of features required for analysis and computation. Secondly, even if higher order objects *are* recognized in terms of features, we have just seen that physical processes such as resonance, far from being unstructured, might, by making possible accident/essence discrimination, etc., provide the necessary structure for higher level analytical operations. Thirdly, it cuts no ice against a neurological (non-symbolic) view that it does not permit further analysis, if this means that perceptual processes are holistic and so cannot be explained in terms of a computer program. What the Gestaltists precisely question is whether or not perception is the sort of phenomenon which is amenable to formal, symbolic analysis.

Of course, it is still possible that the Gestaltists went too far in trying to assimilate thought to the same sort of concrete, holistic brain processes they found necessary to call upon in their account of perception. Thus, even though the exponents of symbolic representation have no account of perceptual processes, they might be right about the mechanism of everyday thinking and learning. Such a model of everyday learning and recognition is proposed by Winston (1975a): For example, given a set of positive and negative instances, Winston's program for learning the structural description of an arch uses a descriptive repertoire to construct a formal description of the class of arches.

But is this a plausible general theory of learning? Winston's commitment to a computer model dictates the conclusion that it must be:

> Although this may seem like a very special kind of learning, I think the implications are far-ranging, because I believe that learning by examples, learning by being told, learning by imitation, learning by reinforcement and other forms are much like one another. In the literature of learning there is frequently an unstated assumption that these various forms are fundamentally different. But I think the classical boundaries between the various kinds of learning will disappear once superficially different kinds of learning are understood in terms of processes that construct and manipulate descriptions.[9]

Yet Winston's program only works if the 'student' is saved the trouble of what Peirce called 'abduction', by being 'told' a set of context-free features and relations—in this case a list of possible spatial relationships of blocks such as 'standing', 'above', and 'supported by'—from which to build up a description. These features are just the sort of perceptual prominences which are built up by repeated experience. Minsky and Papert presuppose that this learning has already been built into the program when they say that 'to eliminate objects which seem atypical. . .the program lists all relationships exhibited by more than half of the candidates in the set'.[10] Without pre-selected features, all the objects share an indefinitely large number of relationships. Thus Winston's program presupposes the sort of learning by training, or being told, which it claims to explain.

If not a theory of learning, is Winston's program at least a plausible theory of categorization? Once it has been given what Winston disarmingly calls a 'good description' and carefully-chosen examples, the program does conclude that an arch is a structure in which a prismatic body is supported by two upright blocks that do not touch one another. Winston admits, however, that having two supports and a top does not begin to capture even the geometrical structure of arches, many of which are curved. So Winston proposes to 'generalize the machine's description attributes to acts and properties required by those acts', adding some *ad hoc* functional predicate like 'something to walk through'.

But it is not at all clear how a 'functional predicate' which refers to implicit knowledge of the bodily skill of 'walking through' is to be formalized. Indeed, Winston himself provides a *reductio ad absurdum* of this facile appeal to formal functional predicates:

> To a human, an arch may be something to walk through, as well as an appropriate alignment of bricks. And certainly, a flat rock serves as a table to a hungry person, although far removed from the image the word 'table' usually calls to mind. But the machine does not yet know anything of walking or eating, so the programs discussed here handle only some of the physical aspects of these human notions. There is no inherent obstacle forbidding the machine to enjoy functional understanding. It is a matter of generalizing the machine's descriptive ability to acts and properties required by those acts. Then chains of pointers can link TABLE to FOOD as well as to a physical image of a table, and the machine will be perfectly happy to draw up its chair to a flat rock with the human given that there is something on that table which it wishes to eat.[11]

Progress on recognition of arches, tables, and so on, must it seems, either wait until we have captured, in an abstract symbolic description, all that human beings implicitly know about walking and eating simply by having a body, or else until computers no longer have to be told what it is to walk and eat, because they have human bodies and appetites themselves!

In the meantime, Winston's proposal cannot be considered a serious contribution to a theory of learning and recognition until he solves the following fundamental problems:

(1) The program can only learn even a simplified geometrical concept like arch if the programmer, using his everyday understanding, makes explicit and preselects a small set of relevant features to 'tell' the program. There is no hint how programs could acquire these features.
(2) To distinguish essential from accidental features, the program preweights its primitives, but Winston gives us no idea how the program could assign these weights. Moreover, once we see how arches function in our everyday activities, there is no

reason to suppose that there are any necessary and sufficient features capable of defining our everyday notion of an arch.

(3) Some prominent characteristics shared by some everyday arches are 'helping to support something while leaving an important open space under it', or 'being the sort of thing one can walk under and through at the same time'. How does Winston propose to capture such contextual characteristics in terms of the context-free features required by a formal representation?

Despite these serious obstacles, Winston claims that 'there will be no contentment with (concept learning) machines that only do as well as humans'. It is noteworthy that Winston's work is eight years old and there has been little progress in machine learning, induction, or concept formation. Indeed, Minsky and Papert admit that 'we are still far from knowing how to design a powerful yet subtle and sensitive inductive learning program'.[12] What is surprising is that they add 'but the schemata developed in Winston's work should take us a substantial part of the way'. The lack of progress since Winston's work was published, plus the total dependence of the program on a human programmer to provide the primitives from which it can produce its rigid, restricted, and largely irrelevant descriptions, makes it hard to understand in what way the program is a substantial first step.

Moreover, if Winston claims to 'shed some light' on the question: How do we recognize examples of various concepts? his theory must, like any psychological theory, be subject to empirical test. Contrary to Winston's claims, recent evidence collected and analyzed by Eleanor Rosch on just this subject has tended to establish that recognition of basic objects such as tables and chairs does not depend on finding which formal features define their concept, but on seeing each object as more or less distant from an imagined paradigm:

> Many experiments have shown that categories appear to be coded in the mind neither by means of lists of each individual member of the category, nor by means of a list of formal criteria necessary and sufficient for category membership, but, rather, in terms of a prototype of a typical category number. The most economical cognitive code for a category is, in fact, a *concrete image* of an average category member.[13]

This research suggests that Winston's approach of looking for criterial features is a dead end, and that, perhaps, Minsky's proposal for using frames or prototypes to represent everyday knowledge is more promising. Minsky's proposal, however, is not without its own problems; indeed a paragraph from Minsky's influential paper, 'A Framework for Representing Knowledge', can be used to pin-point many of the unsolved problems in this area:

> There are many forms of chairs, for example, and one should choose carefully the chair-description frames that are to be the major capitols of chair-land. These are used for rapid matching and assigning priorities to the various differences. The lower priority *features* of the *cluster* center then serve. . .as properties of the chair *types* . . .[14]

There is no argument why we would expect to find elementary context-free 'features' characterizing a chair type, nor any suggestion as to what these features might be. They certainly cannot be legs, back, seat, etc., since these are aspects of already recognized chairs, not context-free features defined apart from chairs, which then cluster in a chair representation. Minsky continues:

> Difference could be functional as well as geometric. Thus, after rejecting a first try at 'chair' one might try the functional idea of 'something one can sit on' to explain an unconventional form.[15]

But a function so defined is not abstractable from human embodied know-how and cultural practices. If it is treated merely as an additional symbolic descriptor along with physical features, function cannot even distinguish conventional chair shapes from thrones, saddles, and toilets. Minsky concludes:

> Of course, that analysis would fail to capture toy chairs, or chairs of such ornamental delicacy that their actual use would be unthinkable. These would be better handled by the method of excuses, in which one would bypass the usual geometrical or functional explanation in favour of responding to *contexts* involving *art* or *play*.[16]

This is what is required all right, but by what elementary features are these contexts to be recognized? There is no reason at all to suppose that one can avoid the difficulty of formally representing our knowledge of chairs by abstractly representing even more holistic, concrete, culturally determined, and loosely organized human practices such as art and play.

This passage and observations such as 'trading normally occurs in a social context of law, trust and convention. Unless we also represent these other facts, most trade transactions will be meaningless'[17] show that Minsky has understood my argument (1972) that intelligent behaviour requires as a background the totality of practices which make up the human way of being in the world. But Minsky seems oblivious to the hand waving character of his proposal that frames will enable workers in AI to represent this background in symbolic descriptions, as if the programmers could make explicit the totality of activities which they have picked up by training—activities which pervade their lives as water encompasses the life of a fish. Without this background of tacit know-how AI programs will continue to be *ad hoc* game-like tricks, and the capability for providing such a background is, at present, beyond the horizon.

REPRESENTATION AND PARADIGMS

AI's new cognitive scientists might retrench once more, however, and claim that although commonsense categorization of chairs, tables, and arches is too concrete and tied in with human practices to be amenable to formal representation at this time, one might begin by producing a formal model of pure thought. In that case, science would seem to be an ideal subject for computer simulation, since as a detached theoretical enterprise it deals with context-free attributes, whose law-like relations can in principle be grasped by any sufficiently powerful intellect, whether human, Martian, digital, or divine.

Yet according to the latest theory accepted by historians of science, even scientific research requires concrete examples for its successes. Just as everyday problem solving and more developed forms of technology take place in a practical context which makes possible *insight* into which aspects of objects are *significant* for the task at hand, so all appeal to attributes whether practical or theoretical requires 'abduction' (in Peirce's sense of the word) to exclude from consideration all but a limited number of possibly *relevant* factors. In science, selective attention is directed by an implicitly-agreed-upon example of successful scientific practice which leads the scientist to notice only a limited number of facts and events. Otherwise, the scientist is as hopelessly lost as a Martian or computer. As Thomas Kuhn (1970) notes: 'In the absence of a paradigm or some candidate for a paradigm, all the facts that could possibly pertain to the development of a given science are likely to seem equally relevant'.[18]

In his frame article Minsky claims that 'the frame idea is in the tradition of. . .the 'paradigms' of Kuhn', so it is appropriate to ask whether a theory of formal representation such as Minsky's can do justice to Kuhn's analysis. After quoting Kuhn's description of a 'paradigm induced Gestalt switch', Minsky interprets as follows:

> According to Kuhn's model of scientific evolution, 'normal' science proceeds by using established *descriptive schemes*. Major changes result from new 'paradigms', new ways of describing things. . . Whenever our customary viewpoints do not work well, whenever we fail to find effective frame systems items in memory, we must construct new ones that bring out the right *features*.[19]

But what Minsky leaves out is precisely Kuhn's claim that a paradigm, as used by scientists, is not an abstract descriptive scheme utilizing formal features, but rather a set of shared concrete exemplars.

> The practice of normal science depends on the ability, acquired from exemplars, to group objects and situations into similarity sets which are primitive in the sense that the grouping is done without an answer to the question. 'Similar with respect to what'.[20]

Kuhn explicitly repudiates any formal reconstruction which claims that the scientist must be using symbolic descriptions:

> I have in mind a manner of knowing which is misconstrued if reconstrued in terms of rules that are first abstracted from exemplars and thereafter function in their stead.[21]

Indeed, Kuhn sees his book as raising and answering just those questions which Minsky refuses to face:

> Why is the *concrete* scientific achievement, as a locus of professional commitment, prior to the various concepts, laws, theories, and points of view which may be *abstracted* from it? In what sense is the shared paradigm a fundamental unit for the student of scientific development, a unit that *cannot* be fully reduced to logically *atomic components* which might function in its stead?[22]

His answer is that seeing things in terms of exemplars and analogies enables scientists to agree on what is relevant while still holding different interpretations:

> Scientists can agree that a Newton, Lavoisier, Maxwell, or Einstein has produced an apparently permanent solution to a group of outstanding problems and still disagree. . .about the particular abstract characteristics which make those solutions permanent. They can, that is, agree in their *identification* of a paradigm without agreeing on, or even attempting to produce, a full *interpretation* or *rationalization* of it.[23]

Thus, although it is the job of scientists to find abstractable, exact, symbolic descriptions, and the subject matter of science consists of such formal accounts, the thinking of scientists themselves does not seem to be amenable to this sort of analysis. Indeed, if each scientist had internalized a fixed, formal description of a particular stage of his discipline, this scheme would, as Minsky remarks, require explicit 'redefining of 'normal" for each modification of scientific practice. But, according to Kuhn, it is precisely the advantage of 'global paradigms' that this need not occur.

What can we conclude concerning the contribution of MIT's AI Laboratory to the science of psychology? No one can deny Minsky and Papert's claim that 'Computer Science has brought a flood of. . .ideas, well defined, and experimentally implemented, for thinking about thinking. . .' But all of these ideas involve the construction and manipulation of symbolic descriptions and, as we have seen, the notion that human cognition can be explained in terms of formal representations does not seem at all obvious in the face of actual research on perception, everyday concept formation, and abstract scientific thought. Even Minsky and Papert show a new modesty with respect to their former claims for AI. They admit that AI is still in its embryonic stages and that the much-heralded 'breakthrough' still lies in the future:

> Just as astronomy succeeded astrology, following Kepler's discovery of planetary regularities, the discoveries of these many principles in empirical explorations of intellectual processes in machines should lead to a science, eventually.[24]

Moreover, 'should' has replaced 'will' in their predictions. But AI's current contribution to psychology suggests an even more modest hope: As more psychologists, like Goldmeier, are frustrated by the limitations of formal computer models, and others, like Shepard and Rosch, continue to investigate the function of images as opposed to symbolic representations, the limited success of AI may come to be seen as an important disconfirmation of the information-processing approach. At that point artificial intelligence may enter a new era and relinquish its preoccupation with digital simulations, based on symbolic representations, despite the methodological advantages afforded by them. Eventually, the very failure of such models may provide the impetus required by the AI community to take a serious look at non-symbolic experience and its underlying neurological foundations.

NOTES

1. Marvin Minsky and Seymour Papert, *Artificial Intelligence*, Condon Lectures, Oregon State System of Higher Education, Eugene, Oregon (1974).
2. Minsky (1968) p.7.
3. Minsky and Papert (1974) p.6.
4. Winston (1975) p.2.
5. R.N. Shepard and B. Metzler, 'Mental rotation of three-dimensional objects', *Science* (1971) 701-703. Minsky recognizes in his frames article that 'Many psychologists feel that the experiments of Shepard on matching rotated objects indicate that humans perform continuous operations upon picture-like images' (p.273), but he dismisses this view as only one possible account of the evidence. However, he gives no reason for rejecting Shepard's plausible account, nor any empirical argument for

preferring his frame version. For a more serious attempt to save formal representations in the face of the latest findings concerning images, see Zenon Pylyshyn's paper, 'Imagery and artificial intelligence', *Minnesota Studies in the Philosophy of Science*, Vol. IX.

6. Minsky and Papert (1974) p.34.
7. Minsky (1975) p.215.
8. ibid. p.275.
9. Winston (1975(a)) p.185.
10. Minsky and Papert (1974) p.54.
11. Winston (1975(a)) pp. 193-194.
12. Minsky and Papert (1974) p.56.
13. Rosch (preprint) p.41.
14. Minsky (1975) p.255; (My italics).
15. ibid., loc. cit.
16. ibid., loc. cit. (my italics).
17. ibid., p.240.
18. Kuhn (1970) p.15
19. Minsky (1975) p.261 (my italics).
20. Kuhn (1970) p.200.
21. ibid., p.192.
22. ibid., p.11 (my italics).
23. ibid., p.44.
24. Minsky and Papert (1974) p.25.

REFERENCES

Dreyfus, H.L. *What Computers Can't Do*, New York (Harper and Row, 1972).

Minsky, M. and Papert, S. *Artificial Intelligence*, Eugene, (Oregon State System of Higher Education 1974).

Winston, P.H. (ed) *The Psychology of Computer Vision*, New York (McGraw Hill, 1975).

Winston, P.H. (ed) 'Learning structural description from examples'. In *The Psychology of Computer Vision*, (McGraw Hill, 1975) Ch.5.

Minsky, M. (ed) *Semantic information processing*, Cambridge, Mass., (MIT Press, 1968).

Minsky, M. 'A Framework for representing knowledge'. In P.H. Winston (ed) *The Psychology of Computer Vision*, New York (McGraw Hill, 1975).

Rosch, E. (preprint) 'Human categorization'. In N. Warren (ed), *Advances in Cross-Cultural Psychology* (Vol.I), London, (Academic Press, New York).

Goldmeier, E. *Similarity in Visually Perceived Forms*, New York (International Universities Press, 1972).

Kuhn, T.S. *The Structure of Scientific Revolutions*, 2nd edition, (University of Chicago Press, 1970).

PART IV
HUMAN MENTALITY AND COMPUTER SIMULATIONS

CHAPTER 7
THE SIMULATION OF EPISTEMIC ACTS
Kenneth M. Sayre

PHILOSOPHIC METHOD AND ARTIFICIAL INTELLIGENCE

Why should philosophers be interested in artificial intelligence? A presumptuous answer would be that philosophers are concerned with all branches of knowledge, artificial intelligence being a case in point. Besides being presumptuous, this answer is factually inaccurate. Although artificial intelligence has its own journal, its own research institutes, and its own learned spokesmen, I do not believe it has achieved the status of a branch of knowledge. Equally presumptuous, I might add, is the notion that philosophers are competent to pass judgment on the status artificial intelligence might someday achieve as a field of inquiry. Granted that the present has not fulfilled the predictions of the previous decade, it is not the philosopher's business to prejudge the future.

A more common motive stems from the philosopher's preoccupation with doctrinal issues. If machines can be shown capable of mental activities—the argument goes—then there is no reason why the mental activity of man should not likewise be conceived as merely mechanical. Success in computer simulation is thus taken as support for materialism. For reasons examined elsewhere, however, I think the drift of this argument is basically mistaken. The fact that minds and machines both can recognize patterns, for example, no more implies that minds are material, than the fact that birds and aeroplanes both fly implies that aeroplanes are oviparous. By reverse token, even if it were shown that certain forms of mentality cannot be simulated, it would remain a possibility nonetheless that the mind is material; for after all there are physical systems that human technology cannot duplicate. In my opinion at least, a philosopher's interest in artificial intelligence ought to be carefully disengaged from doctrinal 'isms'.

The value of artificial intelligence to philosophy, rather, is methodological. For artificial intelligence is a form of modelling, and modelling is a technique of conceptual analysis. To illustrate, I might repeat a passage recorded ten years ago in *Philosophy and Cybernetics*.

> A sign of the thoroughness with which the operations of mathematical calculation are understood is the considerable skill which has been demonstrated in programming computers to perform these operations without subsequent human intervention. One of the main reasons we are not able to program the creative skill of the poet or composer into the computer, on the other hand, is that we do not understand these skills as well as those of the mathematical reckoner. In the attempt to achieve rudimentary creative skills with a computer, however, we will become able to identify more precisely those aspects of the creative process of which our understanding is most inadequate, and will be able consequently to improve our understanding through analytic attention more carefully directed upon these puzzling features.

The passage concluded with the suggestion, slightly paraphrased, that a mark of our understanding a mental activity is our ability either to duplicate such activity in a properly programmed computer or to specify exactly and without philosophic jargon why such activity cannot be duplicated.

Guided by this method, an interdisciplinary research group under my direction undertook in the early 1960s to develop a computer program capable of recognizing hand-written words in an atemporal context. Conceptual groundwork for the project was provided by the book *Recognition*[3] in which it was emphasized that this activity is a matter more of information detection than of symbol classification. Programming began in 1966, and after several false starts and six years' work, a system was achieved capable of recognizing approximately 80 percent of a test set of 84 words from ten different penmen. These results were approximately equivalent, percentagewise, to the best previously made known in the literature, with the significant difference that our program, unlike the others, was not dependent upon information about stroke sequence during the act of inscription. The results thus demonstrated for the first time the feasibility of the mechanical recognition of words previously inscribed on a written page. A full report of this project was published in September 1973.[4]

I mention this project, and the methodological conception by which it was guided, as a point of departure for a series of remarks outlining how my conception of the philosophic usefulness of artificial intelligence has changed during the present decade. The changes represent a generalization of the methodology described above, rather than, in any basic sense, a repudiation. In the second half of the paper, I relate this more general conception of method to the recent publication *Cybernetics and the Philosophy of Mind*[5], and move on to consider applications that have not yet been reported.

In the course of designing the recognition program previously mentioned, it soon became apparent that more was being learned from conceptual exploration than from actual coding. Late in 1967, for example, a basic flaw was discovered in the program's use of statistical information, requiring extensive adjustments in the program years before the opportunity arose to begin experimenting with a fully coded version. Even more valuable to me personally was the preliminary conceptual analysis reported in the book *Recognition*, of which the eventual success of the program was only one reward. More important vindication came in the form of an extension to other puzzling philosophic issues of the conceptual framework upon which that analysis proceeded. This conceptual framework was based upon communication theory.

The relevance of communication theory to the pattern recognition project appeared initially in the fact that letter recognition is the fulfillment of a communication transaction between two language users, in which one recovers the information encoded in the other's symbols. Since communication theory is the general theory of information transferal, it is applicable in particular to such transactions. The feature of the communication-theoretic framework which linked it directly to the project of computer simulation, of course, is that its basic categories are completely definable in mathematical terms, and hence fully programmable on a digital computer. It appears in retrospect that the philosophically most instructive result of the pattern recognition project was not the successful simulation of script-recognition in a computer program, but rather the fact that this function proved analysable in terms of categories admitting articulation with mathematical rigour. Although the clarity and distinctness of mathematics does not constitute a mark of truth, as

Descartes seems sometimes to have thought, these qualities do provide a criterion of conceptual precision that certifies a theory ready for serious testing. To put it succinctly, the heuristic value of artificial intelligence appears to lie not in the actual programming, but in the conceptual articulation that makes programming possible. In the case of the recognition project, this articulation was based upon communication theory.

Publication of the book, *Consciousness*, in 1969, marked for me a new departure in philosophic method. Although explicitly the book was an exploration of the topic of machine consciousness, the matter of actually simulating the conscious response never came under discussion. The primary thrust of the book was rather to show that the type of neuronal-response-patterning that underlies the conscious activity of a human organism could occur as well in a mechanical system. And the argument intended to achieve this result, in its simplest possible form, was that the response patterns supporting human consciousness can be formulated in the mathematics of communication theory and hence could be programmed into a digital computer. Having developed this argument to the best of my ability, I considered the project of the book complete with its publication. It was only as an afterthought, some years later, that it occurred to me to seek funds for the development of a proto-conscious mechanism. Not unexpectedly, this search was unrewarded. But I did not consider the project any less successful for this reason, as a venture either in philosophy or in artificial intelligence.

There is another aspect of this shift in emphasis from mechanical simulation to mathematically-based conceptual analysis that deserves careful discussion. According to what I take to be the standard conception, a necessary condition for the computer simulation of a mental (or any other) activity is that this activity consist of a set of specific responses to specific inputs. Simulation amounts to devising a set of transformations to be performed mechanically which will associate particular inputs with appropriate outputs. Thus MacKay has stated, for instance, that:

> any pattern of observable behaviour which can be specified in terms of unique and precisely-definable reactions to precisely-definable situations can in principle be imitated mechanically.[6]

According to *Recognition*, likewise:

any mental function which is such that (1) its input and output can be specified with precision, and (2) the transformation it performs can be approximated by equations which express a determinate relationship between input and output, can for these reasons alone be simulated with some degree of adequacy.[7]

I think now, however, that there is a mistake in this way of viewing simulation—if not a mistake at least an oversimplification. The trouble stems from the fact that there are various mental activities which, in their natural form, do not involve specific responses to specific stimulus situations. Yet these activities, I believe, are not thereby excluded from performance by wholly mechanical systems.

This can be illustrated with reference to perceptual consciousness. As described in my book, *Consciousness*, the conscious response is a pattern of neuronal activities which adapt in their configuration to changing stimulus situations, maintaining the organism ready to deal with environmental contingencies with a minimum expenditure of information-processing capacities. The input to the agency of consciousness, as it were, is not a set of determinate sensory stimuli, but rather a complex field of sensory data specific sectors of which vary from moment to moment in their significance for the guidance of the behaving organism. Rather than responding to specific sets of determinate stimuli, the agency of consciousness has, as a primary function, to discriminate the stimuli to which the organism responds. This data-processing operation is a function, in turn, not only of the organism's present and past record of stimulation, but also of the organism's changing needs and interests, and of other forms of data processing in which it is currently involved. The output of consciousness, in turn, is not merely a set of neuronal patterns enacted in response to input stimuli. It is rather a variable array of efferent messages enabling the organism to cope with environmental uncertainties. That is to say, the conscious response is a function not only of input stimuli but also of demands imposed by behavioural circumstances. Just as there are indefinitely many environmental circumstances under which the conscious organism must be able to maintain stability through its sensory faculties, so there are indefinitely many states, both input and output, that would have to be represented in a simulated consciousness. In brief, if a simulation of the conscious response is ever achieved, it will not come in the form of a mere transformation between determinate sets of input and output data.

Another facet of the predicament appears as we reflect on the fact that certain mental acts reach full status only in relationship with states of affairs in the world at large. What I mean by this can be illustrated with reference to a use of the term 'conscious' in which we say that we are conscious *that* such and such is the case. In this sense, 'conscious that' is closely synonymous with 'aware that' and 'realize that'. Thus one might say indiffently 'I am aware that my shoe is untied' or 'I am conscious that my shoe is untied'; but in either case what is said would be correct only if in fact the shoe is untied. To be conscious that one's shoe is untied, in effect, is more than enacting in one's cortical areas a certain patterned response capable of guiding one's behaviour successfully in changing environmental circumstances; it is in addition for the neuronal structures which effect that guidance to stand in a relationship of correspondence with an actual state of affairs. A question arises which has been perennially puzzling. How is it possible for the human cortex—to say nothing of a mechanical model—to correspond to the structure of the world around it?

This puzzle of mind-object correspondence is more commonly discussed with reference to such plainly epistemic terms as 'believe', 'think', and 'perceive'. Such terms are called 'epistemic' because of the involvement of their referents with a state of knowledge. To perceive that something is so, for example, amounts to knowing it on the basis of current perceptual evidence. Other epistemic terms are 'conclude' and 'notice', and of course the paradigm 'know' itself. A common characteristic of epistemic terms is that they accept propositional objects ('I perceive that John is present'), often convertible without radical change in meaning to objects of a nonpropositional nature ('I perceive John').

A subset of epistemic verbs refer to mental achievements with the puzzling feature, noted above, of achieving status only in correspondence with certain states of affairs. Both knowing that John is present and perceiving that John is present are achievements requiring that John in fact is present. By way of contrast, one may believe, think or conclude that John is present, without its being the case that in fact he is. While there is no oddity in the conjunction of claims 'I believe that John is present but he may in fact be elsewhere', the conjunction 'I perceive that John is present but he may be elsewhere' has about it the air of self-refutation. For a human organism to attain a state of perception with this particular epistemic character—for convenience let us refer to it as a state of 'perceptual knowing'—it is necessary to be in a condition of perceptual consciousness. But it is necessary as well that the organism's state of perceptual knowing correspond to an existing state of affairs.

SIMULATING THE CONDITIONS OF PERCEPTUAL KNOWING

The problem I wish to pose is how this correspondence between mental structure and extramental reality can be conceived in a way that would make simulation possible. Even granting, as we may for the sake of discussion, that the analysis of perceptual consciousness given in the book *Consciousness* is adequate, the question remains unanswered what it would be for an artifact to be capable of a state of consciousness the structures of which correspond to a state of affairs beyond it. To put the question in this form, of course, is only superficially different from asking what it is for a human mind to attain correspondence with the world beyond. By posing the question in terms of an artificial system, we may hope to achieve additional insight into the mental structures of the human organism.

This problem has faced philosophers for over two millenia, and has received a variety of imaginative resolutions. Aristotle's answer, in the context of his doctrine of act and potency, was to maintain that the sense faculty and the sensory object, although distinct in potency, in actuality become one and the same (*De Anima*, 425b 26-426a 20). That is, perceptual act and perceptual object are somehow literally identical. Kant attempted to resolve the problem by making principles of thought constitutive of all experiential objects, in effect claiming identity between structure of thought and structure of whatever can be empirically known. A more recent expedient has been the invention of the proposition, which in some mysterious way both is object of thought and corresponds to fact in objective reality. It should not take much argument to be convinced that one could not profitably undertake to devise an artifact capable of actualizing its sensory faculties identically with sensible objects, or of constituting objects according to its principles of thought, to say nothing of entertaining propositions that are somehow objects of thought while isomorphic with the structure of empirical reality. Nonetheless, the conception of mind-object correspondence that I want to advance has recognizable affinities with these classical solutions.

Since this conception relies upon the cybernetic framework we should review some basic categories of communication theory. An information channel consists of an input alphabet $A = (a_i)$, $i = 1, 2, ..., m$, and an output alphabet $B = (b_j)$, $j = 1, 2, ..., n$, associated by conditional probabilities $P(b_j/a_i)$ for all i and j. $P(b_j/a_i)$ is the probability that the output symbol b_j occurs (will be 'received') if the input symbol a_i occurs (is 'sent'). This relationship between A and B can be perspicuously represented by the schema

$$\left\{ \begin{array}{c} a_1 \\ a_2 \\ a_3 \\ \cdot \\ \cdot \\ \cdot \\ a_m \end{array} \right\} -P(b_j/a_i) \rightarrow \left\{ \begin{array}{c} b_1 \\ b_2 \\ b_3 \\ \cdot \\ \cdot \\ \cdot \\ b_n \end{array} \right\}$$

Given $P(a_i)$ and $P(b_j/a_i)$ for all i and j, $P(b_j)$ can be directly calculated, and with it $P(a_i/b_j)$ by Bayes' equality

$$\text{(I)} \quad P(a_i/b_j) = \frac{P(b_j/a_i)\, P(a_i)}{P(b_j)}$$

A related equality is

$$\text{(II)} \quad P(a_i, b_j) = P(b_j/a_i)\, P(a_i)$$

giving the probability of the joint occurence of a_i and b_j.

The capacity of the channel A-B to transmit information varies directly with the *self-information* (variety) of the input set A, according to the formula

(III) $H(A) = \sum_A P(a_i) \log 1/P(a_i)$

and with the reliability of B as an indicator of A. The reliability of B as an indicator of A varies inversely with the *equivocation* of A with respect to B, expressed formally

(IV) $H(A/B) = \sum_{A/B} P(a_i, b_j) \log 1/P(a_i/b_j)$

That is, the more reliable B is generally as an indicator of A, the lower the equivocation of A to B. The capacity of channel A-B as a transmitter of information thus is given by the quantity

(V) $I(A;B) = H(A) - H(A/B)$

which is designated the *mutual information* of the channel A-B.

Human visual perception takes place over a cascade of information channels, so related that the output of one is the input of the next for each pair of channels within the series. In the afferent sequence, there is the channel from lens to retina, from retina to chiasma, from chiasma to geniculate body, and so forth into the visual cortex. In the efferent phase, there is a comparably articulated sequence extending from the cortex to the muscle fibers that effect the organism's interaction with its external environment. The requirements of behavioural guidance, as it were, constitute the load placed upon the afferent system, to which the latter responds by passing information from receptors to cortex in the amount and form necessary to maintain visual control. As should be expected, the informational processes occurring at crucial points in this series can be characterized in terms of communication theory.

In its overall dynamics, the visual information-processing system proceeds according to what elsewhere has been called 'the postulate of perceptual efficiency'.[8] This postulate is a corollary of Shannon's Tenth Theorem, which states in effect that the capacity of a guidance system to correct deviations from an optimal state is limited by the amount of information present at the system's input. An immediate entailment of this theorem is that the (evolutionary or artifactual) development of increasingly more versatile capacities for environmental adaption must be accompanied by the development of increasingly more discriminatory sensory mechanisms. The corollary in question is that organisms under selective pressure to increase their capacities for environmental adaption will be under pressure, as a consequence, to increase the efficiency of their perceptual channels. The effect is that highly evolved organisms tend to expend as little of their information-processing capacities on a task requiring perceptual guidance as is compatible with its successful pursuit. This tendency, I maintain, is the basis of human perceptual awareness. The dynamics of the perceptual response are such that it seeks to maintain a balance between steady control of the organism's perceptual projects and a minimum expenditure of its limited capacity for perceptual information processing. By this expedient, the organism is enabled to pursue a variety of perceptual projects simultaneously when none involves excessive novelty, but at the same time remains prepared to cope with situations involving stress or challenge by focusing all its informational resources around a single venture.

A measure of information-handling capacity committed at a given stage in the afferent process is the range of different system states that can be discriminated at that point—the self-information of that stage as defined in (III) above. The signal that additional capacity is needed at a particular juncture comes in the form of increased equivocation across that link in the perceptual cascade, defined in formula (IV) above and appearing phenomenologically as perceptual vagueness or disorientation, or perhaps as incipient lapse of the perceptual field. Since effective perceptual control is adequate mutual information across the cascade of channels, and since mutual information is the difference between self-information and equivocation, the dynamics of perceptual consciousness are summarized symbolically by the basic equation (V) of communication theory. Interpreted along the lines sketched above, this equation shows that the information-processing activity ($H(A)$) of a given channel in the perceptual cascade varies in response to changes in equivocation ($H(A/B)$), but that when demands upon the perceptual system ($I(A;B)$) and its equivocation remain relatively constant this activity itself will remain relatively stable.

In conditions of perceptual equilibrium, the afferent information-processing activities of the organism thus hold their set by a kind of inertia that enables the organism to maintain perceptual control with minimum expenditure of its processing capacities. Afferent sets of this sort are what I have termed previously 'patterned visual responses'[9], and what in the following will be referred to simply as 'percepts'. Among the expedients by which the organism maintains afferent control with minimum outlay of its informational resources are various operations of smoothing, sorting, and data reduction, all reproducible in mechanical systems. Among the features of perceptual patterns resulting from these operations are the conscious phenomena of constancy, persistence and gap-indifference, along with other phenomena studied by gestalt psychology.

So much by way of summary of material treated elsewhere. The purpose of this summary has been to prepare the way for an account in communication theoretic terms of that correspondence between mind and object by which visual awareness achieves the status of perceptual knowing. For this purpose we shall retain the concept of the perceptual process as a series of neuronal events taking place over a cascade of information channels, each stage of which is related to its immediate successor by a determinate measure of mutual information. The role of the process overall is to sustain a degree of mutual information across the afferent sequence sufficient for behavioural control in a changing environment.

Although the perceptual process itself may be rightly conceived as beginning with events at the sensory periphery of the perceiving organism, however, it is clear that these events constitute the output of a cascade of channels tracing ultimately (in the case of vision) to the sun itself. A distinguishable stage occurs at each juncture in the physical process where the informational structure of the incoming signal is altered in transmission to subsequent stages. This may occur as the signal enters a different medium (the earth's atmosphere, water vapour, optical lenses), or where the medium is subject to irregular distortion. Most importantly, however, it occurs when the physical nature of the signal itself is altered at the surface of a visible object. By a selective process of absorption and reflection, the signal takes on a set of informational features unique to the object that has deflected its progress. Although these informational structures are conveyed by light of certain wavelengths, the structures in question are not the lightwaves themselves. These structures rather take the form of probability functions characterizing the distribution of certain wavelengths in certain regions. In similar fashion, the data impinging on the periphery of the sensory system yielding awareness of objects in the form of a patterned response is not the stimulation of certain receptors by certain wavelengths; it is rather the probabilistic features of such activity in retinal space and time. A common but basic mistake in scientifically inspired thinking about the perceptual process is to construe lightwaves as objects of colour vision. But light waves in no way serve as objects of vision. They serve instead as the medium for the conveyance of coded messages, the informational features of which evoke the patterns of visual perception.

Consider now the relationship between visual pattern and object. A characteristic of any cascade of information channels is the presence of some degree of mutual information between the first and last members of the series. Like a chain of physically connected parts, a cascade possesses mutual information no greater than that of its weakest link. Yet even the weakest member must possess some degree of mutual information if the sequence is to qualify as an informational cascade. Mutual information, we recall, is the measure of a channel's capacity for the reliable indication of events at the input, by events occurring at the channel's output. Maximum capacity is present in a channel completely free from equivocation, in which case the output provides an indication that is completely reliable of all events at the channel's input. Such a series is known technically as a noiseless channel, with all the information present at its input also present at its output.

This same feature is possible in a cascade of information channels. If all channels in the cascade are noiseless, then this same property attaches to the channel itself. In a noiseless cascade of information channels, that is to say, the information present at its input is identically present at its output also. The configuration of events occurring at the output literally reproduces in probability distribution—that is, in informational structure—the configuration occurring at the channel's input. In most practical instances, of course, an informational cascade is far from noiseless, and hence is less than perfectly reliable in information transfer. As long as some degree of mutual information exists across the cascade, however, there is at least a partial identity of information present at input and output.

An answer to our previous question is near at hand. The correspondence between mind and object that gives perceptual awareness the status of perceptual knowing occurs—as Aristotle foresaw—in the form of an identity. Perhaps one could even retain the metaphors of act and potency: whereas potentially many different sets of events could occur both at input and output, in the perceptual cascade the informational structure of events actually occurring at both input and output is identical to the extent of its mutual information. Rather than refurbish an old manner of speaking, however, it is better to speak in terms of communication theory, guaranteeing reproducibility in an artificial system. A person perceives an object in the epistemic sense, requiring the object's presence, if and only if (1) the person is perceptually conscious, and (2) his awareness is structured around perceptual patterns informationally identical with the structures at the surface of the object.

A case of perceptual knowing *ipso facto* is a case of veridical perception. Illusory perception, on the other hand, occurs in cases of extreme equivocation, due to anomalous transmission or processing malfunction, where perceptual patterns are set up in the subject's cortex which lack correspondence with external conditions. We should note in passing that, whereas veridical perception usually implicates three dimensional objects in our immediate environment—since these are the objects we must cope with in the normal run of beahviour—there is no reason why perception should not be focused at other junctures of the external cascade. By attending to the image of the sun cast through a pin-hole on a smooth white surface, for instance, we are perceptually aware of the gross features of the sun itself; and by concentrating on the convection waves above a hot highway we perceive a characteristic of what, in other circumstances, would count as a medium with anolmalous features. In any case, the object of awareness in the act of perception is the object we are prepared to deal with in our concurrent behaviour. For it belongs to the nature of the perceptual process that it respond to the organism's need for guidance in an uncertain environment.

CYBERNETICS AND THE NATURE OF THE REASONING PROCESS

I turn now to a topic requiring treatment of a more technical nature, a topic of importance for the understanding of human reason. Perhaps because of its considerable difficulty, it is also a topic largely ignored by recent philosophers. In its practically-oriented and informal application, reason manifests itself as a faculty for tracing out causal relations, and for anticipating effects before they actually occur. In its formal manifestations, on the other hand, reason proceeds by tracing out relationships of logical connection, with no reference at all to cause and effect. An unsolved problem of epistemology is how the logical connections of formal reasoning relate to the causal connections among states of affairs. The idealist solution—which is scarcely intelligible—is to construe causal relatedness in terms of logical connections. No more promising is the approach of those empiricists who treat logical inference as a case of causal relatedness. So crucial is the problem of understanding the relation between causation and reason, however, that we find an empiricist like Sellars agreeing with the idealists in maintaining that 'serious consequences for morals and the life of reason follow from the denial that logical necessity is involved in causal relations'.[10]

Even more puzzling, if that is possible, is the almost entirely unexplored problem of specifying how the neuronal events of the reasoning process relate to the structures of logical inference. The neuronal capacity for rational inference, which in its higher forms appears unique to the human species, obviously developed prior to any technique of formal reasoning. Hence understanding the latter's role in the guidance of human behaviour would be served by any understanding we could gain of the former.

Thus we face the challenge of comprehending the interrelationships not only between the connectives of causation and logic, but also between causation and logic and the neuronal structures of the reasoning process. In exploring the resources cybernetics can bring to these problems, I must rely further upon a summary of accounts developed in *Cybernetics and the Philosophy of Mind*.

Percepts, in the sense outlined above, are stable patterns of afferent neuronal activity which regulate the organism's behaviour with minimum outlay of informational capacity, and which structure its field of perceptual awareness. Such patterns are elicited by stimulation at the sensory periphery, hence are controlled by physical events in the external environment. A related account can be given of meanings, which in effect are percepts freed from perceptual control. Let us conceive meanings as neuronal patterns, either afferent or efferent, which like percepts are formally definable in terms of informational characteristics, and which can be instantiated identically in different cortexes. Meanings are shared originally through the vocalizations of language, whereby informationally equivalent patterns can be activated in different organisms.

Although primarily under the control of vocal stimuli, meanings also become subject to relationships of redundance. The meaning 'ripe', applied for instance to bananas, is compounded of the meanings 'yellow' and 'handlength', in such a fashion that applicability of the former assures applicability of the latter. Application of 'ripe' thus renders the application of 'yellow' redundant. By reverse token, applicability of 'yellow' is necessary for the application of 'ripe', thus controlling the latter in a restrictive sense.

Concepts can be conceived as meanings thus removed from direct stimulus control, either by vocalization or by the perceptual presence of objects, and brought under the control of other meanings. Whereas the percept 'yellow', for example, is normally activated only by yellow objects, the meaning may be activated by the sound 'yellow' as well; and the concept 'yellow' may be activated not only by the sound and the object, but also by the meaning 'yellow' itself. Thus understood, percepts, meanings and concepts alike are structures of neuronal activity, distinguished primarily with respect to source of control. The control of a concept is a function of its redundancy relationships, which can be defined in terms of communication theory. Consider the relationships between concepts M and N such that applicability of M renders N applicable also. In this case, applicability of M to a stimulus situation precludes application of any concept not applicable conjointly with N, while nonapplicability of N, in turn, precludes the application of M itself. Each concept is determinate by way of being either necessary or sufficient for application of the other, but may be indeterminate in either respect relative to yet other concepts. Whereas 'ripe', for instance, may be indeterminate with respect to 'mottled', 'yellow' may be indeterminate with respect to 'handlength'.

Now in the ordinary sense of equivocation, a concept is equivocal in a given field of application to the extent that it is indeterminate with respect to the applicability of other potentially relevant concepts. The concept M is less equivocal than N if all concepts precluded by N are precluded by M also, but M precludes other concepts besides. The concept 'ripe' thus is less equivocal with respect to edible bananas than the concept 'yellow', but no further decrease in equivocation is achieved by the concepts 'ripe' and 'yellow' combined. When 'ripe' and 'yellow' are related in this fashion, then the application of 'ripe' renders 'yellow' redundant. But these relationships, intuitively obvious in the ordinary sense, can be formulated also in terms of the equivocation of communication theory.

If 'ripe' is less equivocal with respect to 'edible banana' than 'yellow', but no more equivocal than 'ripe' and 'yellow' combined, then the following communication theoretic relationships hold: (a) H('edible banana'/'ripe') < H('edible banana'/'yellow'), and (b) H('edible banana'/'ripe') = H('edible banana'/'yellow', 'ripe'). This relationship is one defined elsewhere[11] as the 'masking' relationship. In general, D masks C with respect to E if and only if (a) H(E/D) < H(E/C) (the equivocation of E with respect to D is less than the equivocation of E with respect to C), and (b) H(E/D) = H(E/CD) (no further decrease in equivocation with respect to E would follow from the combination of C and D). We will symbolize this masking relationship by the expression 'M(D,C),E', read 'D masks C with respect to E'.

The definition of redundancy among concepts is now straightforward and simple. When M masks N with respect to Q, then in that application M renders N redundant. Thus 'ripe' masks 'yellow' with respect to 'edible banana', and hence renders 'yellow' redundant in that respect. Since not all ripe things are yellow, however, 'ripe' masks 'yellow' only with reference to particular applications. By contrast, all squares are rectangular without limitation of applicability. If the relationship M(A,B),C holds for all C indiscriminately, then we shall say that A masks B without qualification, symbolized simply 'M(A,B)'.

Another result follows at this point which, although not directly related to the theme of this paper, is of sufficient philosophic interest to warrant mention. The masking relationship provides a definition of analyticity that is neither circular nor dependent upon equally vague notions. If M(A,B) without qualification, then it is the case that all A is B, that this is true on the basis of meanings, and that a statement to this effect is necessarily true, hence analytic.

The masking relationship holds among concepts, hence among neural structures involved in the reasoning process. The capacity of these structures to support the procedures of formal inference is illuminated by the fact that the logical structure of the paradigm syllogism 'Barbara', Figure 1, as seen below

$$\text{All M is P}$$
$$\underline{\text{All S is M}}$$
$$\therefore \text{All S is P}$$

can be formulated in terms of the masking relationship, and further by the fact that the syllogism thus formulated can be shown to be valid on the basis of equations from communication theory.

To the universal affirmative proposition 'All S is P' corresponds the neuronal relationship M(S,P) and to the universal negative 'No S is P' the relationship M(S, not-P). 'Some S is P' corresponds to not-M(S, not-P), while 'Some S is not P' goes over into not-M(S,P).[12] The denial of a concept such as not-P signifies its nonapplicability, the denial of a masking relationship its failure to hold. These renditions, we may note, preserve fidelity to the basic relationships of the square of opposition, in line with the customary understanding that particular but not universal propositions have existential import.

The grounds for validity of Barbara, Figure 1, can be shown on the basis of these renditions. Barbara, Figure 1, can be construed as the argument form 'if M(M,P) and M(S,M), then M(S,P)'. The demonstration requires a formal definition of a cascade of information channels, toward which we can move with the following observations. As noted previously, two information channels A-B and B-C are cascaded when the output of the first is the input of the second. In such an arrangement, an output event c_k indicates an input event a_i only derivatively through an intermediate event bj. $P(c_k)$ thus depends directly upon $P(bj)$, and upon $P(a_i)$ only as this latter affects $P(bj)$. This property of a cascaded channel can be written

(VI) $P(c_k/bj, a_i) = P(c_k/bj)$ for all i, j, and k (subscripts henceforth omitted.)

From (VI) and (II) we derive

$$\frac{P(a,b,c)}{P(b,a)} = \frac{P(c,b)}{P(b)}$$

$$P(a/b, c) = \frac{P(a,b,c)}{P(b,c)}$$

$$= \frac{P(a,b,c)\,P(b,a)}{P(a,b,c)\,P(b)}$$

(VII) $P(a/b,c) = P(a/b)$

Since equations (VI) and (VII) hold for all and only for cascades A-B-C, they may be taken as defining what is meant by the cascade of channels A-B and B-C.[13]

With these resources, our task is to prove that if M(M,P) and M(S,M), then M(S,P). That is, given for all reference classes R (by definition of the masking relationship):

H(R/M) < H(R/P); H(R/M) = H(R/MP); and

$H(R/S) < H(R/M)$; $H(R/S) = H(R/SM)$; our task is to prove $H(R/S) < H(R/P)$; $H(R/S) = H(R/SP)$.

That $H(R/S) < H(R/P)$ follows directly from transitivity of the '$<$' relation. To show that $H(R/S) = H(R/SP)$ requires more work. Since $H(R/M) = H(R/MP)$, it follows by (IV) that

$$\underset{RM}{\Sigma}\ P(r,m) \log 1/P(r/m) = \underset{RMP}{\Sigma} P(r,m,p) \log 1/P(r/p,m)$$

Since in general $P(a) = \underset{B}{\Sigma}P(a/b)P(b) = \underset{B}{\Sigma} P(a,b)$

$$\text{hence } \underset{A}{\Sigma}P(a) = \underset{AB}{\Sigma} P(a,b)$$

we have $\quad \underset{RMP}{\Sigma}P(r,m,p) \log 1/P(r/m) = \underset{RMP}{\Sigma}P(r,m,p) \log 1/P(r/p,m)$,

and $\quad P(r/m) = P(r/m,p)$

By parallel reasoning, $H(R/S) = H/R/SM)$ yields
$$P(r/s) = P(r/s,m)$$

The latter two results identify the cascades R-M-P and R-S-M by (VII). But if S is intermediate in a cascade between R and M, and M is intermediate in a cascade between R and P, then S is intermediate in a cascade between R and P. Hence $P(r/s) = P(r/s,p)$ by (VII), which leads to the desired conclusion by (IV) as follows:

$$\underset{RSP}{\Sigma P(r,s,p)} \log 1/P(r/s) \quad = \quad \underset{RSP}{\Sigma P(r,s,p)} \log 1/P(r/s,p)$$

$$\underset{RS}{\Sigma P(r,s)} \log 1/P(r/s) \quad = \quad \underset{RSP}{\Sigma P(r,s,p)} \log 1/P(r/s,/p)$$

$$H(R/S) = H(R/SP) \qquad \text{Q.E.D.}$$

This derivation shows that the neuronal structures (concepts) postulated as underlying syllogistic inference stand in the same relation of necessary dependence as the logical structures through which they are expressed in formal reasoning. In answer to the question how logical inference is related to the neuronal processes involved in reasoning, we may say, in the case of Barbara, Figure 1, at least, that in a literal sense they proceed according to equivalent relationships of dependency and consequence.

The final problem posed above concerns the relationship between causation and reason. The response we are now prepared to give may be brief without being programmatic. According to the analysis of causation developed, defended and extensively deployed in *Cybernetics and the Philosophy of Mind*[14] the causal relation also can be understood in terms of the masking relationship. A set of events C is causally related to another set E if and only if (i) for every event in E is there at least one in C such that the probability of the former given the latter is greater than the probability of the former alone (for each e_i there is a c_j such that $P(e_i c_j) > P(e_i)$) and (ii) there is no other set D such that D masks C with respect to E (there is no D such that $M(D,C)E$). The temporal ordering of C and E in this account is determined by the communication theoretic equivalent of the thermodynamic principle that entropy tends to increase with advancing time. A mathematical consequence of this account is that deterministically associated causal events are ordered with cause temporally prior to effect. One advantage of the account, however, is that it provides for the possibility of other relationships in which the cause is temporally posterior, as seemingly required by microphysics and biology. This result, I may hasten to add, does not suggest causal influences running backwards in time, but merely establishes that explanatory variables in some empirical sciences may be temporally posterior to be events they explain.

Another advantage of this account of causation is that it shows how causal sequences can be mirrored in the processing of reasoning. Both causation and reason are founded on the masking relationship. The only difference in formal structure between the two lies in the additional features of causal relatedness, first that the probability of the effect given the cause is greater than that of the effect alone, and second that cause and effect are temporally related. In a literal sense, syllogistic reasoning is an image of causal relatedness, abstracted from particularities of time and place. By reverse token, causation is an order among events in nature answering to the forms of logical inference.

Whereas most philosophers have found unintelligible the idealist's notion that logical relations literally are part of natural causal processes, these results show a clear and fully intelligible sense in which reason and causation may be conceived as congruent. The utility of reasoning in the discovery of causal relationships may be understood as following from this congruence of structure. And it is by virtue of this utility that reason must be presumed to have evolved and to have gained mankind precedence in natural selection.

By way of a final remark, it may be re-emphasized that these latter results, although not touching directly upon artificial intelligence, stem from a research program motivated by the guiding principle that what is fully understood can be artificially simulated. If my observations at the beginning of the essay are correct, these results thus further testify to the value of artificial intelligence as a method of philosophical analysis, apart from any attempt actually to simulate the reasoning processes in question.

NOTES AND REFERENCES

1. Sayre, K.M. *Consciousness,* NY (Random House, 1969) ch.8. See also Sayre, K. *Moonflight,* University of Notre Dame Press (1977).
2. Sayre, K.M. and Crosson, F.J. (eds) *Philosophy and Cybernetics.* University of Notre Dame Press (1967) ix-x.
3. Sayre, K.M. *Recognition* (University of Notre Dame Press, 1965).
4. Sayre, K.M. 'Machine recognition of handwritten words: A project report', *Pattern Recognition, 5* (1973) 213-228.
5. Sayre, K.M. *Cybernetics and the Philosophy of Mind,* New York (Humanities Press, 1976).
6. MacKay, D.M. 'Mindlike behavior in artifacts'. *British Journal for the Philosophy of Science,* (1951) p.108.
7. Sayre (1965) p.17.
8. Sayre (1976) p.146.
9. Sayre (1969) Ch. 7.
10. Sellars, W. 'Actions and Events', *Nous, 7,* (May, 1972) p.179.
11. Sayre, (1976) Ch.5.

12. This change in representation from *Cybernetics and the Philosophy of Mind* I owe to James Garson.

13. Abramson, N. (1963) *Information Theory and Coding*, New York (McGraw-Hill, 1963) p.114.

14. See also: Sayre, K.M. (1977) 'Statistical models of causal relations', *Philosophy of Science*, *44*, *2* (June, 1977) 203-214.

CHAPTER 8
ASCRIBING MENTAL QUALITIES
TO MACHINES
John McCarthy

To ascribe certain 'beliefs', 'knowledge', 'free will', 'intentions', 'consciousness', 'abilities' or 'wants' to a machine or
computer program is legitimate when such an ascription expresses the same information about the machine that it expresses about a person. It is useful when the ascription helps us
understand the structure of the machine, its past or future
behaviour, or how to repair or improve it. It is perhaps never
logically required even for humans, but expressing reasonably
briefly what is actually known about the state of a machine in a
particular situation may require mental qualities or qualities
isomorphic to them.[1] Theories of belief, knowledge and wanting
can be constructed for machines in a simpler setting than for
humans and later applied to humans. Ascription of mental
qualities is most straightforward for machines of known structure such as thermostats and computer operating systems, but is
most useful when applied to entities whose structure is very
incompletely known.

These views are motivated by work in artificial intelligence[2].
They can be taken as asserting that many of the philosophical
problems of mind take a concrete form when one takes seriously
the idea of making machines behave intelligently. In particular,
AI raises two issues for machines that have heretofore been
considered only in connection with people.

First, in designing intelligent programs and looking at them
from the outside we need to determine the conditions under
which specific mental and volitional terms are applicable. We
can exemplify these problems by asking when it might be
legitimate to say about a machine, *'It knows I want a
reservation to Boston, and it can give it to me, but it won't'*.

Second, when we want a generally intelligent[3] computer

161

program, we must build into it a general view of what the world is like, with especial attention to facts about how the information required to solve problems is to be obtained and used. Thus we must provide it with some kind of metaphysics or general world-view, and epistemology (theory of knowledge) however naive.

As much as possible, we will ascribe mental qualities separately from each other instead of bundling them into a concept of mind. This is necessary because present machines have rather varied little minds; the mental qualities that can legitimately be ascribed to them are few and differ from machine to machine. We will not even try to meet objections like, 'Unless it also does X, it is illegitimate to speak of its having mental qualities'.

Machines as simple as thermostats can be said to have beliefs, and having beliefs seems to be a characteristic of most machines capable of problem solving performance. However, the machines mankind has so far found it useful to construct rarely have beliefs about beliefs, although such beliefs will be needed by computer programs that reason about what knowledge they lack and where to get it. Mental qualities peculiar to human-like motivational structures[4], such as love and hate, will not be required for intelligent behaviour but we could probably program computers to exhibit them if we wanted to, because our common sense notions about them translate readily into certain program and data structures. Still other mental qualities, like humour and appreciation of beauty, seem much harder to model. While we will be quite liberal in ascribing some mental qualities even to rather primitive machines, we will try to be conservative in our criteria for ascribing any particular quality.

The successive sections of this paper will give philosophical and AI reasons for ascribing beliefs to machines, two new forms of definition that seem necessary for defining mental qualities and examples of their use, examples of systems to which mental qualities are ascribed, some first attempts at defining a variety of mental qualities, some comments on other views on mental qualities, notes, and references.

This paper is exploratory and its presentation is non-technical. Any axioms that are presented are illustrative and not part of an axiomatic system proposed as a serious candidate for

AI or philosophical use. This is regrettable for two reasons. First, AI use of these concepts requires formal axiomatization. Second, the lack of formalism focuses attention on whether the paper correctly characterizes mental qualities rather than on the formal properties of the theories proposed. I think we can attain a situation like that in the foundations of mathematics, wherein the controversies about whether to take an intuitionist or classical point of view have been mainly replaced by technical studies of intuitionist and classical theories and the relations between them. In future work, I hope to treat these matters more formally along the lines of McCarthy (1977a) and (1977b). This will not eliminate controversy about the true nature of mental qualities, but I believe that their eventual resolution requires more technical knowledge than is now available.

WHY ASCRIBE MENTAL QUALITIES?

Why should we want to ascribe beliefs to machines at all? This is the converse question to that of reductionism. Instead of asking how mental qualities can be reduced to physical ones, we ask how to ascribe mental qualities to physical systems.

Our general motivation for ascribing mental qualities is the same as for ascribing any other qualities, namely to express available information about the machine and its current state. To have information, we must have a space of possibilities whether explicitly described or not. The ascription must therefore serve to distinguish the present state of the machine from past or future states, or from the state the machine would have in other conditions, or from the state of other machines. Therefore, the issue is whether ascription of mental qualities is helpful in making these discriminations in the case of machines.

To put the issue sharply, consider a computer program for which we possess complete listings. The behaviour of the program in any environment is determined from the structure of the program and can be found out by simulating the action of the program and the environment without having to deal with any concept of belief. Nevertheless, there are several reasons for ascribing belief and other mental qualities:

1. Although we may know the program, its state at a given moment is usually not directly observable, and the facts we can obtain about its current state may be more readily expressed by ascribing certain beliefs and goals than in any other way.

2. Even if we can simulate its interaction with its environment using another more comprehensive program, the simulation may be a billion times too slow. Also we may not have the initial conditions of the environment or the environment's laws of motion in a suitable form, whereas it may be feasible to make a prediction of the effects of the beliefs we ascribe to the program without any computer at all.

3. Ascribing beliefs may allow the derivation of general statements about the program's behaviour that could not be obtained from any finite number of simulations.

4. The belief and goal structures we ascribe to the program may be easier to understand than the details of the program as expressed in its listing.

5. The belief and goal structure is likely to be close to the structure the designer of the program had in mind, and it may be easier to debug the program in terms of this structure than directly from the listing. In fact, it is often possible for someone to correct a fault by reasoning in general terms about the information in a program or machine, diagnosing what is wrong as a false belief, and looking at the details of the program or machine only sufficiently to determine how the false belief is represented and what mechanism caused it to arise.

6. The difference between this program and another actual or hypothetical program may best be expressed as a difference in belief structure.

All the above reasons for ascribing belief's are epistemological; i.e. ascribing beliefs is needed to adapt to limitations on our ability to acquire knowledge, use it for prediction, and establish generalizations in terms of the elementary structure of the program. Perhaps this is the general reason for ascribing higher levels of organization to systems.

Computers give rise to numerous examples of building a higher structure on the basis of a lower and conducting subsequent analysis using the higher structure. The geometry of the electric fields in a transistor and its chemical composition give rise to its properties as an electric circuit element. Transistors are combined in small circuits and powered in standard ways to make logical elements such as ANDs, ORs, NOTs, and flip-flops. Computers are designed with these logical elements to obey a desired order code, the designer usually needn't consider the properties of the transistors as circuit elements. When writing a compiler from a higher level language, one works with the order code and doesn't have to know about the ANDs and ORs; the user of the higher order language needn't know the computer's order code.

In the above cases, users of the higher level can completely ignore the lower level, because the behaviour of the higher level system is completely determined by the values of the higher level variables; e.g. in order to determine the outcome of a computer program, one needn't consider the flip-flops. However, when we ascribe mental structure to humans or goals to society, we always get highly incomplete systems; the higher level behaviour cannot be fully predicted from higher level observations and higher level 'laws' even when the underlying lower level behaviour is determinate. Moreover, at a given state of science and technology, different kinds of information can be obtained from experiment and theory building at the different levels of organization.

In order to program a computer to obtain information and co-operation from people and other machines, we will have to make it ascribe knowledge, belief, and wants to other machines and people. For example, a program that plans trips will have to ascribe knowledge to travel agents and to the airline reservation computers. It must somehow treat the information in books, perhaps by ascribing to them a passive form of knowledge. The more powerful the program is in interpreting what it is told, the less it has to know about how the information it can receive is represented internally in the teller and the more its ascriptions of knowledge will look like human ascriptions of knowledge to other humans.

TWO METHODS OF DEFINITION AND THEIR APPLICATION TO MENTAL QUALITIES

In our opinion, a major source of problems in defining mental and intensional concepts is the weakness of the methods of definition that have been explicitly used. We introduce two kinds of definitions: *definition relative to an approximate theory* and *second order structural definition* and apply them to defining mental qualities.

1. Definitions relative to an approximate theory

It is commonplace that most scientific concepts are not defined by isolated sentences of natural languages but rather as parts of theories, and the acceptance of the theory is determined by its fit to a large collection of phenomena. We propose a similar method for explicating mental and other common sense concepts, but a certain phenomenon plays a more important role than with scientific theories: the concept is meaningful only in the theory, and cannot be defined with more precision than the theory permits.

The notion of one theory approximating another needs to be formalized. In the case of physics, one can think of various kinds of numerical or probabilistic approximation. I think this kind of approximation is untypical and misleading and will not help to explicate such concepts as intentional action as meaningful in approximate theories. Instead it may go something like this:

Consider a detailed theory T that has a state variable s. We may imagine that s changes with time. The approximating theory T' has a state variable s'. There is a predicate $atp(s,T')$ whose truth means that T' is applicable when the world is in state s. There is a relation $corr(s,s')$ which asserts that s' corresponds to the state s. We have

$$(1) \quad \forall s.(atp(s,T') \supset \exists s'.corr(s,s')).$$

Certain functions $f1(s)$, $f2(s)$, etc. have corresponding functions $f1'(s')$, $f2'(s')$ etc. We have relations like

(2) $\forall s\, s'.(corr(s,s') \supset f1(s) = f1'\,(s')\,)$.

However, the approximate theory T' may have additional functions $g1'(s')$ etc. that do not correspond to any functions of s. Even when it is possible to construct gs corresponding to the g's, their definitions will often seem arbitrary, because the common sense user of $g1'$ will only have used it within the context of T'. Concepts whose definition involves counterfactuals provide examples.

Suppose we want to ascribe *intentions* and *free will* and to distinguish a *deliberate action* from an occurrence. We want to call an output a *deliberate action* if the output would have been different if the machine's intentions had been different. This requires a criterion for the truth of the counterfactual conditional sentence, 'If its intentions had been different the output wouldn't have occurred', and we require what seems to be a novel treatment of counterfactuals.

We treat the 'relevant aspect of reality' as a Cartesian product so that we can talk about changing one component and leaving the others unchanged. This would be straightforward if the Cartesian product structure existed in the world; however, it usually exists only in certain approximate models of the world. Consequently no single definite state of the world as a whole corresponds to changing one component. The following paragraphs present these ideas in greater detail.

Suppose A is a theory in which some aspect of reality is characterized by the values of three quantities x, y and z. Let f be a function of three arguments, let u be a quantity satisfying $u = f(x,y,z)$, where $f(1,1,1) = 3$ and $f(2,1,1) = 5$. Consider a state of the model in which $x = 1$, $y = 1$ and $z = 1$. Within the theory A, the counterfactual conditional sentence '*u = 3, but if x were 2 then u would be 5*' is true, because the counterfactual condition means changing x to 2 and leaving the other variables unchanged.

Now let's go beyond the model and suppose that x,y and z are quantities depending on the state of the world. Even if $u = f(x,y,z)$ is taken as a law of nature, the counterfactual need not be taken as true, because someone might argue that if x were 2, then y would be 3 so that u might not be 5. If the theory A has a sufficiently preferred status we may take the meaning of the counterfactual in A to be its general meaning, but it may sometimes be better to consider the counterfactual as defined solely in the theory, i.e. as *syncategorematic*.

A common sense example may be helpful: Suppose a ski instructor says, 'He wouldn't have fallen if he had bent his knees when he made that turn', and another instructor replies, 'No, the reason he fell was that he didn't put his weight on his downhill ski'. Suppose, further, that on reviewing a film, they agree that the first instructor was correct and the second mistaken. I contend that this agreement is based on their common acceptance of a theory of skiing, and that *within the theory*, the decision may well be rigorous even though no-one bothers to imagine an alternate world as much like the real world as possible but in which the student had put his weight on his downhill ski.

We suggest that this is often (I haven't yet looked for counter-examples) the common sense meaning of a counterfactual. The counterfactual has a definite meaning in a theory, because the theory has a Cartesian product structure, and the theory is sufficiently preferred that the meaning of the counterfactual in the world is taken as its meaning in the theory. This is especially likely to be true for concepts that have a natural definition in terms of counterfactuals, like the concept of *deliberate action* with which we started this section.

In all cases that we know about, the theory is approximate and incomplete. Provided certain propositions are true, a certain quantity is approximately a given function of certain other quantities. The incompleteness lies in the fact that the theory doesn't predict states of the world but only certain functions of them. Thus a useful concept like deliberate action may seem to vanish if examined too closely, when we try to define it in terms of states of the world and not just in terms of certain functions of these states.

REMARKS:

1.1. The known cases in which a concept is defined relative to an approximate theory involve counterfactuals. This may not always be the case.

1.2. It is important to study the nature of the approximations.

l.3. McCarthy and Hayes (1969) treats the notion of *X can do Y* using a theory in which the world is regarded as a collection of interacting automata. That paper failed to note that sentences using 'can' cannot necessarily be translated into single assertions about the world.

1.4. The attempt by old fashioned introspective psychology to analyse the mind into an interacting *will*, *intellect* and other components cannot be excluded on the methodological grounds used by behaviourists and positivists to declare them meaningless and exclude them from science. These concepts might have precise definitions within a suitable approximate theory.

1.5. The above treatment of counterfactuals in which they are defined in terms of the Cartesian product structure of an approximate theory may be better than the 'closest possible world' treatments discussed by Lewis (1973). The truth values are well defined within the approximate theories, and the theories can be justified by evidence involving phenomena not mentioned in isolated counterfactual assertions.

1.6. Definition relative to approximate theories may help separate questions, such as some of those concerning counterfactuals, into *internal* questions within the approximate theory and the *external* question of the justification of the theory as a whole. The internal questions are likely to be technical and have definite answers on which people can agree even if they have philosophical or scientific disagreements about the external questions.

2. Second Order Structural Definition

Structural definitions of qualities are given in terms of the state of the system being described while behavioural definitions are given in terms of its actual or potential behaviour.[5]

If the structure of the machine is known, one can give an *ad hoc* 'first order structural definition'. This is a predicate $B(s,p)$ where *s* represents a state of the machine and *p* represents a sentence in a suitable language, and $B(s,p)$ is the assertion that when the machine is in state s, it believes the sentence p. (The considerations of this paper are neutral in deciding whether to regard the object of belief as a sentence or to use a modal operator or to admit *propositions* as abstract objects that can be believed. The paper is written as though sentences are the objects of belief, but I have more recently come to favour propositions, which I discuss in McCarthy, (1977a).)

A general 'first order' structural definition of belief would be a predicate $B(W,M,s,p)$ where W is the 'world' in which the machine M whose beliefs are in question is situated. I do not see how to give such a definition of belief, and I think it is impossible. Therefore we turn to second order definitions. [6]

A second order structural definition of belief is a second order predicate $\beta(W,M,B)$. $\beta(W,M,B)$ asserts that the first order predicate B is a 'good' notion of belief for the machine M in the world W. Here 'good' means that the beliefs that B ascribes to M agree with our ideas of what beliefs M would have, not that the beliefs themselves are true. The axiomatizations of belief in the literature are partial second order definitions.

In general, a second order definition gives criteria for criticizing an ascription of a quality to a system. We suggest that both our common sense and scientific usage of not-directly-observable qualities corresponds more loosely to second order structural definition than to any kind of behavioural definition. Note that a second order definition cannot guarantee that there exist predicates B meeting the criterion β or that such a B is unique. Some qualities are best defined jointly with related qualities, for example, beliefs and goals may require joint treatment.

Second order definitions criticize whole belief structures rather than individual beliefs. We can treat individual beliefs by saying that a system believes p in state s provided all 'reasonably good' B's satisfy $B(s,p)$. Thus we are distinguishing the 'intersection' of the reasonably good B's.

An analogy with cryptography may be helpful. We solve a cyptogram by making hypotheses about the structure of the cipher and about the translation of parts of the cipher text. Our solution is complete when we have 'guessed' a cipher system that produces the cryptogram from a plausible plaintext message. Though we never prove that our solution is unique, two different solutions are almost never found except for very short cryptograms. In the analogy, the second order definition β corresponds to the general idea of encipherment, and B is the particular system used. While we will rarely be able to prove uniqueness, we don't expect to find two Bs both satisfying β.

It seems to me that there should be a metatheorem of mathematical logic asserting that not all second order definitions can be reduced to first order definitions and further theorems characterizing those second order definitions that admit such reductions. Such technical results, if they can be found, may be helpful in philosophy and in the construction of formal scientific theories. I would conjecture that many of the informal philosophical arguments that certain mental concepts cannot be reduced to physics will turn out to be sketches of arguments that these concepts require second (or higher) order definitions.

Here is an approximate second order definition of belief. For each state s of the machine and each sentence p in a suitable language L, we assign truth to $B(s,p)$ if and only if the machine is considered to believe p when it is in state s. The language L is chosen for our convenience, and there is no assumption that the machine explicitly represents sentences of L in any way. Thus we can talk about the beliefs of Chinese, dogs, corporations, thermostats, and computer-operating systems without assuming that they use English or our favourite first order language. L may or may not be the language we are using for making other assertions, e.g. we could, writing in English, systematically use French sentences as objects of belief. However, the best choice for artificial intelligence work may be to make L a subset of our 'outer' language, restricted so as to avoid the paradoxical self-references of Montague (1963).

We now subject $B(s,p)$ to certain criteria; $\beta(B,W)$ is considered true provided the following conditions are satisfied:

2.1. The set $Bel(s)$ of beliefs, i.e. the set of p's for which $B(s,p)$ is assigned true when M is in state s contains sufficiently 'obvious' consequences of some of its members.

2.2. $Bel(s)$ changes in a reasonable way when the state changes in time. We like new beliefs to be logical or 'plausible' consequences of old ones, or to come in as 'communications' in some language on the input lines, or to be 'observations', i.e.

beliefs about the environment, the information for which comes in on the input lines. The set of beliefs should not change too rapidly as the states changes with time.

2.3. We prefer the set of beliefs to be as consistent as possible. (Admittedly, consistency is not a quantitative concept in mathematical logic – a system is either consistent or not – but it would seem that we will sometimes have to ascribe inconsistent sets of beliefs to machines and people. Our intuition says that we should be able to maintain areas of consistency in our beliefs and that it may be especially important to avoid inconsistencies in the machine's purely analytic beliefs.)

2.4. Our criteria for belief systems can be strengthened if we identify some of the machine's beliefs as expressing goals, i.e if we have beliefs of the form 'It would be good if. . . .' Then we can ask that the machine's behaviour be somewhat 'rational' i.e. *it does what it believes will achieve its goals.* The more of its behaviour we can account for in this way, the better we will like the function $B(s,p)$. We also would like to regard internal state changes as changes in belief insofar as this is reasonable.

2.5. If the machine communicates, i.e. emits sentences in some language that can be interpreted as assertions, questions and commands, we will want the assertions to be among its beliefs unless we are ascribing to it a goal or subgoal that involves lying. We will be most satisfied with our belief ascription, if we can account for its communications as furthering the goals we are ascribing.

2.6. Sometimes we shall want to ascribe introspective beliefs, such as a belief that it does not know how to fly to Boston or even that it doesn't know what it wants in a certain situation.

2.7. Finally we will prefer a more economical ascription B to a less economical one. The fewer beliefs we ascribe and the less they change in state consistent with accounting for the behaviour and the internal state changes, the better we will like it. In particular, if $\forall s\ p.(B1(s,\ p) \supset B2\ (s,\ p))$, *but not conversely, and* $B1$ accounts for all the state changes and outputs that $B2$ does, we will prefer $B1$ to $B2$. This insures that we will prefer to assign no beliefs to stones that don't change and don't behave. A belief predicate that applies to a family of machines is preferable to one that applies to a single machine.

The above criteria have been formulated somewhat vaguely. This would be bad if there were widely different ascriptions of beliefs to a particular machine that all met our criteria or if the criteria allowed ascriptions that differed widely from our intuitions. My present opinion is that more thought will make the criteria somewhat more precise at no cost in applicability, but that they *should* still remain rather vague, i.e. we shall want to ascribe belief in a 'family' of cases. However, even at the present level of vagueness there probably won't be radically different, equally 'good' ascriptions of belief for systems of practical interest. If there were, we would notice unresolvable ambiguities in our ascriptions of belief to our acquaintances.

While we may not want to pin down our general idea of belief to a single axiomatization, we will need to build precise axiomatizations of belief and other mental qualities into particular, intelligent computer programs.

EXAMPLES OF SYSTEMS WITH MENTAL QUALITIES

Let us consider some examples of machines and programs to which we may ascribe belief and goal structures.

1. Thermostats

Ascribing beliefs to simple thermostats is unnecessary for the study of thermostats, because their operation can be well understood without it. However, their very simplicity makes it clearer what is involved in the ascription, and we maintain (partly as a provocation to those who regard attribution of beliefs to machines as mere intellectual sloppiness) that the ascription is legitimate.[7]

First consider a simple thermostat that turns off the heat when the temperature is a degree above the temperature set on the thermostat, turns on the heat when the temperature is a degree below the desired temperature, and leaves the heat as is when the temperature is in the two degree range around the desired temperature. The simplest belief predicate $B(s,p)$ ascribes belief to only three sentences: 'The room is too cold', 'The room is too hot', and 'The room is OK', the beliefs being assigned to states of the thermostat in the obvious way. We ascribe to it the goal, 'The room should be ok'. When the thermostat believes the room is too cold or too hot it sends a message saying so to the furnace. A slightly more complex belief predicate could also be used in which the thermostat has a belief about what the temperature should be and another belief about what it is. It is not clear which is better, but if we wished to consider possible errors in the thermometer, then we would ascribe beliefs about what the temperature is. We do not ascribe to it any other beliefs, it has no opinion even about whether the heat is on or off or about the weather or about who won the Battle of Waterloo. Moreover, it has no introspective beliefs; i.e. it doesn't believe that it believes the room is too hot.

Let us compare the above $B(s,p)$ with the criteria of the previous section. The belief structure is consistent, because all the beliefs are independent of one another, they arise from observation, and they result in action in accordance with the ascribed goal. There is no reasoning and only commands (which we have not included in our discussion) are communicated. Clearly, assigning beliefs is of modest intellectual benefit in this case. However, if we consider the class of possible thermostats, then the ascribed belief structure has greater constancy than the mechanisms for actually measuring and representing the temperature.

The temperature control system in my house may be described as follows: thermostats upstairs and downstairs tell the central system to turn on or shut off hot water flow to these areas. A central water-temperature thermostat tells the furnace to turn on or off thus keeping the central hot water reservoir at the right temperature. Recently it was too hot upstairs, and the question arose as to whether the upstairs thermostat mistakenly *believed* it was too cold upstairs or whether the furnace thermostat mistakenly *believed* the water was too cold. It turned out that neither mistake was made; the downstairs controller *tried* to turn off the flow of water but *couldn't*, because the valve was stuck. The plumber came once and found the trouble, and came again when a replacement valve was ordered. Since the services of plumbers are increasingly expensive, and microcomputers are increasingly cheap, one is led to design a temperature control system that would *know* a lot more about the thermal state of the house and its own state of health.

In the first place, while the present system *couldn't* turn off the flow of hot water upstairs, there is no reason to ascribe to it the 'knowledge' that it couldn't, and *a fortiori* it had no ability to communicate this fact or to take it into account in controlling the system. A more advanced system would know whether the *actions* it *attempted* had succeeded, and it would communicate failures and adapt to them. We adapted to the failure by turning off the whole system until the house cooled off and then letting the two parts warm up together. The present system has the *physical capacity* of doing this even if it hasn't the *knowledge* or the *will*.

While the thermostat believes 'The room is too cold', there is no need to say that it understands the concept of 'too cold'. The internal structure of 'The room is too cold' is a part of our language, not its.

Consider a thermostat whose wires to the furnace have been cut. Shall we still say that it knows whether the room is too cold? Since fixing the thermostat might well be aided by ascribing this knowledge, we would like to do so. Our excuse is that we are entitled to distinguish, in our language, the concept of a broken temperature control system from the concept of a certain collection of parts, i.e. to make intensional characterizations of physical objects.

2. Self-reproducing intelligent configurations in a cellular automaton world

A *cellular automaton system* assigns a finite automaton to each point of the plane with integer co-ordinates. The state of each automaton at time $t + 1$ depends on its state at time t and the states of its neighbours at time t. An early use of cellular automata was by von Neumann, who found a twenty-seven state automaton whose cells could be initialized into a self-reproducing configuration that was also a universal computer. The basic automaton in von Neumann's system had a 'resting' state 0, and a point in state 0 whose four neighbours were also in that state would remain in state 0. The initial configurations considered had all but a finite number of cells in state 0, and, of course, this property would persist although the number of non-zero cells might grow indefinitely with time.

The self-reproducing system used the states of a long strip of non-zero cells as a 'tape' containing instructions to a 'universal constructor' configuration that would construct a copy of the configuration to be reproduced, but with each cell in a passive state that would persist as long as its neighbours were also in passive states. After the construction phase, the tape would be copied to make the tape for the new machine, and then the new system would be set in motion by activating one of its cells. The new system would then move away from its mother, and the process would start over. The purpose of the design was to demonstrate that arbitrarily complex configurations could be self-reproducing, the complexity being assured by also requiring that they be universal computers.

Since von Neumann's time, simpler basic cells admitting self-reproducing universal computers have been discovered. The simplest so far is the two-state Life automaton of John Conway (Cf. Gosper, 1976). The state of a cell at time $t + 1$ is determined by its state at time t and the states of its eight neighbours at time t. Namely, a point whose state is 0 will change to state 1 if exactly three of its neighbours are in state 1. A point whose state is 1 will remain in state 1 if two or three of its neighbours are in state 1. In all other cases the state becomes or remains 0.

Although this was not Conway's reason for introducing them, Conway and Gosper have shown that self-reproducing universal computers could be built up as Life configurations.

Consider a number of such self-reproducing universal computers operating in the Life plane, and suppose that they have been programmed to study the properties of their world and to communicate among themselves about it and pursue various goals co-operatively and competitively. Call these configurations Life robots. In some respects their intellectual and scientific problems will be like ours, but in one major respect they live in a simpler world than ours seems to be. Namely, the fundamental physics of their world is that of the life automaton, and there is no obstacle to each robot *knowing* this physics, and being able to simulate the evolution of a life configuration given the initial state. Moreover, if the initial state of the robot world is finite it can have been recorded in each robot in the beginning or else recorded on a strip of cells that the robots can read. (The infinite regress of having to describe the description is avoided by providing that the description is not separately described, but can be read *both* as a description of the world *and* as a description of itself.)

Since these robots know the initial state of their world and its laws of motion, they can simulate as much of its history as they want, assuming that each can grow into unoccupied space so as to have memory to store the states of the world being simulated. This simulation is necessarily slower than real time, so they can never catch up with the present – let alone predict the future. This is obvious if the simulation is carried out straightforwardly by updating a list of currently active cells in the simulated world according to the Life rule, but it also applies to any clever mathematical method that might predict millions of steps ahead. Some Life configurations, e.g. static ones or ones containing single 'gliders' or 'cannon', can have their distant futures predicted with little computing. Namely, if there were an algorithm for such prediction, a robot could be made that would predict its own future and then disobey the prediction. The detailed proof would be analogous to the proof of unsolvability of the halting problem for Turing machines.

Now we come to the point of this long disquisition. Suppose we wish to program a robot to be successful in the Life world in competition or co-operation with the others. Without any idea of how to give a mathematical proof, I will claim that our robot will need programs that ascribe purposes and beliefs to its fellow robots and predict how they will react to its own actions by assuming that *they will act in ways that they believe will achieve their goals*. Our robot might acquire these mental theories in several ways: First, we might design the universal machine so that they are present in the initial configuration of the world. Second, we might program it to acquire these ideas by induction from its experience and even transmit them to others through an 'educational system'. Third, it might derive the psychological laws from the fundamental physics of the world and its knowledge of the initial configuration. Finally, it might discover how robots are built from Life cells by doing experimental 'biology'.

Knowing the Life physics without some information about the initial configuration is insufficient to derive the 'psychological' laws, because robots can be constructed in the Life world in an infinity of ways. This follows from the 'folk theorem' that the Life automaton is universal in the sense that any cellular automaton can be constructed by taking sufficiently large squares of Life cells as the basic cell of the other automaton.[8]

Men are in a more difficult intellectual position than Life robots. We don't know the fundamental physics of our world, and we can't even be sure that its fundamental physics is describable in finite terms. Even if we knew the physical laws, they seem to preclude precise knowledge of an initial state and precise calculation of its future both for quantum mechanical reasons and because the continuous functions needed to represent fields seem to involve an infinite amount of information.

This example suggests that much of human mental structure is not an accident of evolution or even of the physics of our world, but is required for successful problem solving behaviour and must be designed into or evolved by any system that exhibits such behaviour.

3. Computer time-sharing systems

These complicated computer programs allocate computer time and other resources among users. They allow each user of the computer to behave as though he had a computer of his own, but also allow them to share files of data and programs and to communicate with each other. They are often used for many years with continual small changes, and the people making the changes and correcting errors are often different from the original authors of the system. A person confronted with the task of correcting a malfunction or making a change in a time-sharing system can often conveniently use a mentalistic model of the system.

.Thus suppose a user complains that the system will not run

his program. Perhaps the system believes that he doesn't want to run, perhaps it persistently believes that he has just run, perhaps it believes that his quota of computer resources is exhausted, or perhaps it believes that his program requires a resource that is unavailable. Testing these hypotheses can often be done with surprisingly little understanding of the internal workings of the program.

4. Programs designed to reason

Suppose we explicitly design a program to represent information by sentences in a certain language stored in the memory of the computer and decide what to do by making inferences, and doing what it concludes will advance its goals. Naturally, we would hope that our previous second order definition of belief will 'approve of' a $B(p,s)$ that ascribed to the program believing the sentences explicitly built in. We would be somewhat embarrassed if someone were to show that our second order definition approved as well, or better, of an entirely different set of beliefs.

Such a program was first proposed in McCarthy (1959), and here is how it might work: information about the world is stored in a wide variety of data structures. For example, a visual scene received by a TV camera may be represented by a *512x512x3* array of numbers representing the intensities of three colours at the points of the visual field. At another level, the same scene may be represented by a list of regions, and at a further level there may be a list of physical objects and their parts, together with other information about these objects obtained from non-visual sources. Moreover, information about how to solve various kinds of problems may be represented by programs in some programming language.

However, all the above representations are subordinate to a collection of sentences in a suitable, first order language that includes set theory. By subordinate, we mean that there are sentences that tell what the data structues represent and what the programs do. New sentences can arise by a variety of processes: inference from sentences already present, by computation from the data structures representing observations, and by interpreting certain inputs as communications in one or more languages.

The construction of such a program is one of the major approaches to achieving high level artificial intelligence, and, like every other approach, it faces numerous obstacles. These obstacles can be divided into two classes, *epistemological* and *heuristic*. The epistemological problem is to determine what information about the world is to be represented in the sentences and other data structures, and the heuristic problem is to decide how the information can be used effectively to solve problems. Naturally, the problems interact, but the epistemological problem is more basic and also more relevant to our present concerns. We would regard it as solved if we knew how to express the information needed for intelligent behaviour so that the solution to problems logically followed from the data. The heuristic problem of actually obtaining the solutions would remain.

The information to be represented can be roughly divided into general information about the world and information about particular situations. The formalism used to represent information about the world must be 'epistemologically adequate', i.e. it must be capable of representing the information that is actually available to the program or can be deduced from its sensory apparatus. Thus it could not handle available information about a cup of hot coffee if its only way of representing information about fluids was in terms of the positions and velocities of the molecules. Even the hydrodynamicist's Eulerian distributions of density, velocity, temperature and pressure would be useless for representing the information actually obtainable from a television camera. These considerations are further discussed in McCarthy and Hayes (1969).

Here are some of the kinds of general information that will have to be represented:

1. Narrative. Events occur in space and time. Some events are extended in time. Partial information must be expressed about what events begin or end during, before and after others. Partial information about places and their spacial relations must be expressible. Sometimes dynamic information such as velocities are better known than the space-time facts in terms of which they are defined.

2. Partial information about causal systems. Quantities have values and later have different values. Causal laws relate these values.

3. Some changes are results of actions by the program and other actors. Information about the effects of actions can be used to determine what goals can be achieved in given circumstances.

4. Objects and substances have locations in space. It may be that temporal and causal facts are prior to spatial facts in the formalism.

5. Some objects are actors with beliefs, purposes and intentions.

Of course, the above English description is no substitute for an axiomatized formalism, not even for philosophy, but *a fortiori* when computer programs must be written. The main difficulties in designing such a formalism involve deciding how to express partial information. McCarthy and Hayes (1969) use a notion of 'situation' wherein the situation is never known, only facts about situations are known. Unfortunately, the formalism is not suitable for expressing what might be known when events are taking place in parallel with unknown temporal relations. It also only treats the case in which the result of an action is a definite new situation and therefore isn't suitable for describing continuous processes.

GLOSSARY OF MENTAL QUALITIES

In this section we give short 'definitions' for machines of a collection of mental qualities. We include a number of terms which give us difficulty with an indication of what the difficulties seem to be. We emphasize the place of these concepts in the design of intelligent robots.

1. Introspection and self-knowledge

We say that a machine introspects when it comes to have beliefs about its own mental state. A simple form of introspection takes place when a program determines whether it has certain information and, if not, asks for it. Often an operating system will compute a check sum of itself every few minutes to verify that it hasn't been changed by a software or hardware malfunction.

In principle, introspection is easier for computer programs than for people, because the entire memory in which programs and data are stored is available for inspection. In fact, a computer program can be made to predict how it would react to particular inputs provided it has enough free storage to perform the calculation. This situation smells of paradox, and there is one. Namely, if a program could predict its own actions in less time than it takes to carry out the action, it could refuse to do what it has predicted for itself. This only shows that self-simulation is necessarily a slow process, and this is not surprising.

However, present programs do little interesting introspection. This is just a matter of the undeveloped state of artificial intelligence; programmers don't yet know how to make a computer program look at itself in a useful way.

2. Consciousness and self-consciousness

Suppose we wish to distinguish the self-awareness of a machine, animal or person from its awareness of other things. We explicate awareness as belief in certain sentences, so in this case we want to distinguish those sentences or those terms in the sentences that may be considered to be about the self. We also don't expect that self-consciousness will be a single property that something either has or hasn't but rather there will be many kinds of self-awareness with humans posessing many of the kinds we can imagine.

Here are some of the kinds of self-awareness:

2.1 Certain predicates of the situation, propositional fluents in the terminology of McCarthy and Hayes (1969), are directly observable in almost all situations, while others often must be inferred. The almost always observable fluents may reasonably be identified with the senses. Likewise the values of certain fluents are almost always under the control of the being and can be called motor parameters for lack of a common language term. We have in mind the positions of the joints. Most motor parameters are both observable and controllable. I am inclined to regard the posession of a substantial set of such constantly observable or controllable fluents as the most primitive form of self-consciousness, but I have no strong arguments against someone who wished to require more.

2.2 The second level of self-consciousness requires a term *I* in the language denoting the self. *I* should belong to the class of persistent objects and some of the same predicates should be applicable to it as are applicable to other objects. For example, like other objects *I* has a location that can change in time. *I* is also visible and impenetrable like other objects. However, we don't want to get carried away in regarding a physical body as a necessary condition for self-consciousness. Imagine a distributed computer whose sense and motor organs could also be in a variety of places. We don't want to exclude it from self-consciousness by definition.

2.3. The third level comes when *I* is regarded as an actor among others. The conditions that permit *I* to do something are similar to the conditions that permit other actors to do similar things.

2.4. The fourth level requires the applicability of predicates such as 'believes', 'wants' and 'can' to *I*. Beliefs about past situations and the ability to hypothesize future situations are also required for this level.

3. Language and thought

Here is a hypothesis arising from artificial intelligence concerning the relation between language and thought. Imagine a person or machine that represents information internally in a huge network. Each node of the network has references to other nodes through relations. If the system has a variable collection of relations, then the relations have to be represented by nodes, and we get a symmetrical theory if we suppose that each node is connected to a set of pairs of other nodes. We can imagine this structure to have a long term part, and also extremely temporary parts, representing current 'thoughts'. Naturally, each being has its own network depending on its own experience. A thought is then a temporary node currently being referenced by the mechanism of consciousness. Its meaning is determined by its references to other nodes which, in turn refer, to yet other nodes. Now consider the problem of communicating a thought to another being.

Its full communication would involve transmitting the entire network that can be reached from the given node, and this would ordinarily constitute the entire experience of the being. More than that, it would be necessary to also communicate the programs that take action on the basis of encountering certain nodes. Even if all this could be transmitted, the recipient would still have to find equivalents for the information in terms of its own network. Therefore, thoughts have to be translated into a public language before they can be communicated.

A language is also a network of associations and programs. However, certain of the nodes in this network (more accurately a *family* of networks, since no two people speak precisely the same language) are associated with words or set phrases. Sometimes the translation from thoughts to sentences is easy, because large parts of the private networks are taken from the public network, and there is an advantage in preserving the correspondence. However, the translation is always approximate, in a sense that still lacks a technical definition, and some areas of experience are difficult to translate at all. Sometimes this is for intrinsic reasons, and sometimes because particular cultures don't use language in this area. (It is my impression that cultures differ in the extent to which information about facial appearance that can be used for recognition is verbally transmitted.) According to this scheme, the 'deep structure' of a publicly expressible thought is a node in the public network. It is translated into the deep structure of a sentence as a tree whose terminal nodes are the nodes to which words or set phrases are attached. This 'deep structure' then must be translated into a string in a spoken or written language.

The need to use language to express thought also applies when we have to ascribe thoughts to other beings, since we cannot put the entire network into a single sentence.

4. Intentions

We are tempted to say that a machine 'intends' to perform an action when it believes it will and also believes that it could do otherwise. However, we will resist this temptation and propose that a predicate *intends (actor, action, state)* be suitably axiomatized where one of the axioms says, that the machine intends the action if it believes it will perform the action and could do otherwise. Armstrong (1968) wants to require an element of servo-mechanism in order that a belief that an action will be performed be regarded as an intention, i.e. there should be a commitment to do it one way or another. There may be good reasons to allow several versions of intention to co-exist in the same formalism.

5. Free will

When we program a computer to make choices intelligently after determining its options, examining their consequences, and deciding which is most favourable or most moral or whatever, we must program it to take an attitude towards its freedom of choice essentially isomorphic to that which a human must take to his own. A program will have to take such an attitude towards another unless it knows the details of the other's construction and present state.

We can define whether a particular action was free or forced *relative to a theory* that ascribes beliefs and within which beings do what they believe will advance their goals. In such a theory, action is precipitated by a belief of the form 'I should do X now'. We will say that the action was free if changing the belief to 'I shouldn't do X now' would have resulted in the action not being performed. This requires that the theory of belief have sufficient Cartesian product structure so that changing a single belief is defined, but it doesn't require defining what the state of the world would be if a single belief were different.

It may be possible to separate the notion of a 'free action' into a technical part and a controversial part. The technical part would define freedom relative to an approximate co-ordinate system, giving the necessary Cartesian product structure.

Relative to the co-ordinatization, the freedom of a particular action would be a technical issue, but people could argue about whether to accept the whole co-ordinate system.

This isn't the whole free will story, because moralists are also concerned with whether praise or blame may be attributed to a choice. The following considerations would seem to apply to any attempt to define the morality of actions in a way that would apply to machines:

5.1. There is unlikely to be a simple behavioural definition. Instead there would be a second-order definition, criticizing predicates that ascribe morality to actions.

5.2. The theory must contain at least one axiom of morality that is not just a statement of physical fact. Relative to this axiom, moral judgments of actions can be factual.

5.3. The theory of morality will presuppose a theory of belief in which statements of the form 'It believed the action would harm someone' are defined. The theory must ascribe beliefs about others' welfare and perhaps about the being's own welfare.

5.4. It might be necessary to consider the machine as imbedded in some kind of society in order to ascribe morality to its actions.

5.5. No present machines admit such a belief structure, and no such structure may be required to make a machine with arbitrarily high intelligence in the sense of problem-solving ability.

5.6. It seems unlikely that morally judgeable machines or machines to which rights might legitimately be ascribed should be made if and when it becomes possible to do so.

6. Understanding

It seems to me that understanding the concept of 'understanding' is fundamental and difficult. The first difficulty lies in determining what the operand is. What is the 'theory of relativity' in 'Pat understands the theory of relativity'? What does 'misunderstand' mean? It seems that understanding should involve knowing a certain collection of facts including the general laws that permit deducing the answers to questions. We probably want to separate understanding from issues of cleverness and creativity.

7. Creativity

This may be easier than 'understanding', at least if we confine our attention to reasoning processes. Many problem solutions involve the introduction of entities not present in the statement of the problem. For example, proving that an 8 by 8 square board with two diagonally opposite squares removed cannot be covered by dominoes each covering two adjacent squares involves introducing the colours of the squares and the fact that a dominoe covers two squares of opposite colour. We want to regard this as a creative proof even though it might be quite easy for an experienced combinatorist.

OTHER VIEWS ABOUT MIND

The fundamental difference in point of view between this paper and most philosophy is that we are motivated by the problem of designing an artificial intelligence. Therefore, our attitude towards a concept like *belief* is determined by trying to decide what ways of acquiring and using beliefs will lead to intelligent behavior. Then we discover that much that one intelligence can find out about another can be expressed by ascribing beliefs to it.

A negative view of empiricism seems to be dictated by the apparent artificiality of designing an empiricist computer program to operate in the real world. Namely, we plan to provide our program with certain senses, but we have no way of being sure that the world in which we are putting the machine is constructable from the sense impressions it will have. Whether it will ever 'know' some fact about the world is contingent, so we are not inclined to build into it the notion that what it can't know about doesn't exist.

The philosophical views most sympathetic to our approach are some expressed by Carnap in some of the discursive sections of Carnap (1956).

Hilary Putnam (1961) argues that the classical mind-body problems are just as acute for machines as for men. Some of his arguments are more explicit than any given here, but in that paper, he doesn't try to solve the problems for machines.

D.M. Armstrong (1968) 'attempts to show that there are no valid philosophical or logical reasons for rejecting the identification of mind and brain'. He does this by proposing definitions of mental concepts in terms of the state of the brain. Fundamentally, I agree with him and think that such a program of definition can be carried out, but it seems to me that his methods for defining mental qualities as brain states are too weak even for defining properties of computer programs. While he goes beyond behavioural definitions as such, he relies on dispositional states.

This paper is partly an attempt to do what Ryle (1949) says can't be done and shouldn't be attempted, namely to define mental qualities in terms of states of a machine. The attempt is based on methods of which he would not approve; he implicitly requires first order definitions, and he implicitly requires that definitions be made in terms of the state of the world and not in terms of approximate theories.

His final view of the proper subject matter of epistemology is too narrow to help researchers in artificial intelligence. Namely, we need help in expressing those facts about the world that can be obtained in an ordinary situation by an ordinary person. The general facts about the world will enable our program to decide to call a travel agent to find out how to get to Boston.

Donald Davidson (1973) undertakes to show, 'There is no important sense in which psychology can be reduced to the physical sciences'. He proceeds by arguing that the mental qualities of a hypothetical, artificial man could not be defined physically even if we knew the details of its physical structure.

One sense of Davidson's statement does not require the arguments he gives. There are many universal computing elements, relays, neurons, gates and flip-flops, and physics tells us many ways of constructing them. Any information-processing system that can be constructed of one kind of element can be constructed of any other. Therefore, physics tells us nothing about what information processes exist in nature or can be constructed. Computer science is no more reducible to physics than is psychology.

However, Davidson also argues that the mental states of an organism are not describable in terms of its physical structure, and I take this to assert also that they are not describable in terms of its construction from logical elements. I would take his arguments as showing that mental qualities don't have what I have called first order, structural definitions. I don't think they apply to second order definitions.

D.C. Dennett (1971) expresses views very similar to mine about the reasons for ascribing mental qualities to machines. However, the present paper emphasizes criteria for ascribing particular mental qualities to particular machines rather than the general proposition that mental qualities may be ascribed. I think that the chess programs Dennett discusses have more limited mental structures than he seems to ascribe to them. Thus their 'beliefs' almost always concern particular positions, and they 'believe' almost no general propositions about chess, and this accounts for many of their weaknesses. Intuitively, this is well understood by researchers in computer game playing, and providing the program with a way of representing general facts about chess and even general facts about particular positions is a major unsolved problem. For example, no present program can represent the assertion 'Black has a backward pawn on his Q3 and white may be able to cramp black's position by putting pressure on it'. Such a representation would require rules that permit such a statement to be derived in appropriate positions and would guide the examination of possible moves in accordance with it.

One must also distinguish between believing the laws of logic and merely following them (see Dennett, p.95). The former requires a language that can express sentences about sentences and which contains some kind of reflexion principle. Many present, problem-solving programs can use *modus ponens* but cannot reason about their own ability to use new facts in a way that corresponds to believing *modus ponens*.

NOTES

1. McCarthy and Hayes (1969) defines an *epistemologically adequate* representation of information as one that can express the information actually available to a subject under given circumstances. Thus when we see a person, parts of him are

occluded, and we use our memory of previous looks at him and our general knowledge of humans to finish off a 'picture' of him that includes both two and three dimensional information. We must also consider *metaphysically adequate* representations that can represent complete facts, ignoring the subject's ability to acquire the facts in given circumstances. Thus Laplace thought that the positions and velocities of the particles in the universe gave a metaphysically adequate representation. Metaphysically adequate representations are needed for scientific and other theories, but artificial intelligence and a full philosophical treatment of common sense experience also require epistemologically adequate representations. This paper might be summarized as contending that mental concepts are needed for an epistemologically adequate representation of facts about machines, especially future intelligent machines.

2. Work in artificial intelligence is still far from showing how to reach human-level intellectual performance. Our approach to the AI problem involves identifying the intellectual mechanisms required for problem solving and describing them precisely. Therefore we are at the end of the philosophical spectrum that requires everything to be formalized in mathematical logic. It is sometimes said that one studies philosophy in order to advance beyond one's untutored naive world-view, but unfortunately for artificial intelligence, no-one has yet been able to give a description of even a naive world-view, complete and precise enough to allow a knowledge-seeking program to be constructed in accordance with its tenets.

3. Present AI programs operate in limited domains e.g. play particular games, prove theorems in a particular logical system, or understand natural language sentences covering a particular subject matter and with other semantic restrictions. General intelligence will require general models of situations changing in time, actors with goals and strategies for achieving them, and knowledge about how information can be obtained.

4. Our opinion is that human intellectual structure is substantially determined by the intellectual problems humans face. Thus a Martian or a machine will need similar structures to solve similar problems. Dennett (1971) expresses similar views. On the other hand, the human motivational structure seems to have many accidental features that might not be found in Martians and that we

would not be inclined to program into machines. This is not the place to present arguments for this viewpoint.

5. Behavioural definitions are often favoured in philosophy. A system is defined to have a certain quality if it behaves in a certain way or is *disposed* to behave in a certain way. Their virtue is conservatism; they don't postulate internal states that are unobservable to present science and may remain unobservable. However, such definitions are awkward for mental qualities, because, as common sense suggests, a mental quality may not result in behaviour, because another mental quality may prevent it; I may think you are thick-headed, but politeness may prevent my saying so. Particular difficulties can be overcome, but an impression of vagueness remains. The liking for behavioural definitions stems from caution, but I would interpret scientific experience as showing that boldness in postulating complex structures of unobserved entities, provided it is accompanied by a willingness to take back mistakes, is more likely to be rewarded by understanding of and control over nature than is positivistic timidity. It is particularly instructive to imagine a determined behaviourist trying to figure out an electronic computer. Trying to define each quality behaviourally would get him nowhere; only simultaneously postulating a complex structure including memory, arithmetic unit, control structure, and input-output would yield predictions that could be compared with experiment. There is a sense in which operational definitions are not taken seriously even by their proposers. Suppose someone gives an operational definition of length (e.g. involving a certain platinum bar), and a whole school of physicists and philosophers becomes quite attached to it. A few years later, someone else criticizes the definition as lacking some desirable property, proposes a change, and the change is accepted. This is normal, but if the original definition expressed what they really meant by the length, they would refuse to change, arguing that the new concept may have its uses, but it isn't what they mean by 'length'. This shows that the concept of 'length' as a property of objects is more stable than any operational definition. Carnap has an interesting section in *Meaning and Necessity* entitled 'The concept of intension for a robot' in which he makes a similar point saying,

> It is clear that the method of structural analysis, if applicable, is more powerful than the behaviouristic method, because it can

supply a general answer, and, under favourable circumstances, even a complete answer to the question of the intension of a given predicate.

The clincher for AI, however, is an 'argument from design'. In order to produce desired behaviour in a computer program, we build certain mental qualities into its structure. This doesn't lead to behavioural characterizations of the qualities, because the particular qualities are only one of many ways we might use to get the desired behaviour, and anyway the desired behaviour is not always realized.

6. Putnam (1970) also proposes second order definitions for psychological properties.

7. Whether a system has beliefs and other mental qualities is not primarily a matter of complexity of the system. Although cars are more complex than thermostats, it is hard to ascribe beliefs or goals to them, and the same is perhaps true of the basic hardware of a computer, the part of the computer that executes the program without the program itself.

8. Our own ability to derive the laws of higher levels of organization from knowledge of lower level laws is also limited by universality. While the presently accepted laws of physics allow only one chemistry, the laws of physics and chemistry allow many biologies, and, because the neuron is a universal computing element, an arbitrary mental structure is allowed by basic neurophysiology. Therefore, to determine human mental structure, one must make psychological experiments, or determine the actual anatomical structure of the brain and the information stored in it. One cannot determine the structure of the brain merely from the fact that the brain is capable of certain, problem-solving performances. In this respect our position is similar to that of the Life robot.

9. Philosophy and artificial intelligence. These fields overlap in the following way. In order to make a computer program behave intelligently its designer must build into it a view of the world in general, apart from what they include about particular sciences. (The skeptic who doubts whether there is anything to say about the world apart from the particular sciences should try to write a computer program that can figure out how to get to Timbuktoo, taking into account not only the facts about travel in general but also facts about what people and documents have what

information, and what information will be required at different stages of the trip and when and how it is to be obtained. He will rapidly discover that he is lacking a 'science of common sense'. He will be unable to formally express and build into his program 'what everybody knows'. Maybe philosophy could be defined as an attempted science of common sense, or else the science of common sense should be a definite part of philosophy).

Artificial intelligence has another component which philosophers have not studied, namely *heuristics*. Heuristics is concerned with: given the facts and a goal, how should it investigate the possibilities and decide what to do. On the other hand, artificial intelligence is not much concerned with aesthetics and ethics.

Not all approaches to philosophy lead to results relevant to the artificial intelligence problem. On the face of it, a philosophy that entailed the view that artificial intelligence was impossible would be unhelpful, but besides that, taking artificial intelligence seriously suggests some philosophical points of view. I am not sure that all I shall list are required for pursuing the AI goal – some of them may be just my prejudices – but here they are:

9.1. The relation between a world view and the world should be studied by methods akin to metamathematics, in which systems are studied from the outside. In metamathematics we study the relation between a mathematical system and its models. Philosophy (or perhaps 'metaphilosophy') should study the relation between world structures and systems within them, that seek knowledge. Just as the metamathematician can use any mathematical methods in this study and distinguishes the methods he uses from those being studied, so the philosopher should use all his scientific knowledge in studying philosphical systems from the outside.

Thus the question 'How do I know?' is best answered by studying 'How does it know', getting the best answer that the current state of science and philosophy permits, and then seeing how this answer stands up to doubts about one's own sources of knowledge.

9.2. We regard metaphysics as the study of the general structure of the world and epistemology as studying what knowledge of the world can be had by an intelligence with given opportunities to observe and experiment. We need to distinguish what can be determined about the structure of humans and machines by scientific research, over a period of time, and experimenting with many individuals, from what can be learned in a particular situation with particular opportunities to observe. From the AI point of view, the latter is as important as the former, and we suppose that philosophers would also consider it part of epistemology. The possibilities of reductionism are also different for theoretical and everyday epistemology. We could imagine that the rules of everyday epistemology could be deduced from a knowledge of physics and the structure of the being and the world, but we can't see how one could avoid using mental concepts in expressing knowledge actually obtained by the senses.

9.3 It is now accepted that the basic concepts of physical theories are far removed from observation. The human sense organs are many levels of organization removed from quantum mechanical states, and we have learned to accept the complication this causes in verifying physical theories. Experience in trying to make intelligent computer programs suggests that the basic concepts of the common-sense world are also complex and not always directly accessible to observation. In particular the common-sense world is not a construct from sense data, but sense data play an important role. When a man or a computer program sees a dog, we will need both the relation between the observer and the dog and the relation between the observer and the brown patch in order to construct a good theory of the event.

9.4 In spirit this paper is materialist, but it is logically compatible with some other philosophies. Thus cellular automaton models of the physical world may be supplemented by supposing that certain complex configurations interact with additional automata called souls that also interact with each other. Such 'interactionist dualism' won't meet emotional or spiritual objections to materialism, but it does provide a logical niche for any empirically argued belief in telepathy, communication with the dead and other psychic phenomena. A person who believed the alleged evidence for such phenomena and still wanted a scientific explanation could model his beliefs with auxiliary automata.

REFERENCES

Armstrong, D.M. *A Materialist Theory of the Mind*. London and New York, (Routledge and Kegan Paul, 1968).

Carnap, Rudolf. *Meaning and Necessity*, (University of Chicago Press, 1956).

Davidson, Donald. 'The material mind'. *Logic, Methodology and Philosophy of Science IV*, P. Suppes, L. Henkin, C. Moisil, and A. Joja (eds). Amsterdam, (North-Holland, 1973).

Dennett, D.C. 'Intentional systems'. *Journal of Philosophy 68, 4* (1971).

Gosper, R.W. (1976) 'Private communication'. (Much information about Life has been printed in Martin Gardner's column in *Scientific American*, and there is a magazine called *Lifeline*).

Lewis, David. *Counterfactuals*, (Harvard University Press, 1973).

McCarthy, John. 'Programs with common sense'. *Mechanisation of Thought Processes, Volume I*. London (HMSO, 1959).

McCarthy, J. and Hayes, P.J. 'Some philosophical problems from the standpoint of artificial intelligence'. *Machine Intelligence 4*, (Edinburgh University Press, 1969) 463-502.

McCarthy, John. *First Order Theories of Individual Concepts*, Stanford Artificial Intelligence Laboratory (Forthcoming, 1977 (a)).

McCarthy, John. *Circumscription – A Way of Jumping to Conclusions*, Stanford Artificial Intelligence Laboratory (Forthcoming, 1977 (b)).

Montague, Richard. 'Syntactical treatments of modality, with corollaries on reflexion principles and finite axiomatizability, *Acta Philosophica Fennica 16* (1963) 153-167.

Moore, E.F. 'Gedanken experiments with sequential machines'. *Automata Studies*. (Princeton University Press, 1956).

Putnam, Hilary. 'Minds and machines'. In *Dimensions of Mind*, Sidney Hook (ed) New York, (Collier Books, 1962)

Putnam, Hilary. 'On Properties'. In *Essays in Honor of Carl G. Hempel*, Dordrecht, Holland (D. Reidel, 1970).

Ryle, Gilbert. *The Concepts of Mind*, London (Hutchinson and Company, 1949).

CHAPTER 9
NATURAL LANGUAGE, PHILOSOPHY, AND ARTIFICIAL INTELLIGENCE
Roger C. Schank

INTRODUCTION

Artificial intelligence is a field that is not exactly sure what it is about. Nilsson (1974) describes AI as a field whose successes cease to be AI when they are achieved. It is easy to think of problems that were considered to be part of AI ten years ago that are not now, and of parts of AI now that were part of some other field ten years ago. For example, pattern recognition and theorem proving dominated the First International Joint Conference on Artificial Intelligence in 1969, now natural language and knowledge representation seem to prevail.

It is even more of a problem because people in other fields cannot agree on either the relevance or the place of AI with respect to their own fields. Is AI psychology? Is it philosophy? Many computer scientists not in AI feel sure it isn't computer science. Is the work in natural language processing linguistics? Linguists feel certain that it isn't even in any way relevant. (See Dresher and Hornstein (1977).)

To make matters worse, AI people have to put up with people who state that we are trying to do things which are, in principle, impossible. Consider the following passages. The first is from the late philosopher, Yehoshua Bar-Hillel (1960):

> 'Little John was looking for his toy box. Finally he found it. *The box was in the pen.* John was very happy.'

> Assume, for simplicity's sake, that pen in English has only the following two meanings: (1) a certain writing utensil, (2) an enclosure where small children can play. I now claim that no existing or imaginable program will enable an electronic computer to determine that the word pen in the given sentence within the

given context has the second of the above meanings, whereas every reader with a sufficient knowledge of English will do this quite automatically.

The second passage is from the newsletter SIGART (June, 1974):

> Dreyfus accepted McCarthy's challenge at the end to define the 'simplest' problem requiring intelligence that he felt could not be done in principle on a digital computer. He posed the *summarization problem* (originally suggested by Professor Zadeh) as being in this category, even if he wasn't sure this was the 'simplest' such problem. It goes as follows:

> Read and summarize in a few sentences a lengthy story (such as might be found in a newspaper or magazine) so that practically anyone would agree that your summary did abstract the important features of the story.

In this paper I shall attempt to at least put straight what we can do and are doing in natural language processing. I shall concentrate on the work being done in my own laboratory at Yale, but there is of course other relevant work (Cf. Norman and Rumelhart (1975), Bobrow and Winograd (1977), Rieger (1977), Wilks (1975), and Charniak (1977)). I shall talk about what we can do first, and then I shall present some general comments on what AI is about.

THE PROGRAMS

Sam

SAM (Script Applier Mechanism) is a program running at Yale that was designed to understand stories that rely heavily on scripts. A script is a data structure that describes in detail the events that make up a standard situation. Thus all the events that make up a restaurant, together with options for what to do when something goes wrong and choice points that depend on the kind of restaurant you are in, make up the restaurant script. Because scripts describe mundane situations the stories processed by SAM tend to be fairly commonplace stories, for which a rich knowledge base is available. Story 1 below, relies on multiple knowledge bases, called scripts, as well as having a complication arise in one script as a result of an odd occurrence in a previous one. Story 2 is an actual newspaper story that SAM has processed.

SAM understands these stories and others like them. By 'understand' we mean SAM can create a linked causal chain of conceptualizations that represent what took place in each story. SAM parses the story into input conceptualizations using Riesbeck's analyser (Riesbeck, 1975). These are then fed to a program that looks for script applicability (Cullingford, 1976). When a script seems to be applicable, it is used by the script applier to make inferences about events that must have occurred between events specifically mentioned.

The final, internal representation is a language-free network of concepts and their interrelations. SAM generates paraphrases that are longer than the original. This is possible since inferences made by the script applier are retained. We also generate 1) paraphrases that are shorter and closer to the original and 2) summaries that rely on measures of the relative importance of events within a script.

In addition, we have developed a program that can query the obtained representation so as to answer questions about the input story (see Lehnert, 1977).

Since the representation language that we use (conceptual dependency, see Schank (1975)) is intended to be interlingual, generation in English is no harder for us than in any other language. Thus, we have also written generation programs that translate the stories we understand into Chinese, Russian, Dutch and Spanish. The translation programs work by taking the output from the script applier and encoding it according to the rules of the target language.

Thus, we come to the point where the two passages quoted above are relevant. Bar-Hillel's statement regarding the impossibility of mechanical translation was based on his assessment of the problem of encoding knowledge into a computer program. The argument does not, in fact, reveal a basic impossibility but merely a pragmatic difficulty. To the degree to which scripts are available, understanding, and therefore translation, is possible. It should be clear that translation from one natural language to another is no harder than computer understanding of language in general. Both tasks depend on the ability of a machine to analyse semantic content. Scripts provide a partial solution to the knowledge encoding problem. To the extent that scripts apply in a given understanding task, understanding and translation are possible.

These programs would seem also to be relevant to the statement made by Dreyfus. SAM *does* process stories directly from newspapers. At the conference at which this paper was presented, however, Dreyfus demonstrated that he could move faster than our programs by stating that he had been misquoted and that what we could never do was handle stories that were not script-based. In his own paper (of this volume) Dreyfus demonstrates his continued skepticism over the recent accomplishment in AI. Later on in this paper, however, we shall present the results of a program which handles non-script-based story input. It is hard to believe that this will satisfy Dreyfus either but neither is it clear that that matters.

STORY 1

INPUT:

John went to New York by bus. On the bus he talked to an old lady. When he left the bus, he thanked the driver. He took the subway to Leone's. On the subway his pocket was picked. He got off the train and entered Leone's. He had some lasagna. When the check came, he discovered he couldn't pay. The management told him he would have to wash dishes. When he left, he caught a bus to New Haven.

OUTPUT:

Long paraphrase: JOHN WENT TO A BUS STOP. HE WAITED AT IT A FEW MINUTES. HE ENTERED A BUS. THE DRIVER GOT THE TICKET FROM JOHN. HE WENT TO A SEAT. HE SAT DOWN IN IT. WHILE JOHN WAS ON THE BUS AN OLD LADY AND JOHN TALKED. THE DRIVER TOOK JOHN TO NEW YORK. HE WENT TO THE DRIVER. WHEN GETTING OFF

THE BUS JOHN THANKED THE DRIVER. JOHN GOT OFF IT.

HE ENTERED A STATION. HE PUT A TOKEN INTO THE TURNSTILE. HE WENT TO THE PLATFORM. HE WAITED AT IT A FEW MINUTES. HE ENTERED A SUBWAY CAR. A THIEF WENT TO JOHN. THE THIEF PICKED JOHN'S POCKET. HE WENT. JOHN WENT TO THE SEAT. HE SAT DOWN IN IT. THE DRIVER TOOK JOHN TO LEONE'S. HE LEFT THE SUBWAY CAR. HE LEFT THE STATION.

HE ENTERED LEONE'S. HE LOOKED AROUND INSIDE IT. HE SAW HE COULD GO TO A TABLE. HE WENT TO IT. HE SAT DOWN IN THE SEAT. HE ORDERED SOME LASAGNA. THE WAITER INDICATED TO THE CHEF JOHN WOULD LIKE HIM TO PREPARE SOMETHING. THE CHEF PREPARED THE LASAGNA. THE WAITER GOT IT FROM THE CHEF. THE WAITER WENT TO THE TABLE. HE SERVED THE LASAGNA TO JOHN. HE ATE IT. HE BECAME FULL.

HE ASKED THE WAITER FOR THE CHECK. JOHN GOT IT FROM THE WAITER. JOHN READ THE CHECK. JOHN DISCOVERED HE WAS UNABLE TO PAY THE CHECK. HE INDICATED TO THE WAITER HE WAS UNABLE TO PAY THE CHECK. THE MANAGEMENT TOLD JOHN HE WOULD HAVE HAD TO WASH DISHES. HE ENTERED THE KITCHEN. HE WASHED DISHES. HE LEFT LEONE'S.

HE WENT TO THE BUS STOP. HE WAITED AT IT A FEW MINUTES. HE ENTERED THE BUS. THE DRIVER GOT THE TICKET FROM JOHN. HE WENT TO THE SEAT. HE SAT DOWN IN IT. THE DRIVER TOOK JOHN TO NEW HAVEN. HE GOT OFF THE BUS.

(Paragraphing has been added to the computer output for ease of reading.)

Short paraphrase: JOHN TOOK A BUS TO NEW YORK. HE TOOK THE SUBWAY TO LEONE'S. ON THE SUBWAY A THIEF PICKED JOHN'S POCKET. JOHN

ENTERED LEONE'S. HE ORDERED SOME LASAGNA. HE ATE IT. HE DISCOVERED HE WAS UNABLE TO PAY THE CHECK. THE MANAGEMENT TOLD JOHN HE WOULD HAVE TO WASH DISHES.

Below are questions asked to SAM (in English), which have been answered by SAM:

Q1: Why did John go to New York?
A1: BECAUSE JOHN WANTED TO GO TO LEONE'S.

Q2: How did John get to Leone's?
A2: JOHN TOOK A BUS TO NEW YORK AND THEN HE TOOK THE SUBWAY TO LEONE'S.

Q3: Did anything unusual happen on the bus?
A3: I DON'T REMEMBER ANYTHING.

Q4: Did anything unusual happen on the subway?
A4: A THIEF PICKED JOHN'S POCKET.

Q5: What did John order?
A5: JOHN ORDERED LASAGNA.

Q6: Did anything unusual happen at the restaurant?
A6: JOHN DISCOVERED THAT HE COULDN'T PAY THE CHECK AND SO HE HAD TO WASH DISHES.

Q7: Why couldn't John pay the check?
A7: BECAUSE JOHN DID NOT HAVE ANY MONEY.

Q8: Why didn't John have any money?
A8: BECAUSE A THIEF PICKED JOHN'S POCKET.

Q9: How did John get back to New Haven?
A9: JOHN WENT FROM LEONE'S BY SUBWAY AND THEN HE WENT TO NEW HAVEN BY BUS.

Q10: How was John able to take the bus to New Haven?
A10: PROBABLY JOHN HAD A TICKET.

Below is the Chinese translation of Story 1 produced by SAM:

John tzuoh charng twu chih che daw Neou Iue chiuh le. Ta tzay charng twu chi che lii. Ta gen i wey lao tay tay tarn i tarn. Ta tsorng charng twu chih che lii chiuh chuh le. Ta shieh shieh sy ji. Ta tzuoh dih shiah huoo che daw Leone's chiuh le. Ta tzay dih shiah tiee luh che lii. I ge par shoou tou le chyan. Ta tsorng dih shiah tiee luh che chuh chiuh le. Ta jinn le Leone's. Ta chr le i da li tsay. Ta tsorng char farng nadaw i ge janq dhan. Ta fa shyann ta bu kee yii fu chyan. Char farng jiaw to bih shiu yaw shii bei tz. Ta tsorng fang guar lii chu chiuh le. Ta tzuoh charng tu chi che daw Sin Gang chiuh le.

Story 2 was obtained from the New Haven Register.

STORY 2:

A New Jersey man was killed on Friday evening when the car in which he was riding swerved off Route 69 and struck a tree. David Hall, 27, was pronounced dead at the scene by Dr. Dana Blanchard, medical examiner. Frank Miller, 16, of 593 Foxon Road, operator of the vehicle, was taken by Flanagan Ambulance to Yale-New haven Hospital. He was treated and released. The Branford Fire Department extricated the passenger from the vehicle. No charges were made. Patrolman Robert Onofrio is continuing the investigation.

QUESTION-ANSWERING OUTPUT:

Q1: Was anyone killed?
A1: YES, DAVID HALL DIED.

Q2: Was anyone hurt?
A2: YES, FRANK MILLER WAS SLIGHTLY INJURED.

Q3: Why was Frank Miller hurt?
A3: BECAUSE THE AUTOMOBILE HIT A TREE.

Q4: Did Frank Miller go to the hospital?
A4: YES, HE WAS IN YALE-NEW HAVEN.

Q5: How did Frank Miller get to the hospital?
A5: AN AMBULANCE TOOK HIM TO YALE-NEW HAVEN.

Summary:

AN AUTOMOBILE HIT A TREE NEAR HIGHWAY 69 FOUR DAYS AGO. DAVID HALL, AGE 27, RESIDENCE IN NEW JERSEY, THE PASSENGER, DIED. FRANK MILLER, AGE 16 RESIDENCE AT 593 FOXON ROAD IN NEW HAVEN, CONNECTICUT, THE DRIVER, WAS SLIGHTLY INJURED. THE POLICE DEPARTMENT DID NOT FILE CHARGES.

Frump

Another newspaper-story-reading program operating at Yale is FRUMP (Fast Reading and Understanding Memory Program). FRUMP is a program that is intended to skim a newspaper quickly while looking for things it is interested in. FRUMP uses simpler, less detailed scripts than SAM. Furthermore, its parsing is done directly from the scripts. After a story has been identified to be relevant to a domain of interest, the particular items that are interesting to FRUMP in that domain are predicted. Special purpose expectations are set up to look for the concepts around which FRUMP's expectations are organized. Sentences are never completely parsed. When a relevant concept is found, rules of English are used to find the information that FRUMP wants to know.

FRUMP is a very fast program compared to SAM. While SAM often takes a few minutes of CPU time to read a long story, FRUMP rarely takes more than a few seconds to read the same story. SAM is set up to understand a domain fully enough so that it can detect problems or unusual circumstances and understand the kinds of complications that can arise in a story, as it did in Story 1. However, for very static newspaper stories describing ordinary events, we have come to believe that the full power of SAM is a hindrance at times. FRUMP can do no more than skim a newspaper story about which it has knowledge, but it is very fast at what it does.

FRUMP also has an update mode in which it can read stories that are follow-ups to stories it has already read. In update mode FRUMP only notices: (a) pieces of information connected with things it was interested in at the first reading that were left undetermined; and (b) standard follow up information. FRUMP is described in DeJong (1977).

STORY 3.

INPUT

A passenger train carrying tourists, including some Americans, collided with a freight train in the rugged Sierra Madre of Northern Mexico, killing at least seventeen persons and injuring 45, the police reported today.

They said that at least five of the injured were Americans, and there were unofficial reports that one of the dead was from New York City.

Some of the passengers were travel agents, most from Mexico City, making the trip as part of a tourism promotion, the police said.

The American Society of Travel Agents had been meeting in Guadalajara, though it was not known whether any of the group were aboard the train.

One observation car on the railroad to the Pacific tumbled into a 45 foot canyon when the passenger train smashed into the freight yesterday afternoon near the village of Pittorreal about 20 miles west of Chihuahua City and 200 miles south of the United States border, the police said.

They said that rescue workers were still trying to pry apart the car's wreckage to reach passengers trapped inside. The rescue squads could not use cutting torches on the wreckage because spilled diesel fuel might ignite, the police reported.

RUSSIAN SUMMARY:

V ZHELEZNODOROZHNOI KATASTROFE V MEKSIKE 17 CHELOVEK BYLO UBITO I 45 RANENO.

SPANISH SUMMARY:

HUBO 17 MUERTOS Y 45 HERIDOS CUANDO UN

FERROCARRIL CHOCO CONTRA UN FERROCARRIL
EN MEXICO.

ENGLISH SUMMARY:

17 PEOPLE WERE KILLED AND 45 WERE INJURED
WHEN A TRAIN CRASHED INTO A TRAIN IN MEX-
ICO.

STORY 4

INPUT:

A severe earthquake struck Northeastern Italy last night,
collapsing entire sections of towns northeast of Venice near the
Yugoslav border killing at least 95 persons and injuring at least
1000, the Italian interior ministry reported.

In the city of Udine alone, a government spokesman said they
feared at least 200 dead under the debris. The city, on the main
railroad between Rome and Vienna, has a population of about
90,000.

The spokesman for the Caribinieri, the paramilitary national,
police force, said there had been reports of severe damage from
half a dozen towns in the foothills of the Alps, with whole
families buried in building collapses. Communications with a
number of points in the area were still out.

The earthquake was recorded at 6.3 on the Richter scale,
which measures ground motion. In populated areas, a quake
registering 4 on that scale can cause moderate damage, a reading
of 6 can be severe and a reading of 7 indicates a major
earthquake.

RUSSIAN SUMMARY:

ZEMLETRYASENIE SREDNEI SILY PROIZOSHLO V
ITALII. CILA ZEMLETRYASENIYA OPREDELENA V
6.3 BALLA PO SHKALE RIKHTERA. PRI ZEM-
LETRYASENII 95 CHELOVEK BYLO UBITO I 1000
RANENO.

SPANISH SUMMARY:

HUBO 95 MUERTOS Y 1000 HERIDOS EN UN TER-REMOTO FUERTE EN ITALIA. EL TERREMOTO MIDIO 6.3 EN LA ESCALA RICHTER.

ENGLISH SUMMARY:

95 PEOPLE WERE KILLED AND 1000 INJURED IN A SEVERE EARTHQUAKE THAT STRUCK ITALY. THE QUAKE REGISTERED 6.3 ON THE RICHTER SCALE.

Pam

Not all stories are based on scripts. Thus, some more general and more powerful mechanisms are sometimes necessary in order to understand a story.

PAM (Plan Applier Mechanism) is a program running at Yale that is intended to understand more general, plan-based stories. (PAM is described in Schank and Abelson (1977) and in Wilensky (1976)). Stories (5) and (6) below were processed by PAM.

A plan-based story is one in which the central characters must develop fairly novel plans to deal with problems and interferences that have occurred with respect to goals that they are interested in attaining. Truly interesting stories are plan-based rather than script-based.

Over the past two years we have been developing a theory of how people understand such complex stories (see Schank and Abelson (1977)). PAM was an early test of some of those theories. PAM uses knowledge about goals, themes, and planboxes, to figure out the intentions of all the characters it hears about. The program's job is to keep track of the goals of each of the characters in a story and to interpret their actions as means of achieving those goals. Below is Story 5, followed by the output PAM produces after processing it.

> John loved Mary but she didn't want to marry him. One day, a
> dragon stole Mary from the castle. John got on top of his horse

and killed the dragon. Mary agreed to marry him. They lived happily ever after.

OUTPUT:

Paraphrase:

JOHN WAS IN LOVE WITH MARY. SHE DID NOT WANT TO MARRY HIM. A DRAGON TOOK HER FROM A CASTLE. HE LEARNED THAT THAT DRAGON HAD TAKEN HER FROM THE CASTLE. HE MOUNTED A HORSE. IT TOOK HIM TO HER. HE KILLED THE DRAGON. SHE WAS INDEBTED TO HIM. SHE TOLD HIM SHE WAS GOING TO MARRY HIM. HE MARRIED HER. HE AND SHE WERE HAPPY THEREAFTER.

Questions:

Q1: Why did John get on his horse?
A1: BECAUSE HE WANTED TO BE NEAR MARY.

Q2: Why did Mary agree to marry John?
A2: BECAUSE SHE WAS INDEBTED TO HIM.

Q3: Why did John kill the dragon?
A3: BECAUSE HE WANTED MARY NOT TO DIE.

Below is Story 6 and the output PAM creates for it:

INPUT:

John disliked his job as the bank janitor. One day, a thief tried to rob the bank. John jumped on the thief and knocked him out. The bank president made John the bank guard. John enjoyed his new job.

OUTPUT:

Paraphrase:

JOHN DISLIKED BEING A BANK JANITOR. A THIEF TRIED TO ROB THE BANK. JOHN LEARNED THE

THIEF HAD ROBBED IT. JOHN WANTED THE THIEF TO NOT HAVE THE BANK'S MONEY. JOHN KNOCKED THE THIEF OUT. THE BANK WAS INDEBTED TO JOHN. THE PRESIDENT MADE JOHN A BANK GUARD. HE LIKED BEING IT.

Questions:

Q1: Why did John knock the thief out?
A1: BECAUSE HE WANTED THE THIEF NOT TO HAVE THE BANK'S MONEY.

Q2: Why did the bank president make John the bank guard?
A2: BECAUSE THE BANK WAS INDEBTED TO JOHN.

In order to understand these stories, PAM, like SAM, must make implicit inferences to connect up the sentences of the story it is processing. The following are some of the inferences PAM makes for Story 5:

John wanted to marry Mary.
Mary was endangered by the dragon.
John learned that the dragon had kidnapped Mary.
John wanted to save Mary from the dragon.
John rode his horse to where Mary was.
Mary became grateful to John for rescuing her.
John and Mary got married.

Many of these inferences are dependent on knowledge about how goals can be achieved. For example, to understand why John killed the dragon, we must know that killing a captor is a way to free a captive. In addition, we must know that in order to rescue Mary, John must first be near her, that riding a horse is a way of changing one's location, and that to ride a horse, it is necessary to mount it. Without this knowledge, we could not understand why John got on his horse.

Talespin

Another task that indicates what computers can do when knowledge is made available to them is the creation of stories.

TALESPIN is a program written by Jim Meehan and described in Meehan (1976), which makes up stories by simulating a world, assigning goals to some characters and saying what happens when these goals interact with events in the simulated world. The reader/user supplies much of the information about the initial state of the world, such as the choice of characters and the relationships between one character and another.

Below are two stories written by TALESPIN. Story 7 is in an interactive mode where the user makes decisions. Story 8 is told with no user interaction. Upper case output is from the program, either as part of the story ('JOHN BEAR ATE THE HONEY'), or as part of the question/answer dialogue ('HOW HUNGRY IS IRVING BIRD'). Our answers to these questions are typed when an asterisk (*) appears.

STORY 7:

WELCOME TO TALESPIN
CHOOSE ANY OF THE FOLLOWING CHARACTERS
FOR THE STORY:
(BEAR BEE BOY GIRL FOX CROW ANT HEN LION
DOG WOLF MOUSE CAT GOAT CANARY)

*(BEAR BEE BOY CANARY)
IRVING BEE IS AT THE BEEHIVE
SOME HONEY IS AT THE BEEHIVE.
IRVING BEE HAS THE HONEY.
SAM ADAMS IS AT A HOUSE.
WILMA CANARY IS AT A NEST.

CHOOSE ANY OF THE FOLLOWING PROPS:
(BREADCRUMBS CHEESE BASEBALL)

*NIL

CHOOSE ANY OF THE FOLLOWING MISCEL-
LANEOUS ITEMS:
(BERRIES FLOWER RIVER WORM)
*(BERRIES WORM)

SOME BLUEBERRIES ARE AT A BUSH.
A WORM IS AT A PATCH OF GROUND.

WHO KNOWS ABOUT THE BLUEBERRIES?
1: WILMA CANARY 2: SAM ADAMS 3: IRVING BEE 4:
JOHN BEAR
*4

JOHN BEAR THINKS THAT THE BLUEBERRIES ARE
AT THE BUSH.

HOW HUNGRY IS JOHN BEAR?
1: VERY 2: SOMEWHAT 3: NOT VERY 4: NOT AT ALL
*4

JOHN BEAR IS NOT VERY HUNGRY.

WHO KNOWS ABOUT THE WORM?
1: WILMA CANARY 2: SAM ADAMS 3: IRVING BEAR 4:
JOHN BEAR
*2

SAM ADAMS THINKS THAT THE WORM IS AT THE
PATCH OF GROUND.

THIS IS A STORY ABOUT . . .
1: WILMA CANARY 2: SAM ADAMS 3:IRVING BEE 4:
JOHN BEAR
*2

HIS PROBLEM IS THAT HE IS . . .
1: HUNGRY 2: THIRSTY 3: HORNY 4: TIRED
*1

SAM ADAMS IS SOMEWHAT HUNGRY.
SAM ADAMS WANTS TO GET SOME BERRIES.
SAM ADAMS WANTS TO FIND OUT WHERE SOME
BERRIES ARE.

DOES SAM ADAMS LIKE WILMA CANARY?
1: A LOT 2: A LITTLE 3: NOT MUCH 4: NOT AT ALL
*2

SAM ADAMS WANTS WILMA CANARY TO TELL SAM ADAMS WHERE SOME BERRIES ARE.

DOES SAM ADAMS FEEL DECEPTIVE TOWARDS WILMA CANARY?

1: A LOT 2: A LITTLE 3: NOT MUCH 4: NOT AT ALL
*4

DOES SAM ADAMS FEEL COMPETITIVE TOWARDS WILMA CANARY?

1: A LOT 2: A LITTLE 3: NOT MUCH 4: NOT AT ALL
*2

SAM ADAMS DECIDES THAT WILMA CANARY MIGHT WANT SAM ADAMS TO GIVE WILMA CANARY A WORM. SAM ADAMS WANTS TO ASK WILMA CANARY WHETHER WILMA CANARY WILL TELL SAM ADAMS WHERE SOME BERRIES ARE IF SAM ADAMS GIVES WILMA CANARY A WORM. SAM ADAMS WANTS TO GET NEAR WILMA CANARY. SAM ADAMS WALKS FROM THE HOUSE TO THE GROUND BY THE REDWOOD TREE BY GOING THROUGH A VALLEY THROUGH A MEADOW. SAM ADAMS IS AT THE GROUND BY THE REDWOOD TREE. WILMA CANARY THINKS THAT SAM ADAMS IS AT THE GROUND BY THE REDWOOD TREE. SAM ADAMS ASKS WILMA CANARY WHETHER WILMA CANARY WILL TELL SAM ADAMS WHERE SOME BERRIES ARE IF SAM ADAMS GIVES WILMA CANARY A WORM.

DOES WILMA CANARY FEEL DECEPTIVE TOWARDS SAM ADAMS?
1: A LOT 2: A LITTLE 3: NOT MUCH 4: NOT AT ALL
*1

WILMA CANARY TELLS SAM ADAMS THAT WILMA CANARY WILL TELL SAM ADAMS WHERE SOME

BERRIES ARE. SAM ADAMS THINKS THAT WILMA CANARY WILL TELL SAM ADAMS WHERE SOME BERRIES ARE. SAM ADAMS WANTS TO GET A WORM. SAM ADAMS WANTS TO GET NEAR THE WORM.

IN CREATING A VALLEY, WE CAN MAKE UP A NEW ONE OR USE AN OLD ONE. DO YOU WANT TO USE ANY OF THESE?

1: *VALLEY* 0   2: *VALLEY* 1
DECIDE: *YES
PLEASE TYPE AN INTEGER BETWEEN 1 AND 2
*2

SAM ADAMS WALKS FROM THE GROUND BY THE REDWOOD TREE TO THE PATCH OF GROUND BY GOING THROUGH THE MEADOW THOUGH WILMA CANARY THINKS THAT SAM ADAMS ISN'T AT THE GROUND BY THE REDWOOD TREE. SAM ADAMS TAKES THE WORM. SAM ADAMS WANTS TO GET NEAR WILMA CANARY. SAM ADAMS WALKS FROM THE PATCH OF GROUND TO THE GROUND BY THE REDWOOD TREE BY GOING THROUGH THE MEADOW THROUGH THE VALLEY THROUGH THE MEADOW. WILMA CANARY THINKS THAT SAM ADAMS IS AT THE GROUND BY THE REDWOOD TREE. SAM ADAMS GIVES WILMA CANARY THE WORM. WILMA CANARY THINKS THAT SAM ADAMS GAVE WILMA CANARY THE WORM. WILMA CANARY THINKS THAT WILMA CANARY HAS THE WORM.

HOW HUNGRY IS WILMA CANARY?
1: VERY 2: SOMEWHAT 3: NOT VERY 4: NOT AT ALL
*1

WILMA CANARY EATS THE WORM. THE WORM IS GONE. WILMA CANARY IS NOT VERY HUNGRY. WILMA CANARY TELLS SAM ADAMS THAT SAM

ADAMS IS NOT AT ALL SMART. SAM ADAMS LIKES WILMA CANARY NOT AT ALL. SAM ADAMS TRUSTS WILMA CANARY NOT AT ALL. SAM ADAMS DECIDES THAT WILMA CANARY MIGHT WANT SAM ADAMS TO GIVE WILMA CANARY SOME CHEESE. SAM ADAMS ASKS WILMA CANARY WHETHER WILMA CANARY WILL TELL SAM ADAMS WHERE SOME BERRIES ARE IF SAM ADAMS GIVES WILMA CANARY SOME CHEESE. WILMA CANARY TELLS SAM ADAMS THAT WILMA CANARY WILL TELL SAM ADAMS WHERE SOME BERRIES ARE. SAM ADAMS WANTS TO GET SOME CHEESE. SAM ADAMS WANTS TO FIND OUT WHERE SOME CHEESE IS.

DOES SAM ADAMS LIKE IRVING BEE?
1: A LOT 2: A LITTLE 3: NOT MUCH 4: NOT AT ALL
*4

DOES SAM ADAMS LIKE JOHN BEAR?
1: A LOT 2: A LITTLE 3: NOT MUCH 4: NOT AT ALL
*4

SAM ADAMS DIDN'T FIND OUT WHERE SOME CHEESE IS.
SAM ADAMS DOESN'T GET SOME CHEESE

DOES SAM ADAMS DOMINATE WILMA CANARY?
1: A LOT 2: A LITTLE 3: NOT MUCH 4: NOT AT ALL
*3

SAM ADAMS STRIKES WILMA CANARY. WILMA CANARY IS NOT AT ALL HEALTHY. WILMA CANARY WON'T TELL SAM ADAMS WHERE SOME BERRIES ARE. SAM ADAMS DIDN'T FIND OUT WHERE SOME BERRIES ARE. SAM ADAMS DOESN'T GET SOME BERRIES. THE END.

Below is Story 8. It was generated by TALESPIN in a non-interactive mode. That is, TALESPIN itself made all the decisions.

STORY 8

ONCE UPON A TIME GEORGE ANT LIVED NEAR A PATCH OF GROUND. THERE WAS A NEST IN AN ASH TREE. WILMA BIRD LIVED IN THE NEST. THERE WAS SOME WATER IN A RIVER. WILMA KNEW THAT THE WATER WAS IN THE RIVER. GEORGE KNEW THAT THE WATER WAS IN THE RIVER. ONE DAY WILMA WAS VERY THIRSTY. WILMA WANTED TO GET NEAR SOME WATER. WILMA FLEW FROM HER NEST ACROSS A MEADOW THROUGH A VALLEY TO THE RIVER. WILMA DRANK THE WATER. WILMA WAS NOT THIRSTY.

GEORGE WAS VERY THIRSTY. GEORGE WANTED TO GET NEAR SOME WATER. GEORGE WALKED FROM HIS PATCH OF GROUND ACROSS THE MEADOW THROUGH THE VALLEY TO A RIVER BANK. GEORGE FELL INTO THE WATER. GEORGE WANTED TO GET NEAR THE VALLEY. GEORGE COULDN'T GET NEAR THE VALLEY. GEORGE WANTED TO GET NEAR THE MEADOW. GEORGE COULDN'T GET NEAR THE MEADOW. WILMA WANTED GEORGE TO GET NEAR THE MEADOW. WILMA WANTED TO GET NEAR GEORGE. WILMA GRABBED GEORGE WITH HER CLAW. WILMA TOOK GEORGE FROM THE RIVER THROUGH THE VALLEY TO THE MEADOW. GEORGE WAS DEVOTED TO WILMA. GEORGE OWED EVERYTHING TO WILMA. WILMA LET GO OF GEORGE. GEORGE FELL TO THE MEADOW. THE END.

Below are four stories that were generated by TALESPIN which were mistakes. We present them here for two reasons. First, they illustrate the kind of problems that TALESPIN solves in telling its stories. But, more significantly, they indicate why researchers in artificial intelligence use computers. It is very difficult to fully understand and thus to fully specify the complex processes that are part of human intelligence. When we begin to build a model of an intelligent process we start to discover why what we first hypothesized was incomplete or inaccurate. We can then revise our model on the basis of our failures.

STORY 9

HENRY ANT WAS THIRSTY. HE WALKED OVER TO THE RIVER BANK WHERE HIS GOOD FRIEND BILL BIRD WAS SITTING. HENRY SLIPPED AND FELL IN THE RIVER. HE WAS UNABLE TO CALL FOR HELP. HE DROWNED.

STORY 10

HENRY ANT WAS THIRSTY. HE WALKED OVER TO THE RIVER BANK WHERE HIS GOOD FRIEND BILL BIRD WAS SITTING. HENRY SLIPPED AND FELL IN THE RIVER. GRAVITY DROWNED.

STORY 11

ONCE UPON A TIME THERE WAS A DISHONEST FOX AND A VAIN CROW. ONE DAY THE CROW WAS SITTING IN HIS TREE, HOLDING A PIECE OF CHEESE IN HIS MOUTH. HE NOTICED THAT HE WAS HOLDING THE PIECE OF CHEESE. HE BECAME HUNGRY, AND SWALLOWED THE CHEESE. THE FOX WALKED OVER TO THE CROW. THE END.

STORY 12

JOE BEAR WAS HUNGRY. HE ASKED IRVING BIRD WHERE SOME HONEY WAS. IRVING REFUSED TO TELL HIM, SO JOE OFFERED TO BRING HIM A WORM IF HE'D TELL HIM WHERE SOME HONEY WAS. IRVING AGREED. BUT JOE DIDN'T KNOW WHERE ANY WORMS WERE, SO HE ASKED IRVING, WHO REFUSED TO SAY. SO JOE OFFERED TO BRING HIM A WORM IF HE'D TELL HIM WHERE A WORM WAS. IRVING AGREED. BUT JOE DIDN'T KNOW

WHERE ANY WORMS WERE, SO HE ASKED IRVING,
WHO REFUSED TO SAY. SO JOE OFFERED TO BRING
HIM A WORM IF HE'D TELL HIM WHERE A WORM
WAS. . .

POLITICS

Part of the reason that the quotes by Bar-Hillel and Dreyfus are
inaccurate is that they are indicative of a lack of foresight with
respect to the possibilities for the improvement of the methods
of AI over the years. For example, some years ago Abelson
(1966) constructed a program that was intended to be a model of
an ideological cold warrior. It did not work very well largely
because of the lack of understanding at the time of how to
process natural language. With the advent of scripts as used by
SAM, we set out to look at the problem again. Below is the
output of the POLITICS program, (see Carbonell, 1977). The
input to POLITICS is a sentence that one might find in a
headline of a news story. POLITICS is then asked questions
about what it believes underlies the motivations of the actors.
The answers presented here are in accord with one possible
political philosophy. POLITICS has a number of possible
philosophies that can be input to it.

Russia massed troops on the Czech border.
Why did Russia do this?

BECAUSE RUSSIA THOUGHT THAT IT COULD TAKE
CONTROL OF CZECHOSLOVAKIA BY SENDING
TROOPS.

What will Russia do next?

RUSSIA MAY ORDER ITS TROOPS INTO CZECHO-
SLOVAKIA

What can the United States do?

THE UNITED STATES CAN DO NOTHING, IT CAN

INTERVENE MILITARILY IN CZECHOSLOVAKIA BY
SENDING TROOPS, OR IT CAN INTERVENE DIP-
LOMATICALLY BY TALKING TO RUSSIA ABOUT
CZECHOSLOVAKIA.

What should the United States do?

THE UNITED STATES SHOULD INTERVENE
MILITARILY.

Russia sent massive arms shipments to the MPLA in Angola.

Why did Russia do this?

RUSSIA WANTS TO CONTROL ANGOLA THROUGH
THE MPLA.

What will the MPLA use the arms shipments for?

THE MPLA WILL ATTEMPT TO TAKE OVER ANGOLA
USING THE ARMS SHIPMENTS.

What will the other factions in Angola do?

THE OTHER FACTIONS WILL ASK SOME OTHER
COUNTRY FOR ARMS.

Which country?

THE UNITED STATES

Should the US do anything about it?

YES, THE US SHOULD SEND ARMS TO THE OTHER
FACTIONS IN ANGOLA.

What is an AI program and what is AI? It should be clear that
the work at Yale that we have been discussing represents a
significant advance in the capabilities of computers. However
the reader should beware. AI is really no more than a promise

for the future. We are learning things by writing these programs. In fact, that is probably the major reason that we write them. AI represents a method by which we can learn about the nature of knowledge and the nature of man. The programs shown above are not complete, in the sense that they have only limited knowledge and vocabulary. They can easily be fooled. But they represent a sort of experimental epistemology, and viewed in that light they are significant.

In discussing what an AI program should be or can do, it should be pointed out that there is some disagreement among AI researchers themselves as to what makes an AI program different from any other computer program and what exactly AI is all about.

We will now attempt to put our view on this a bit more precisely:

DEFINITION 1: A program is an AI program if it characterizes and uses knowledge in a way that seems to be in accord with the intuitions of people who normally do the tasks that the program is doing.

Many AI researchers would take issue with definition 1. It seems to me that there are the following possible arguments against it:

Argument 1: For some AI issues it is too difficult to worry about using knowledge of how people function. Sometimes that knowledge is hard to find and sometimes it is irrelevant.

Argument 2: We have no proof of how people do much of what is interesting, so that requirement in definition 1 is meaningless in actual test.

Argument 3: Programs that exhibit intelligence are AI programs no matter how they do it.

The first argument might be made by people doing vision research. Since TV cameras are not much like the human eye, this is a reasonable argument for them. However, this argument ought not to be extended to the problems in vision that come after the initial technical problems are taken care of. People clearly have predictive mechanisms that enable them to under-stand what they see (Minsky, 1975). Such predictive mechan-isms are analogous to those used in natural language processing. Thus also in vision research effective human knowledge charac-terization is likely to save the day in the end. Thus I propose definition 1a:

DEFINITION 1a: An exception to definition 1 exists when the input data to a program must come in a form different from the way the data comes in to a human being.

The statement in Argument 2 is true enough. However, while we have little proof of what people actually do we have two very important types of information. First, we have an existence proof. Since we know that people can do these tasks, there exists at least one way to do them. There may, in fact, exist no more than one way to do them, so seeking to model people is probably a good research plan. One could argue that this is no more than a good heuristic to use while doing research. However, for very complex human tasks it has often been quite unrewarding to attempt to seek algorithms that are an improve-ment over human ones.

Second, we know what people do not do. It is unreasonable to postulate solutions to problems that rely on complicated formulae or numerical computations or on making several passes through a problem or, in certain cases, working back-wards through a problem. Such solutions may work on com-puters but they cannot really be considered to be models of human knowledge. I am thinking here of things such as certain theorem-proving and search techniques, as well as natural language programs that make several passes through a sentence. Thus we have definition 1b.

DEFINITION 1b: A program is not an AI program if it uses a technique that people cannot reasonably be expected to have.

Argument 3 is perhaps the most serious of all. In the early history of AI, most programs that were built bore little or no relation to human knowledge characterization. Early chess programs could be argued to be exhibiting some form of intelligent behaviour yet these methods were clearly non-human-like. But of course, it is within the domain of chess that the most powerful argument lies. Many of the problems in building automated chess programs that clearly used to be AI research are just as clearly not AI today. Today, AI research in chess (e.g. Simon and Gilmartin (1974) and Berliner (1975)) is clearly oriented towards the exploitation of principles of human knowledge.

I would like to argue that there are two kinds of AI programs representing two different stages of research in a particular problem. In the early stages of research in an AI problem area, getting a machine to do something that only a person could do before can be characterized as AI with the minimum requirement that the program should work. But in later stages, the general AI community should be able to learn something about the nature of the knowledge required in the field being modelled. Ideally, the characterization and use of that knowledge should, in some manner, tell us something about how to build better programs in other areas of AI. This is why ideas such as productions, from Newell (1973) and frames from Minsky (1975) have been so exciting in recent years. This can be stated as principles I and II.

PRINCIPLE I: A program that solely exhibits intelligent behaviour without respect to how knowledge has been characterized and used, can be considered to be a stage 1 AI program. A stage 1 AI program is an AI program if, and only if, that kind of intelligent behaviour has never been modelled before.

PRINCIPLE II: An AI program is significant only if it tells us something about the form, nature, and use of knowledge. Such a program is a stage 2 AI program.

If we believe all of this then there is a conclusion from it which we state as principle III:

PRINCIPLE III: The ultimate AI program that we are all aiming for is one that specifies the form in which knowledge is to be input to the program, as well as the form of the rules that use that knowledge, and produces a program that effectively models that domain.

This principle is in accord with the general philosophy behind GPS in Newell and Simon (1974). What I am arguing is that we must be able to learn about the nature of knowledge from any AI program. If we cannot learn about knowledge in general, or knowledge of the actual field being modelled in particular from the writing of the program, then the program is probably not one that fits well in AI.

The real argument to be made here is simply this: AI is the study of knowledge. It differs from epistemology in that it addresses the problem of determining the processes of applying knowledge to real-world situations as opposed to addressing more abstract questions. If AI is the study of knowledge, the only question remaining is to determine what kind of knowledge. The answer seems trivial: human knowledge of course, what other kind is there? The only alternative to studying human knowledge is to try to develop representations of knowledge that are improvements over the ones that humans use. But that would first require understanding the nature and form of human knowledge. Thus, it seems reasonable that the first step towards AI is the characterization of the nature, form, and scope of human knowledge. After this is done, AI may change direction again. As for now, the above definition should suffice.

We might at this point consider just what it is that AI has to offer the disciplines of psychology, linguistics, and philosophy. The answer is the possibility of thinking about and testing integrated processes. The above disciplines have in common a reliance on bits and pieces of unrelated evidence about the phenomena they seek to explain. An AI person looking at these same phenomena, attempts to formulate processes that mimic the behaviour of the system he seeks to find out about. The use of knowledge is a fundamental part of the process of understanding. Viewed as a method used in the process of understanding, the problems of knowledge acquisition and knowledge application are more easily attacked.

Do the programs described here shed light on the nature of human thought processes? Obviously I think that they do. By this I mean that they show that script-based understanding can work in principle, and that it is therefore a viable, although not necessarily proven, theory. As it turns out, psychologists have recently shown a great deal of interest in scripts, and a number of experiments have been and are being run. We will have to wait for conclusive evidence, but as of now we can at least say that the interaction between artificial intelligence and psychology is going in the direction that we had in mind.

Perhaps the most important point to be made by this paper is that it is necessary to attempt to clear up the confusion about where AI fits in the academic scene or exactly what AI is attempting to accomplish. Many philosophers of AI have muddied the waters with their analyses of what AI is trying to do. The most recent of these, namely Joseph Weizenbaum, has caused a great deal of confusion by statements such as:

> It may be possible, following Schank's procedures, to construct a conceptual structure that corresponds to the meaning of the sentence, 'Will you come to dinner with me this evening?' But it is hard to see – and I know that this is not an impossibility argument – how Schank-like schemes could possibly understand that same sentence to mean a shy young man's desperate longing for love. Even if a computer could simulate feelings of desperation and of love, is the computer then capable of being desperate and of loving? Can the computer then understand desperation and love? To the extent that those are legitimate questions at all, and that is a very limited extent indeed, the answer is 'no'. And if that is the answer, then the sense in which even the most powerful Schank-like system 'understands' is about as weak as the sense in which ELIZA 'understood'. (Weizenbaum, (1976)).

It is difficult to ascertain what Weizenbaum has in mind here, but it would seem that questions such as 'Can a computer feel love?' are not of much consequence. Certainly we do not understand less about human knowledge if the answer is one way or the other. And more importantly, the ability of a computer to feel love does not seriously affect its ability to understand. The programs shown above do various understanding tasks. To ask whether they *really* understand is beside the point. They do tell us about the nature and form of human knowledge.

People who tell us that it is wrong or not possible to solve some fundamental problems about understanding and creating intelligent machines are part of an established tradition. For most scientific advances there have been those who have said that it could not or should not be done. In the end, the final product tells the story.

REFERENCES

Abelson, R.P. 'Heuristic processes in the human application of verbal structures in new situations'. *Proc. XVIII International Congress of Psychology, Symposium 25.* Moscow (1966).

Bar-Hillel, Y. 'The present status of automatic translation of languages'. In *Advances in Computers,* Volume I, New York (Academic Press, 1960) 91.

Berliner, H.J. *Chess as Problem Solving: The Development of a Tactics Analyzer.* Carnegie-Mellon University, Pittsburgh (1974).

Bobrow, D. and Winograd, T. 'An overview of KRL'. *Cognitive Science 1, 1* (1977).

Carbonell, J.G. 'Ideological belief system simulation'. Submitted to *The Fifth International Joint Conference on Artificial Intelligence,* Cambridge, Massachusetts (1977).

Charniak, E. 'A framed painting: the representation of a common sense knowledge fragment'. *Cognitive Science,* New Jersey (Ablex, to appear).

Cullingford, R.E. 'The application of script-based knowledge in an integrated story understanding system'. Presented at the *International Conference on Computational Linguistics,* (Ottawa, 1976).

Dresher, B.E. and Hornstein, N. 'On some supposed contributions of artificial intelligence to the scientific study of language'. *Cognition. 4:4* (1977).

DeJong, G.F. 'Skimming newspaper stories by computer'. *Research Report 104,* New Haven (Yale University, 1977).

Lehnert, W.G. 'Human and conceptual question answering'. In *Cognitive Science, 1* (1977).

Meehan, J.R. 'The metanovel: writing stories by computer'. Ph.D. Thesis. *Research Report 74,* New Haven (Yale University, 1976).

Minsky, M. 'A framework for representing knowledge'. In P.H. Winston (ed) *The Psychology of Computer Vision.* New York (McGraw-Hill, 1975).

Newell, A. 'Production systems: models of control structures'. In W.G. Chase, (ed), *Visual information processing.* New York (Academic Press, 1973).

Newell, A and Simon, H.A. *Human problem solving.* New Jersey, (Prentice-Hall, 1974).

Nilsson, N.J. 'Artificial intelligence'. Invited Paper. *Information Processing 74.* Amsterdam. (North-Holland, 1974).

Norman, D. and Rumelhart, D. *Explorations in Cognition.* San Francisco (W.H. Freeman, 1975).

Rieger, C.J. 'The representation and selection of commonsense knowledge for natural language comprehension'. *Technical Report 458* (University of Maryland, 1976).

Riesbeck, C.K. 'Conceptual analysis'. In R.C. Schank, (ed) *Conceptual information processing.* Amsterdam (North-Holland, 1975).

Schank, R.C. *Conceptual information processing.* Amsterdam, (North-Holland, 1975).

Schank, R.C. and Abelson, R.P. *Scripts, Plans, Goals and Understanding: An Inquiry into Human Knowledge Structures.* New Jersey, (Lawrence Erlbaum Associates, 1977).

Simon, H.A. and Gilmartin, K. 'A simulation of Memory for Chess Positions', *Cognitive Psychology, 5* (1974) 29-46.

Weizenbaum, J. *Computer Power and Human Reason: From Judgment to Calculation.* San Francisco (W.H. Freeman 1976).

Wilensky, R. 'Using plans to understand natural language'. *Proceedings of the ACM '76,* Houston, Texas (1976).

Wilks, Y. (1975) 'A preferential pattern seeking semantics for natural language inference'. *Artificial Intelligence 6* (1975) 53-74.

CHAPTER 10.
PHILOSOPHICAL OBJECTIONS
TO PROGRAMS AS THEORIES
Thomas W. Simon

Computer simulations are used to study a wide range of activities, including flood potentials in the Ohio River Valley, relationships between lynx and hare populations, international conflicts, and even, in the global simulations of Forrester, Meadows, *et. al.,* the key parameters of the world itself. While these areas of simulation are not without their critics and controversies, heated debate is almost assured when computers are used to simulate the human mind. The pros and cons of cognitive simulation have been the subject of numerous discussions in psychology and philosophy, (e.g., Fodor, (1968) ch. 4), as well as in artificial intelligence, and the outcome of the debate will have a profound effect on our understanding of people and machines.

The philosophical claims against computer simulation divide into three types: impossibility, ethical, implausibility—all addressing a central issue: Are computer programs theories of human activities? Basically, the impossibility claim examined in the next section is that computer programs cannot by their very nature be theories of human activity and experience because programs are rigid (composed of discrete, inflexible instructions), while the behaviour they allegedly explain is flexible. After rejecting this claim we then see how the impossibility argument infects versions of the ethical claim that computer programs ought not to be theories of certain kinds of human activities because a simulation cannot and should not cover the entire range of human behaviours.

Although the implausibility position, citing *prima facie* reasons for computer programs, providing, at best, very restricted theories, stands as the strongest thesis, it also is not very compelling. Nevertheless, the problem of deciphering the adequacy of computer programs as theories remains.

IMPOSSIBILITY CLAIMS

What Computers Can't Do (Dreyfus (1972)) is the bold-faced title of Hubert Dreyfus' influential work. This title may be somewhat misleading because many of his claims, although themselves often disputable, are not cast in the impossibility mode. Nevertheless, it is commonplace throughout the work to find locutions like 'nonprogramm*able* capacities' (197, italics mine) and claims such as : '. . .the computer could not exhibit the flexibility of a human being solving an open-structured problem' (211). The grounds for these impossibility claims seem to be that a rigid, rule-following computer could not adequately simulate nonformal human activities requiring flexibility, insight, and the like. So, Dreyfus proposes:

(1) No computer program can in principle be a theory about nonformal human intelligent activities.

Before unravelling some general features of impossibility arguments let us examine (1) more closely. Any intuitive appeal that (1) might have probably comes from interpreting it along the lines of:

(2) Nothing inflexible can be flexible.

In other words, computers, operating in accordance with rigid, inflexible instructions, could not possibly cope with context-dependent, open-structured situations requiring a flexibility exhibited only by organisms such as humans. Burrell in adopting this position draws a strict distinction between instructions and rules:

> If it were simply a case of recurrent self-contained activity, instructions would suffice to inculcate the habit, but where the activity itself will require to be 'integrated' with many other activities and meet eventualities too numerous to be foreseen, we require a different kind of generality—that of rules (Burrell, 1967, 210).

While instructions are more mechanically (in the pejorative sense) characterized—a finite number of actions, each clearly and exactly executed in a given order to achieve a definite end – rules are flexible, adaptable to novel contents, open-textured, and so on. Yet, contrary to this position, computer 'rules' can be flexible and applicable to novel situations. In order to make this case, 'flexibility' should be more precisely construed as the capacity for an entity to modify its behaviour in accordance with, and/or despite, changes in that entity's environment. Given this definition, a cybernetic machine such as a target-seeking missile can be programmed to change its desired goal state in response to certain relevant features of the environment, giving it the capacity to pursue very different goals, (Simon, 1976). Similarly, by suitably modifying Schank's conceptual dependency program for understanding English, (Schank, 1973), so that in certain cases the context delimits not only the range of possibilities but also the type of expectation, i.e., the type of prediction for the conceptual structure to make, enough flexibility might be built in to yield an understanding of even metaphorical uses such as: 'the idea is in the pen' (Cf. Dreyfus, 1972, 111). Moreover, critics who make this attack on computer flexibility do not seem to realize that the concept of flexibility is itself relative to a given theoretical framework. The behaviour of a rat, within the context of a Skinnerian psychology, is less flexible than that same behaviour analyzed in a Tolmanian conceptual framework, involving teleological notions. For, in the former, whether the rat swims, hops, or runs through the maze has little or no relevance to the analysis, whereas it is of central concern within the latter. The critics, however, wrongly think that there is one sense of 'flexibility' that applies to humans, irrespective of the theoretical framework.

Nevertheless, Dreyfus, seemingly more radical on this issue than Burrell, would not even accept the above counter-argument. According to him, human action, though orderly, is not even rule-governed. Somehow, humans, uniquely 'at home in [their] world, [having] it comfortably wrapped around [them], so to speak' (Dreyfus, 1972: 172), are simply able to pick out relevant features of their environment, while machines must be pre-programmed to accomplish this feat. In reply, each potentially relevant feature of the environment, which would probably approach infinity, does not have to be preprogrammed into the machine, i.e., programmed prior to the actual environmental confrontation, as long as there are concomitant capacities for drawing inferences (in the loose sense of 'inference', including mere association) from given data. With these capabilities a machine could adequately simulate a human decision not to bet on a jockey today because his mother died yesterday (Dreyfus, 1972: 170). Charles Taylor uses this example to allegedly demonstrate the opposite:

> . . .when we store the information that people often do less than their best just after their near relations die, we can't be expected to tag a connection with betting on horses. This information can be relevant to an infinte set of contexts (in Dreyfus, 1972: 170).

But how humans in their already 'prestructured with meaning' world arrive at these decisions, if not by a similar means of drawing inferences from data, or, more precisely, beliefs about data, remains a mystery on Dreyfus' account, which seems to be exactly where Dreyfus wants to leave the matter. Needless to say, a desire to retain the mysterious element in human behaviour does not constitute an argument against computer capabilities.

The overall difficulty with this particular brand of the impossibility claim is that it assumes that a particular domain of activities is inherently intractable to treatment by a machine operating according to discrete steps. But this is an empirical conjecture and not a logical one. The proposal made by simulationists such as Uhr (1973) and Simon (1973), that ill-structured problems can eventually be treated as well-formed problems, is an empirical claim. There is no domain of problem solving activity, including the more creative aspects, that is necessarily ill-formed, and even if there were, this would not preclude the utility of a 'well-structured' machine from ade-quately simulating it. However debatable this claim might be, its resolution will be found through empirical examination of the creative process and not by some *a priori* means.

Until recently, impossibility arguments have been in vogue throughout the philosophical literature for everything from the existence of God to nominalism. The reasons for the recent decline have been due to the repeated failures of impossibility arguments, except in strictly formal areas, as for example, the undecidability of the halting rule, (Weizenbaum, 1976: 66), and to the increasing sensitivity to the contextual nature of many arguments and analyses, particularly with respect to those claims directed at an on-going rapidly changing, research program like computer simulation. If it is claimed that a computer cannot do a specified task within a particular time limit and under certain conditions, then the claim is subject to empirical investigation. However, if it is claimed that computers cannot do task 'x', irrespective of time frames and conditions, then we have a very different claim. What, in addition to an incredible prediction presumption, makes these argument-types tenuous, is that both the nature of computers and the nature of the processes and task under investigation, as well as our understanding of both, are subject to constant change, redefinition, and re-analysis. It is becoming increasingly difficult to have confidence in any analysis laying down adequate, necessary and sufficient conditions for a concept. Simulations are constantly challenging those conditions and meeting just those conditions previously thought impossible.

Of course, the claims of Dreyfus *et. al.* could easily be recast into a mode wherein computer simulation is regarded as highly implausible. Even though Dreyfus' arguments will not be explicitly examined in this fashion, the strategy will soon be addressed. Before that, however, we will turn to a form of argumentation that in some instances surprisingly depends upon impossibility arguments—the ethical arguments against computer simulation.

ETHICAL CLAIMS

Weizenbaum's recent book, *Computer Power and Human Reason: From Judgement to Calculation*, is probably better entitled: *What Computers Ought Not Do*. Weizenbaum argues that even 'if computers could imitate man in every respect—which in fact they cannot, . . there are some acts of thought that ought to be attempted only by humans' (Weizenbaum, 1976: 13). The fact/value distinction seems to be slowly eroding with increasing acceptance of theses to the effect that scientists *qua* scientists make value judgments (Rudner, 1953). Ethical considerations brought to bear on any science are to be applauded. Two types of computer research qualify as ethically objectionable for Weizenbaum: indirect ones whose application would be ethically reprehensible, i.e., 'easily seen to have irreversible and not entirely foreseeable side effects' (Weizenbaum, 1976: 270), and direct ones whose very nature is ethically unacceptable. An example of the former would be automatic, speech-recognition, computer systems. Though innocuous enough on the surface, they would probably have the side effect of leading to more fully automated battlefields, such as voice-commanded war fleets, and to increased surveillance. Being ethically accountable for the purposes and consequences of scientific investigations is a reasonable demand, but Weizenbaum's argument may be stronger than he intends for it would rule out a large portion of research on higher mental functions, including, but not limited to computer science projects.

If the ability to duplicate higher mental functions as well as the ability to explain and predict these in humans constitutes a major goal of computer science research, then an easily forseeable consequence is the potential use of this knowledge for harmful ends. Given this understanding, both machine and human would then be easier to control. On the one hand, due to easier accessibility, society's understandable lack of moral concern for the machine, and so on, the mental function embodied in the machine would be more controllable. On the other hand, humans would become more controllable since control often follows on the footsteps of prediction, another sought-after result of the simulation. A much more advanced General Problem Solver would not only be able to play good chess but also to solve problems such as devising and implementing totalitarian means of controlling the populace. Should all work on computer simulation of problem solving cease because some of the problems solved would result in serious impediments to human liberty? If so, then a strong case can be made for halting all research on higher mental functions. Here, in having no reservations about psycho-physiological research into speech recognition Weizenbaum appears inconsistent. Although understanding derived from computers seems to lead more directly to technological devices which could be used for ill-purposes, understanding from psycho-physiological research could just as likely result in such devices. Psychology is no further removed from technology than is computer science. There is a sense in which ethical judgments of the form:

(3) Computer simulation on x ought not to be carried out because of consequences y,

involve the impossibility claim examined in the last section. Speech recognition computer projects ought to be discontinued not because of any ethical consequences nor because computers cannot possibly recognize speech but because they cannot recognize speech in the full sense of that activity. Recognizing speech is not merely the ability of something to respond to voice commands of a naval officer in an appropriate way, although that might be an important test, but rather it includes a wide repertoire of responses, such as the ability to refuse a command. Likewise, problem solving involves more than the simple regurgitation of appropriate answers to problems in the same way humans do. It also involves utilizing various value judgments, emotions, and the like in the problem. The difficulty with the types of computer projects Weizenbaum objects to lies in their taking a non-integrative, incomplete approach by detrimentally and artificially isolating a particular phase or part of the activity. This may be a good research strategy, but Weizenbaum is correct in warning of the ethical drawbacks. However, if one of these more complete simulations were at hand, then the force of the ethical objection would not be directed against computer simulation as such but rather against the human activity itself. Of course, a stronger ethical case could be made against some of the research in artificial intelligence where doing a task in a human way is not a constraint. This is in no way meant to belittle or undermine the ethical argument but rather to pinpoint those instances, particularly in computer simulation research, where the ethical concern is closely tied to another: whether a computer can successfully do the task in question in a human manner.

Weizenbaum's second direct ethical thesis more directly ties into the impossibility claim; in fact, it reduces to it. Basically, the thesis is:

(4) A computer program ought not to be a theory of certain aspects of the human experience.

Weizenbaum, while admitting their technical feasibility, labels proposals such as Colby's, that computers be installed as psychotherapists as 'simply obscene' (Weizenbaum, 1976: 268). However, contra Weizenbaum, the claim that 'there are some human functions for which computers *ought* not to be substituted' (Weizenbaum, 1976: 270) does indeed have something to do with what computers can or cannot do. Otherwise, Weizenbaum's position is incoherent. According to Weizenbaum, computers that can do psychotherapy ought not to because the computer lacks love, understanding and respect. Then love, understanding, and respect are supposedly necessary and sufficient conditions for doing psychotherapy as well. So, Weizenbaum's claim is really a disguised form of: computers cannot do psychotherapy well, i.e. they cannot love, understand, and respect—the ethical gloss simply adding a dramatic note. Otherwise, if a machine really *can* do psychotherapy well, it is difficult to see how one could argue that a machine *ought not* to do psychotherapy because of some peculiarly human element in psychotherapy. Presumably, the machine would possess that element if it could do the activity well.

Imagine yourself as director of a prestigious funding agency receiving a research proposal from some avid computer scientist who claims to be able to design a computer that could love, understand, and respect psychotherapy clients. Dismissing the request because the undertaking is impossible is unnecessary. A more reasonable tactic is to argue that it is highly implausible, given present techniques, that a computer exhibiting these alleged characteristics of a psychotherapist would be forthcoming unless the computer were made quite humanoid. Alternatively, the proposal might be rejected not on the grounds that the project is ethically reprehensible but on other ethical considerations, including the harmful consequences that would ensue if this design were implemented. Weizenbaum's ethical argument is strengthened by recasting it as: computers ought not to do a task 'x' not because of the nature of x but because of the harmful consequences of the computer doing 'x'. For example, seeing a computer psychotherapist might result in a person having less respect for other people and having more dependence on machines.

Ethical arguments, then, about computers, in many instances hinge on considerations of what computers can or cannot do.

Those that rely on these considerations, as does Weizenbaum's second ethical claim (4), face the same objections raised against the impossibility arguments (1) in the first section. Now we are in a position to examine the less radical implausibility claim:

(5) There are *prima facie* reasons to believe that if computer programs are even considered as programs, then their range of application is severely limited.

IMPLAUSIBILITY ARGUMENTS

Throughout the simulation literature, computer programs are equated with theories (Winston, 1977: 258). Three questions confront this often unexamined assumption. First of all, are programs likely candidates for theories of anything? Secondly, even if programs constitute theories, what are they theories of? Thirdly, do programs provide adequate theories? We shall try to address each of these in turn.

With respect to the first question, theories come in various forms, the most common are verbal and mathematical. Computer programs appear to be a curious anomaly, neither in verbal form, like Freudian psychoanalytic theory nor mathematical, like some versions of learning theory. Furthermore, programs are generally formulated in the imperative mood, 'GO TO', 'DO', while theories are normally couched in the indicative mood. Computer imperatives are, however, translatable into declaratives. These concerns, however, need not occupy our attention too long, for they are really circuitous ways of stating the obvious: computer programs are a different breed of theory. Moreover, as a number of commentators (Reitman, 1965; Sayre, 1965; Weizenbaum, 1976) have pointed out, programs in being more precise have distinct advantages over their verbal counterparts, and, in being able to represent large ranges of functional interrelationships, outstrip many mathematical versions. In fact, Gregg and Simon provide examples of computer simulations which:

(a) provide grounds of plausibility for the stochastic theories,

(b) make predictions of detail not encompassed in the stochastic theories,

(c) make predictions for new experimental conditions to which the stochastic theories do not apply (1971: 146).

Hence, simulations can be stronger and more falsifiable than a mathematical stochastic theory.

Despite the fact that the program/theory equation appears viable, if adopted as a dogmatic maxim, the claim can be misleading in just the same way that a boast can be misleading by making the boaster think he or she has more than he or she does. Although a program can be constructed as a theory by merely substituting declaratives for imperatives, in many cases that is simply not enough; often more needs to be added and subtracted to the story in order to construct a theory.

> Abstracting a theory from a program is not a trivial matter for different groupings of the program can generate different theories. Therefore, to the extent that a program understood as a model embodies one theory it may well embody many theories (Moor, unpublished manuscript, (1976) 12).

Hence, bits and snatches of a program, reconstructed programs, a detailed program in its entirety, or even 'the theory behind the program' could each constitute the theoretical ingredients of a computer simulation. Yet, practically speaking, it is doubtful that a complete computer program ever constitutes a theory. Many elements of a program, such as 'lower order subroutines and a number of technical necessities' (Frijda, 1967: 611) are irrelevant to theory construction. The simulationist must abstract the theoretically relevant features from the program. Unfortunately, the actual presentation of this extended theory is apt to be as vague as the purely verbal theories (Frijda, 1967: 611). Even more problematic is the fact that any number of verbal theories may be extrapolated from the same program. Moreover, simulationists must constantly guard against falling victim to what has been called 'Bonini's paradox' (Dutton and Starbuck, 1971: 4), constructing a program that is more complex than the phenomena being studied. Yet, if we keep these difficulties in mind, it seems legitimate to speak, however loosely, of programs as theories.

However, some commentators, while agreeing that programs might be theories in these restricted senses, nevertheless want to limit their applicability to a certain restricted range of phenomena. Gunderson (1971), for example, maintains:

(6) Computer programs are theories of program-receptive features but not of program-resistant features.

For Gunderson, program-receptive features are primarily cognitive, whereas program resistant features include more immediately experiential items such as 'having of pains, after-images, feeling anxious, being bored, etc.' (Gunderson, 1971: 146). These latter features are things that one has, and not, as is the case with the former tasks, what one does. Accordingly, since no amount of innovative programming is going to yield these features, in order to simulate them, machines will have to be built with the capacities for exhibiting these features. While not being provided with a hint as to how to build these capacities into machines, I presume that what Gunderson has in mind is that in order for a machine to simulate a pain it should be capable of exhibiting those features associated with this sensation such as being able to have its 'body' damaged, being able to say 'ouch', being able to withdraw the damaged part from the stimulus area, and so on. If Gunderson is correct, then not only is a program not merely equated with a theory but computer simulationists must also expand their scope to include building receptor/effector mechanisms, etc. into the computer. Therefore, the degree to which an activity like problem solving utilizes these program-resistant features is the degree to which the simulationist must look beyond the programming.

Gunderson is committing a fundamental error by conflating 'simulating x' with 'having x', which is an instance of unnecessarily confusing simulation with replication (Cf, Sayre, 1965). Certainly, in order for a person or machine to have a pain or any other sensation, he, she, or it must have the 'capacity' for that sensation. However, it does not follow that being equipped with the capacity for exhibiting x is in any way a prerequisite for simulating 'x' (see Fodor, 1968: 122). Having a theory or a program about pain certainly does not entail that the theory or program has pains. Moreover, since one of the most important goals of any computer simulation is explanation of the phenomenon being simulated, it seem quite reasonable *not* to expect the simulation to explain the felt-qualities of these allegedly program-resistant features in the sense of being required to reproduce them. To paraphrase Einstein, it is not the business of science, particularly computer science, to taste soup, feel pains, or even pollute. Moreover, as Moor (1976) and Oppacher (1977) have pointed out, Gunderson's program-receptive/program-resistant distinction presupposes a software/hardware distinction which in its strict form is simply untenable.

More recently, Haugeland (1978) proposed three, potentially serious hurdles to a simulation, or, more broadly, a cognitive research program: moods, skills, and understanding. Even though the analysis of each of these will undoubtedly prove difficult and complicated, there are, contrary to Haugeland, no *prima facie* (not conclusive) reasons for doubting the applicability of the simulationist approach. The simulationist's task includes deciphering the various processes underlying moods, particularly the complex interplay of feelings, beliefs, evaluations, and so on. To the same extent that Haugeland allows for segregating off felt qualities from the simulationist's concerns, they can be segregated off as factors of moods. Skills present a somewhat different problem in that many skills, particularly motor, do not seem to be analysable into discrete mental, or information, processes. Yet, this may only indicate a different kind of information processing, for example, pattern recognition, taking place while one is acquiring a skill. As Simon notes these different types of information processing account for some of the different abilities of, for example, duffer and master chess players:

> . . .the short term memory of the chess master has the same capacity, measured in chunks, as the short-term memory of a duffer, but [the] duffer's chunks consist of individual pieces while the master's chunks consist of configurations of pieces (1976: 80).

Finally, 'understanding' is highly ambiguous contrasted with, for example, ignorance, mere knowing, and misunderstanding (Scriven, 1972: 32), and Haugeland's sense of understanding as insight is no exception. Insight could consist in 'believing or feeling that one understands' (Scriven, 1972: 32) or, among other things, in the ability to specify why something 'makes sense'. Neither of these are beyond the purview of the simulationist. While Haugeland (1978) wants to deny that 'insight is itself some "transcendental" or impenetrable mystery, which we are forever barred from explaining' he still wants to 'admit that the phenomenon of insight is simply mysterious and unexplainable at present'. Some of the mystery surrounding a concept like *insight* is dispelled by providing an analysis, and an analysis would spell out just those antecendent conditions thought to be implausible by Haugeland.

The phenomena cited by Gunderson and Haugeland represent merely a sample of those proposed as obstacles to program simulation (see also, for example, the characteristics-development, emotionality, and multiple motivation set forth by Neisser, 1976). Without cataloguing all of these, some general comments, negative and positive, can be made about this tactic. First of all, the tactic assumes more than it seems able to deliver. For something fairly definitive must be known about the obstacle-phenomenon which makes that phenomenon incompatible with the simulationist research program. For example, saying that insight presents a serious hurdle to simulation presupposes a fairly well-worked out analysis of the constituents of insight. After all, we want to know what it is about insight that creates the problem. Here the dilemma arises. For once that analysis is given, then the phenomenon, in being more manageable and less mysterious, seems more amenable to a simulation treatment. Still, Haugeland (1978) warning that the simulation approach may well be, like behaviourism, over-stepping its fruitful bounds of inquiry, is well worth noting. Yet, in many cases these limitations are discovered only by over-stepping them.

The third question concerning the adequacy of computer programs as theories is much more difficult to answer.

If one of the functions of a theory is explanation and if a critical element of explanation is the formulation of universal laws, then a simulation of x does not entail an explanation of x (Fodor, 1968: 128). According to Fodor,

> . . .for an adequate simulation to be an adequate explanation it must be the case *both* that the behaviours available to the machine correspond to the behaviours available to the organism *and* that the processes whereby the machines produces behaviour simulate the processes whereby the organism does. (Fodor, 1968: 136).

Not only must the actual behaviours of human and machine correspond but also the repertoire of behaviours, i.e. the range of possible behaviours.

Even granting Fodor's stringent criteria, it is dubious whether satisfaction of them constitutes an explanation in the sense of providing general laws. It is easy to envisage someone constructing a device, such as a model automobile, which corresponds in every relevant respect to the available behaviours and internal processes of an actual automobile and which nonetheless, cannot provide any universal laws governing the operation of the automobile. This construction might be good technology but not good science. The technological feats in the computer field, (for example, robotology) should not be confused with scientific ones.

Nevertheless, it may be the requirement of explanations by general laws which is the problem and not the type of understanding or theory, in the broad sense, generated by many computer simulations. Although Feigenbaum's Elementary Perceiver and Memorizer (EPAM), and Simon and Newell's General Problem Solver (GPS) apparently lack law-like generalizations, this does not detract from the understanding provided by such programs. EPAM simulates and generates an explanation of the role of learning of nonsense syllables. Weizenbaum proclaims:

> The property it has which qualifies it as a theory, however, is that it enunciates certain principles from which consequences may be drawn. These principles themselves are in computer-program form, and their consequences emerge in the behaviour of the program, that is, in the computer's reading of the program (Weizenbaum, 1976, 177).

Yet, these 'principles' of, for example, associative memory networks, follow from a prior theory or theories of which this simulation is a model. Explanatory hypotheses such as:

> People forget for a long time not because of information destruction but because learned material gets lost and inaccessible in a large and growing association network (Feigenbaum, 1963, 308),

result from a theoretical interpretation of the simulation.

Moreover, EPAM yields novel predictions, novel in the sense of not being explicit in the program beforehand. One such is its two kinds of interference ('acquisition of a new association with the production of an older one when the syllables involved have closely similar description' (Weizenbaum, 1976: 163-164)) viz., (1) oscillation, 'Associations which are given correctly over a number of trials sometimes are forgotten, only to reappear and later disappear again' (Feigenbaum, 1963: 299), and (2) retroactive inhibition, oscillation with respect to two different lists. Prior to this simulation, these were not considered closely related (Feigenbaum, 1963: 308).

Admittedly there is a paucity of well formulated theories on problem solving, either at the level of the simulation programs themselves, i.e. those generated from the simulations, or those underlying the simulations. The hypotheses generated from GPS are often either descriptive of how a particular person solves a specific problem, subject S solves problem G by employing rules of type M, or they are concerned with the efficiency of the M-rules. Seemingly, then, these hypotheses, at least in Weizenbaum's opinion, evade the 'real' questions such as:

> How is his [the subject's] perception of what a 'problem' is shaped by the experiences that are an integral part of his acquisition of his vocabulary? How do these experiences shape his perception of what 'objects', 'operators', 'differences', 'goals', etc., are relevant to any problems he may be facing? And so on. No theory that sidesteps such questions can possibly be a theory of human problem solving (Weizenbaum, 1976: 179).

On this view, to be an adequate explanation a computer simulation should generate causal hypotheses such as Wason's description of negations in formal logic as 'more difficult to handle than affirmatives because they had acquired an unpleasant connotation through their association with prohibitives' (Wason and Johnson-Laird, 1972: 20).

However cogent these charges may be, they overlook the orientation and function of simulations like GPS compared to those like EPAM. For these represent complementary research strategies. Reitman aptly notes that Feigenbaum's 'model corresponds to a generalized or abstract individual' (1968: 28) and GPS to single individuals. Other than the information-processing models generated by simulationists there are few alternative theories of human, problem solving. GPS, then, is forced to start from scratch, the first step being a sufficientcy analysis (Newell and Simon, 1972: 13) which provides an 'explanation of how it is possible for a human to solve these problems' (Newell, 1973: 27). Not even sure of what the facts are, regarding problem solving, this computer simulation research comprises an important first step in theory construction. Even though successful sufficiency analyses counter impossibility arguments, simulationists do not rest content with them. Given a sufficientcy analysis one wants to zero in by a series of approximations on the mechanisms responsible for the performance of the cognitive task under study. The reason Weizenbaum rejects GPS as a theory is that it does not live up to the standards of Newtonian theory and the universal laws contained therein. But this is more of a problem with that narrow conception of theory than it is a drawback of GPS. Given the recalcitrance and complexity of the problem, GPS has brought us the beginning fruits of understanding.

Nonetheless, frustrations abound when evaluating the theoretical adequacy of a computer program. Not only are there drawbacks to relying on human protocols or introspective reports to determine the simulation operations (See Dennett, 1968), but empirical constraints on simulation such as intermediate state evidence, relative complexity evidence, and component analysis evidence (Pylyshyn, this volume) also seem limited, merely indicating that we are on the right track (but not anywhere near the station) towards uncovering the principles of mentation. Part of this frustration is due to the black-box character of computer simulation theorizing. Only a limited amount of knowledge can be inferred about the inner workings of any black box. Eventually, the black box has to be opened in order to settle disputes about conflicting views of its internal operations. In the meantime, however, we are quite fortunate in that we know more about the cognitive simulationist's black box than any other, for we have intimate access to it.

With many qualifications programs are theories. What programs are theories of is controversial but not an impediment to research. Despite its limitations, computer simulation does provide the first steps towards constructing a theory of the human mind. By examining a number of philosophical objections (impossibility, ethical, and implausibility) against the 'programs-as-theories' thesis, a number of insights into the foundations of computer simulation methodology have been uncovered. At least with respect to the issues examined here the road is relatively clear from philosophical obstruction. Now, the work must begin.

REFERENCES

Burrel, D.B. 'Obeying rules and following instructions'. *In Philosophy and Cybernetics*. Crosson, Frederick J. and Sayre, Kenneth M. (eds) New York, (Simon and Schuster, 1967) 203-232.

Dennett, Daniel C. 'Computers in behavioral science: machine traces and protocol statements', *Behavioral Science, 13:2* (March 1968) 155-161.

Dorf, Richard C. *Computers and Man*. San Francisco (Boyd & Fraser, 1974).

Dreyfus, Hubert L. *What Computers Can't Do: A Critique of Artificial Intelligence*. New York (Harper and Row, 1972).

Dutton, John and Starbuck, William H. 'Introduction'. In *Computer Simulation of Human Behavior*. New York (Wiley, 1971).

Feigenbaum, Edward A. 'The simulation of verbal learning behavior'. In *Computers and Thought*. Feigenbaum, Edward A. and Feldman, Julian (eds), New York (McGraw Hill, 1963).

Fodor, Jerry. *Psychological Explanation*. New York (Random House, 1968).

Frijda, Nicott. 'Problems of computer simulation'. In *Computer Simulation of Human Behavior*. Dutton, John M. and Starbuck, William H. (eds) New York (Wiley, 1971).

Gregg, Lee W. and Simon, Herbert. 'Process models and stochastic theories of simple concept formation'. In *Computer Simulation of Human Behavior*. New York (Wiley, 1971).

Gunderson, Keith. *Mentality and Machines*. New York (Anchor, 1971).

Haugeland, John. 'The nature and plausibility of cognitivism'. In *The Behavioral and Brain Sciences, 1:2* (June 1978) 215-226.

Jackson, Philip C. *Introduction to Artificial Intelligence*. New York (Petrocelli, 1974).

Moor, James. *Three Myths of Computer Science*. (Unpublished manuscript, 1977).

Neisser, Ulric. 'General, academic and artificial intelligence'. *The Nature of Intelligence*. Resnick, Lauren B. (ed) New Jersey (Earlbaum Assoc., 1976).

Newell, Allen and Simon, Herbert A. *Human problem solving*. New Jersey (Prentice-Hall, 1972).

Oppacher, Franz. (*Private communication*).

Pylyshyn, Z. 'Complexity and the study of artificial and human intelligence', in this volume.

Reitman, Walter R. *Cognition and Thought*. New York (Wiley, 1965).

Rudner, Richard. 'The scientist qua scientist makes value judgments', *Philosophy of Science, 20* (1953).

Sayre, Kenneth M. *Recognition*. Notre Dame (University of Notre Dame Press, 1965).

Schank, Roger C. 'Identification of conceptualizations underlying natural language'. In *Computer Models of Thought and Language*. Schank, Roger C. and Colby, Kenneth Mark, (eds) San Francisco (W.C. Freeman, 1973).

Scriven, Michael. 'The concept of comprehension'. In *Language Comprehension and the Acquisition of Knowledge*. Freedle, Roy O. and Carroll, John B. (eds) New York (Wiley, 1972).

Simon, Herbert A. 'Identifying basic abilities underlying intelligent performance of complex tasks'. In *The Nature of Intelligence*. Resnick, Lauren B. (ed) New Jersey (Erlbaum Assoc., 1976).

Simon, Herbert A. 'The structure of ill-structured problems', *Artificial Intelligence, 4* (1973) 181-201.

Simon, Thomas W. 'A cybernetic analysis of goal-directedness', *Proceedings of the Philosophy of Science Association, 1* (1976) 56-70.

Uhr, Leonard. *Pattern recognition, learning and thought*. New Jersey (Prentice-Hall, 1973).

Wason, P.C. and Johnson-Laird, P.N. *Psychology of reasoning*. Cambridge, Mass. (Harvard University Press, 1972).

Weizenbaum, Joseph. *Computer power and human reason*. San Francisco (W.C. Freeman, 1976).

Winston, Patrick Henry. *Artificial Intelligence*. Reading, Mass. (Addison-Wesley, 1977).

Index